BAYOU DILEMMA

Carl A. Brasseaux and Donald W. Davis, series editors

BAYOU DILEMMA

LOUISIANA IN CRISIS AND CHANGE

Edited by Samuel C. Hyde Jr.

University Press of Mississippi / Jackson

This contribution has been supported with funding provided by the Louisiana Sea Grant College Program (LSG) under NOAA Award # NA14OAR4170099. Additional support is from the Louisiana Sea Grant Foundation. The funding support of LSG and NOAA is gratefully acknowledged, along with the matching support by LSU. Logo created by Louisiana Sea Grant College Program.

The University Press of Mississippi is the scholarly publishing agency of the Mississippi Institutions of Higher Learning: Alcorn State University, Delta State University, Jackson State University, Mississippi State University, Mississippi University for Women, Mississippi Valley State University, University of Mississippi, and University of Southern Mississippi.

www.upress.state.ms.us

The University Press of Mississippi is a member of the Association of University Presses.

Any discriminatory or derogatory language or hate speech regarding race, ethnicity, religion, sex, gender, class, national origin, age, or disability that has been retained or appears in elided form is in no way an endorsement of the use of such language outside a scholarly context.

Copyright © 2024 by University Press of Mississippi
All rights reserved
Manufactured in the United States of America

∞

Names: Hyde, Samuel C., 1958– editor.
Title: Bayou dilemma : Louisiana in crisis and change / edited by Samuel C. Hyde Jr.
Other titles: America's third coast.
Description: Jackson : University Press of Mississippi, [2024] | Series: America's third coast series | Includes bibliographical references and index.
Identifiers: LCCN 2024028293 (print) | LCCN 2024028294 (ebook) | ISBN 9781496853776 (hardback) | ISBN 9781496853783 (trade paperback) | ISBN 9781496853790 (epub) | ISBN 9781496853806 (epub) | ISBN 9781496853813 (pdf) | ISBN 9781496853820 (pdf)
Subjects: LCSH: Race discrimination—Louisiana—History. | Crime—Louisiana—History. | Corruption—Louisiana—History. | Law—Louisiana—History. | Flood control—Louisiana. | Brain drain—United States. | Louisiana—History.
Classification: LCC F369 .B39 2024 (print) | LCC F369 (ebook) | DDC 976.3—dc23/eng/20240729
LC record available at https://lccn.loc.gov/2024028293
LC ebook record available at https://lccn.loc.gov/2024028294

British Library Cataloging-in-Publication Data available

CONTENTS

Foreword: Defining Louisiana through the Lens of Challenge vii
    SAMUEL C. HYDE JR.

Acknowledgments xix

SECTION ONE: INEQUALITY

Chapter One: 1896–2022: The Pardon of Homer Plessy
and Its Impact on Racial Justice 5
    GOVERNOR JOHN BEL EDWARDS

Chapter Two: Defenders of Tradition, Champions of Reform:
Louisiana's Faith Communities Confront Civil Rights Change 14
    KEITH M. FINLEY

Chapter Three: A Soldier's Story: The Fight for Equal Rights
and Social Justice in Post–World War II Louisiana. 43
    MARCUS S. COX

SECTION TWO: CORRUPTION, VIOLENCE, AND THE LIMITS OF REFORM

Chapter Four: Public Corruption in Louisiana: Then and Now. 65
    ADAM FAIRCLOUGH

Chapter Five: As Louisiana as Crawfish Pie:
Endemic Violence and the Nonunanimous Jury Verdict 90
    SAMUEL C. HYDE JR.

Chapter Six: Equality for Women in Louisiana:
An Unfinished Revolution 116
    JANET ALLURED

SECTION THREE: WATER AND WEATHER

Chapter Seven: Louisiana's Coastal Crisis, Management,
and Prognosis considering Tipping Points of Change 149
    JOHN A. LOPEZ

Chapter Eight: Small Watersheds, Big Conflicts:
Managing Floods in the Florida Parishes 167
    CRAIG E. COLTEN

SECTION FOUR: DETERMINING WHO WE ARE

Chapter Nine: The Politics of Opportunity:
Education Reform in the Jindal Administration 195
    PEARSON CROSS

Chapter Ten: Should I Stay or Go? The Social, Political,
and Environmental Causes of Louisiana's "Brain Drain". 215
    ROBERT MANN

About the Contributors 229
Index 233

FOREWORD

DEFINING LOUISIANA THROUGH THE LENS OF CHALLENGE

SAMUEL C. HYDE JR.

"Passionate!" The forthright, single-word assertion came in response to a thoughtful question posed during a group discussion: "What lone word best describes Louisiana?" Many different solitary words could have filled the blank. Among those that emerged as the small group of students of the Bayou State continued to chat were "fun," "beautiful," "unique," "corrupt," "wet," and "violent." "Passionate" seemed to incorporate a little of them all, and it provided a pleasingly positive moniker for a state we all knew remains troubled in so many ways.

When most individuals think of their home state, they tend to emphasize the positive qualities, aspects of life and geography that suggest they made a wise choice in their decision to call this particular place home. There are always a few who remain determined to denigrate their home state at virtually any opportunity, insisting that they would happily live anywhere but here. Yet "here" they remain. And, even among this misplaced category of citizens, an intense pride of place will often well up when an "outsider" miscalculates and joins in the scorn, only to see the original abuser go on the defense of their home.

Readers tend to favor studies that make them feel good. Many popular accounts of states or communities accordingly tend to focus on issues that are pleasing or amusing to observers. Especially attractive are curiosities that are unique to the study area, and in this regard, Louisiana is blessed. The Bayou State enjoys an abundance of novelties that separate it from the culture and character of the rest of the nation. Ethnically, the state is more French oriented than any other portion of the United States, a certainty that impacts everything from food, to culture, to methods of fun. Similarly, it is far more Catholic, even in rural areas, than any other region of the country.

Louisiana has parishes, not counties, wards rather than districts, for political and geographic delineations. Justice centers on the civil code rather than the Common Law that is practiced in every other state of the Union. It includes a large African American population along with the largest rural Italian and Hungarian communities in America. It is also arguably the only place in America where every major European power that intruded into the North American wilderness held governmental authority over at least portions of the state, a historical truth that offers seemingly limitless opportunities for study and amusement. The list of unique qualities goes on and on, but just as useful for identifying the character of a state, and the behavior of its people, are the challenges that have confronted a region and how they have been overcome or managed. And when it comes to confronting life-altering problems, Louisiana again remains at the top of many lists.

Louisiana's troubles are not always unique. The Bayou State shares in many of the challenges common to other states of the South and to those of most developed nations. But just as Louisiana is home to such national oddities as Mardi Gras, boudin, nutria, Cajuns, and crawfish boils, so is it home to special challenges—ones that are seminal to understanding how the people of Louisiana behave and how they are perceived by others.

In the fall of 2022, a diverse group of scholars of Louisiana history and culture gathered to present their views on challenges that have defined life in Louisiana. Ten academics, including scientists, historians, political scientists, geographers, and journalists, along with Governor John Bel Edwards, came together at Southeastern Louisiana University for a symposium titled "Louisiana in Continuity and Change: Challenges Past and Present Confronting the Bayou State." The program advertised as its purpose "to provide ground breaking studies of challenges common to the wider Gulf South that prove acute in Louisiana."

Through presentations, scholarly debate, and most importantly a published volume of the included studies, the program promised to provide an enduring guide for how such trials emerged and how they were overcome, or managed, in the past to offer direction for how they may best be addressed in the future. This book is the product of the overall project.

The first section of essays, titled simply "Inequality," highlight one of the most intractable challenges that has confronted Louisiana throughout its history. Racial, religious, and cultural injustice are far from unique to Louisiana. But the character and endurance of many examples of unfairness are indeed inimitable to the Bayou State.

In the first selection, which also served as something of an introduction to the symposium as well as this volume, Governor John Bel Edwards explains his reasoning behind what he describes as one of his proudest moments in service as chief executive of Louisiana. Everyone is familiar with the term "separate but equal" and its application to enforce racial segregation across the South. Fewer people are aware that the *Plessy v. Ferguson* decision, mandating the separate-but-equal standard, originated in a Louisiana case that resulted from an arrest made not thirty miles from the site of the symposium. The Plessy decision carried profound implications for social development in the South. Edwards explains that the saga of Homer Plessy, and the case that made him famous, was a prearranged, carefully staged event that included collusion with railroad authorities and, until recently, an unrealized family secret.

Despite the economic and social burdens the Supreme Court's decision in the Plessy case carried for the states of the South, and even though a later court challenged the ruling's application for public education in the landmark *Brown v. Topeka Board of Education* decision, Homer Plessey remained a convicted criminal. The governor's term of service included period-defining challenges such as an inherited massive budget deficit, once-in-a-century floods, devastating hurricanes, and a global pandemic, all of which gained him accolades for his leadership, but it was the pardon of Homer Plessy that may be remembered as his proudest moment of service. For Edwards, the pardon was not simply a moral mandate, but a privilege, and it corrected a long overdue historical injustice.

The next two selections continue the theme of racial inequality from diverse perspectives. When discussing the civil rights struggle in America, scholars and the general public alike frequently focus on political issues or legal cases. Less spoken about, but no less critical to both sides in the struggle for social justice, were religious figures and institutions. In his contribution, Keith Finley argues that no survey of the civil rights struggle is complete without measured analysis of the roles played by faith communities. Finley focuses on seminal episodes and actors involved in the struggle, including the Baton Rouge bus boycott, the positions taken by the Louisiana Baptist Convention, and the excommunication of key civil rights opponents to reveal the critical contributions made by people and institutions of faith.

Finley reminds that Louisiana is a state shaped by religion. A whopping 46 percent of Louisianians attend religious observations at least once per week; the national average is 22 percent, while another 33 percent attend once or twice a month or at least several times per year. Throughout the state's history, religion has served as the central vector through which the majority of its residents confront the world. As such, Finley maintains that the institutional mechanisms that governed Louisiana's faith communities profoundly shaped the state's response to racial change just as they remain a central force in shaping the people's identity today.

It took many moving parts to construct the vehicle of racial change in Louisiana and the wider South. In the final selection of this segment of the book, Marcus Cox maintains that in addition to politics, legal cases, and religion, it took a war to promote social justice. Cox examines the role of Black soldiers returning from service in World War II in the movement. These men had seen a new world outside the South, including places where they were not treated as second-class citizens. They had also been part of the fight against unimagined ethnic and racial bigotry in the form of Nazism and its allies, only to return to a land that ever reminded them of their inferior status.

Many of these same men refused to accept the status quo at home. Instead, they assumed a prominent role in demanding change. Whether by helping to organize boycotts, sit-ins, or other actions of peaceful resistance to segregation, veterans proved essential to the movement. Others, having learned the lessons of combat, engaged in more forthright, frequently armed action through creation of organizations such as the Deacons for Defense and Justice. Cox argues that through the dual approach of calls for peaceful change and a willingness to confront oppression aggressively, Black veterans provided much of the impetus that led the movement to ultimate success.

The second section of the book highlights enduring problems and behavior that have for generations handicapped Louisiana and made it something of a pariah nationally. Section 2, titled "Corruption, Violence, and the Limits of Reform," reveals a darker side of Louisiana history. During his presentation at the symposium, esteemed Louisiana scholar Adam Fairclough quipped that looking for examples of corruption in Louisiana "was like shooting fish in a barrel." Fairclough identifies the various rationales put forward historically to explain Louisiana's ubiquitous association with corruption before asking if the reputation is deserved. The answer, he found, is nothing less than startling.

Though corruption served as a central feature of Louisiana life since the arrival of the first French colonial government, post-Watergate demands for greater accountability beginning in the 1970s revealed the extent of the problem. Between 1976 and 2019, federal courts convicted hundreds of Louisiana officials for corrupt practices, 697 in the Eastern Judicial District alone. They included some of the most powerful men in Louisiana government. Sheriffs also shared in the disgrace. Scores of the chief parish law officers from across the state were arrested, and convicted, on charges ranging from attempted murder to sex crimes. Between 1976 and 2018, Louisiana led the nation in federal convictions for corruption.

Fairclough's research reveals that Louisiana is an exceptionally corrupt state in a nation marred by corruption. The huge number of elective offices, nonstop electioneering, and absence of any effective limits on political spending will ever provide opportunities for corruption. If convictions represent the tip of the iceberg, we can only wonder how large the submerged portion is. Fairclough warns that the torrent of recent federally funded programs in the wake of newly placed restrictions on undercover "sting" operations are certain to expand the opportunity for theft and fraud, suggesting the last chapter on corruption in Louisiana is far from written.

The recent repeal of a long-standing Louisiana law highlights another enduring challenge for the Bayou State. My own research reveals that Louisiana arguably remains the most violent state in the union. Year after year, the Uniform Crime Reports issued by the FBI substantiate that unpleasant claim. Until very recently, Louisiana, with the singular exception of Oregon, has remained the only state to permit nonunanimous jury verdicts in felony convictions. A recent frenzy of media attention, fueled by an abundance of out-of-state special-interest funding, prompted the legislature, and Louisiana voters, to abruptly call for change of the law.

Critics insisted that the nonunanimous jury-verdict law was nothing but a tool of white supremacy crafted into the organic law of the state by the racist Constitution of 1898, whose sole purpose was to secure Black convict lease laborers for Louisiana's Bourbon Democrat elite. In making this claim, opponents of the law are correct. The 1898 Constitution was irrefutably designed to enshrine white superiority. But the jury-verdict law was more than simply "Jim Crow's last stand." It served as the product of complex behind the scenes maneuvering designed to break the power of the Populist movement that, driven by the votes of desperately poor white and Black farmers, had come within an inch of recasting Louisiana's social and political identity less than two years earlier.

The 1898 constitution, and the resulting nonunanimous jury-verdict law, likewise resulted from the entreaties of desperate prosecutors and sober minded citizens in parishes where conviction of seemingly obviously guilty parties could not be secured. The willingness of many Louisiana jurors to sympathize with the accused, to allow personal proclivities to influence their vote, to embrace "safe obscurity" rather than the risk attached to voting to convict, or simply adhering to the "he had it coming" perspective, all combined to virtually neutralize the legal system in certain Bayou State judicial districts. The numbers included in the study speak for themselves. And they stand as a warning that without substantive social and cultural reform, the scourge of violence and associated criminal behavior will remain with

Louisiana for many years to come. They also remind us to consider all aspects of a critical issue. Simply attaching a convenient, and socially popular label to a historical challenge denies us the opportunity to understand what it more accurately reflects about Louisiana and the problems confronting its people and, most important, how those problems may be addressed and overcome.

The final selection in this segment of the book highlights the challenges confronting the female population of Louisiana. Author Janet Allured, acknowledges the substantive accomplishments achieved by the post–World War II women's liberation movement in Louisiana as well as that of second-wave feminism in the following decades. The use of peaceful methods of protest attracted a larger proportion of the population, which in turn accounted for much of the movement's success. Allured argues that the feminist movement included a wide diversity of types of women and organizations, all committed to eliminating the second-class status assigned to Louisiana's female population.

Despite the successes attained, Allured highlights a great deal that remains to be done if women are to attain true equality. Profound achievements, such as securing Title IX and the right to serve on juries, as well as subtle cultural changes like eliminating sexist language tropes, revealed additional necessary reforms. Some of these reforms will literally prove essential to survival. Challenging taboos about women's sexuality raised awareness about issues previously considered private. Hotly debated matters such as sex education, reproductive rights, and the access to abortion, directly impact not only the quality of life for women, but for many, their very survival.

Of greatest concern, despite decades of progressive activism, in recent years most prowomen legislation has been either delayed, rolled back, or erratically administered due to determined conservative opposition. Allured concludes that the only certain means to improve the quality of life for all Louisianians is to ensure that women have power. Women continue to constitute only a small proportion of elected officials and policy makers in the Bayou State, yet they remain at the forefront of life improving reforms. In Allured's view, the more women influence decision making, the better life will become in Louisiana.

Scientists and other researchers frequently remind us of the futility in challenging nature. A combination of human meddling over the centuries and a natural process of subsidence, or sinking, in a state that ever remains a prime target for fierce hurricanes and other natural disasters requires that we make efforts to contain, or perhaps partner, with nature to ensure that Louisiana remains a viable place to live. Section 3 of this volume focuses on two of the most intractable environmental challenges confronting Louisiana, specifically coastal erosion and flooding.

"Every thirty-eight minutes a football field size portion of Louisiana converts to open water."[1] The somber truth of the statement shocked Louisiana policy planners into confronting a growing problem of cataclysmic proportions. For generations, Louisiana permitted virtually unregulated exploitation of its fragile ecosystem by lumber companies, oil and gas exploration enterprises, and sediment-containing levee building. Until 1970, despite prior scientific understanding that river levees diminished the land-building process, it was still widely assumed that the natural process of coastal maintenance in Louisiana was somehow functional. A scientific study released that year revealed that an environmental disaster was at hand.

In his study, John Lopez traces the history of the challenge and how it has been confronted over time, before offering some projections for the future of coastal Louisiana. Lopez argues that the 2005 Hurricane Katrina disaster served as a "tipping point" that laid bare the crisis. Advanced awareness of the scope of the problem and a sudden infusion of funding made available by yet another environmental catastrophe, the *Deepwater Horizon* explosion, funded determined efforts to contain and roll back coastal erosion. Included in these efforts was Lopez's own initiative, the multiple-lines-of-defense strategy.

From dour reports of a battle already lost, of New Orleans reduced to a leveed sliver of land amid the sea in need of a stockpile of body bags for the next hurricane, came a few signs of hope. Lopez notes that the peak impact of wetland loss from the industrialization period occurred between 1958 and 1985. The period 1980 to 2006, with wetland protection in place, witnessed reduced loss. The most recent period of data, from 2006 to 2016, suggests that no net loss seems possible in the near term. The Mississippi River seems to be helping, accumulating sediment and energy that Lopez argues makes it a river primed to build land. While acknowledging the continuing severity of the problem, Lopez suggests that disciplined, integrated planning may result in a new tipping point that will preserve what remains and could produce net gains in wetlands in coastal Louisiana.

If Louisiana is defined by any natural substance, it is without question water. Louisiana remains indisputably the wettest state in the union. The ubiquitous presence of water has nourished the Bayou State's exotic agricultural bounties, including sugar cane, rice, and crawfish, just as it has attracted curious flora and fauna found few other places in North America. In many regards, water defines the character of the people of Louisiana. To highlight its relevance before an international audience, the 1984 World's Fair at New Orleans was themed simply, "Water."

The same fluid that nourishes and gives rise to the character of the state and its people also remains among its greatest challenges. Controlling floodwaters in southeastern Louisiana's Florida parishes is the focus of the final selection in section 3 of this book. Author Craig Colten examines the dilemma of flood control along several freshwater streams that traverse the Florida parishes. In addition to obvious factors contributing to regional flooding, such as frequent deluge proportions of rainfall and wind pushing lake waters into the mouths of rivers, Colten identifies human use of the land as a decisive contributor. The mass construction of homes by eager developers, public buildings, commercial structures, and infrastructure adjacent to the waterways subject regions to overflow.

Colten argues that disasters are not natural phenomena. Instead, they are the result of human decisions about where to live and work that frequently defy the demands of nature. Historically, Louisiana relied on political territories that frame the reach of jurisdiction to shape local flood risk. Individual parishes relied on local approaches to mitigating flood impacts and guiding development. But what may be good for one political designation could have devastating impacts on its neighbors. Recurring disastrous floods in the era following rapid growth in southeast Louisiana, especially ones in 1983, 2012, and 2016, revealed the limits of existing flood-control methods.

More recently, Louisiana has turned to the watershed approach for managing floodwaters. "Watershed" refers to the topographically determined territory that collects water and funnels it into a stream. Watershed management is not new. Colten notes that as early as 1908, the Louisiana State Board of Engineers recognized the utility of the approach. Yet the state assigned fiscal management to the parishes. Voters in each parish had to approve bond issues to secure funding. Even if the water management plan was coordinated at the watershed scale, political differences frequently stymied the implementation of drainage projects. And in the Florida parishes, each watershed straddles multiple political jurisdictions, including the state border with Mississippi, where the failure of a dam in Percy Quin State Park resulted in disastrous flooding in downstream Louisiana.

In a state that is home to the nation's largest drainage basin and that is downstream from virtually everything, the absence of a coordinated response to flood control bodes ill for Louisiana. Colten argues that the real challenge for watershed management of floods remains a truly unified approach for all of the physical territories within the basins. Those familiar with the historical primacy of local political control in Louisiana, not to mention interstate issues across these basins, can appreciate the challenge flood control will continue to be in the Bayou State.

Among the most shameful conditions in Louisiana, and one that ever sees the state ranked at the bottom of the national list, is its system of education.

Limits of education arguably remain one of the foremost foundational issues undergirding many of the problems discussed in this volume. In Louisiana, those who can send their children to private schools, and with no vested interest in the public school system, they frequently oppose additional taxation to adequately fund education. Low-paid teachers, decrepit infrastructure, lack of parental support, and even rampant campus violence all reflect the dismal status of public education in Louisiana.

At the dawn of the twenty-first century, a new political champion emerged in the Bayou State, a "wunderkind" named Bobby Jindal. Born the son of an Indian couple studying at Louisana State University, Jindal's energy and intelligence allowed him to rise rapidly in political circles. His ambition knew no limits as he rose from commissioner of higher education to Congress, securing the governorship in his second try. Jindal's ultimate goal remained the presidency. Upon securing overwhelming reelection as governor in 2011, Jindal began his campaign for president. Determined to present himself as the archetype fiscal conservative, Jindal repeatedly slashed funding to higher education and cut taxes to the point that a massive budget deficit developed. Surrounded by aides who seemed only concerned with reducing taxes on business and industry, one of whom required his staff to wear blue jeans and t-shirts when meeting with higher education leaders to reflect his contempt for the educated elite, Jindal's star rapidly began to fade. His campaign for president fizzled and by the time he vacated the "campaign headquarters masquerading as a governor's office," as one reporter called it, he endured an approval rating of barely 20 percent among Louisiana voters.

In the final section of the book, "Determining Who We Are," Pearson Cross explains a key, and perhaps less realized, contribution of the Jindal administration. In the beginning days of Jindal's second term, he rapidly pushed through the legislature a series of reforms to public education that Cross contends reflected either his oft-stated desire to break Louisiana's long legacy of poverty, outmigration, and stagnation, his presidential ambition, or conformance to a national conservative education reform agenda. In determining the true motive, Cross examines Louisiana's 2012 education reform as a case study for creating and passing reform legislation.

Cross argues that the "multiple-streams" theory focusing on policy, problems, and politics, as well as policy entrepreneurs and policy windows, offers the best method for understanding education reform in Louisiana. Jindal assembled a team of outsiders, largely policy experts and activists, along with some like-minded reformers in Louisiana, to change the state's system of education. Borrowing from national blueprints, and initiating the effort under the moniker "Leadership for Change," Jindal personally guided the reforms through to passage. Whether a feather in the cap of his presidential ambitions or his stated commitment to improving the quality of life in Louisiana, Cross argues that it could not have occurred without Jindal's complete commitment. The result was the passage of major legislation reshaping public education in Louisiana. Though the reforms failed to secure the presidency for Jindal, whether they improve the quality of life in Louisiana remains to be determined.

It is fitting that this section, and the book entirely, closes with the question asked by author Robert Mann. "Should I Stay or Go?" reflects the dilemma confronting scores of Louisiana residents who endure the challenges outlined in this book along with a myriad of others. In 2017 Mann wrote, "It is time to admit Louisiana is a place with no visible promise and little hope. It's time to admit that Louisiana is sick and dying."[2] He admits his words reflected despair over Louisiana government's decades long refusal to invest in education and other quality-of-life infrastructure improvements.

In 2002, Louisiana ranked forty-ninth in overall child well-being, fiftieth in economic well-being, forty-ninth in education, forty-eighth in health, and forty-ninth in family and community. The figures reflect not merely a lower quality of life, but perilous conditions for habitation. The 2022 needless deaths of several young children in Baton Rouge provoked public outrage over chronic underfunding of the state's Department of Children and Family Services. Nonetheless, Mann laments that under a state government that provides only 17 percent of the funding necessary to sustain its higher education system, little is likely to change. The result has been a "brain drain" of educated and progressive individuals from the state which aggravates the existing problems.

The core problem, according to Mann, is Louisiana's subservience to industry, particularly the oil and gas and chemical industries. Industry lobbyists and their allies in the legislature forthrightly defend the Industrial Tax Credit system that provides a virtual blank check to industry. Despite the moderate reform agenda followed by the administration of Governor John Bel Edwards, even in recent years no state has awarded business and industry more tax incentives per capita. The promises of job and economic growth as concomitants to the tax breaks have proven less than hollow. Mann argues that if low taxes on business and industry were the cure for all the state's ills, Louisiana would be in almost perfect health.

According to Mann, the state's new antiabortion law may encourage out-migration just as Louisiana's failure to address climate change will someday lead residents to face humidity so intense that outdoor work or recreation during the summer months will be dangerous or impossible. Rising seas and government inability to effectively manage flood control has contributed to an insurance crisis in Louisiana, leaving businesses and homeowners unable to obtain or afford effective coverage. In short, Mann argues that without radical adjustment of state government priorities, Louisiana could become an even poorer, depopulated, partly submerged state whose leaders, in the early twenty-first century, remained focused on loyalty to dying industries and strict adherence to backward and discriminatory social policies.

Few of the articles included in this volume offer positive appraisals of a fascinating state. Indeed, it could be argued that this compilation offers a bleak assessment of Louisiana's future. The problems confronting the state do seem daunting. This project was specifically designed to look at the Bayou State through the lens of problems encountered, past and present, to reveal the challenges and offer educated insight into how they have been, or may yet be, managed or overcome. As such, hope lies herein as well. The "Louisiana in Continuity and Change" symposium and the subsequent publication of its product reveal that scholars are actively working to inform and influence thinking regarding the future of what may be our nation's most curious and charismatic state. It is a work in progress—and Louisiana is worth it!

NOTES

1. Brady Couvillion, Holly Beck, Donald Schoolmaster, and Michelle Fischer, "Land Area Change in Coastal Louisiana, 1932–2016," United State Geological Survey, Statistics to Accompany Scientific Investigation Map, 3381 (USGA: Reston, Virginia, 2017), quoted in *American Crisis, American Shame: The National Consequences of Coastal Erosion* (Hammond, LA: Center for Southeast LA. Studies Documentary Film, 2011).

2. *New Orleans Times Picayune*, September 8, 2017.

ACKNOWLEDGMENTS

Hosting a project like the Louisiana in Continuity and Change: Challenges Past and Present Confronting the Bayou State symposium, and completing the resulting publication, involves years of planning and work. I am grateful for the institutional support provided by the administration at Southeastern Louisiana University, especially our provost, Dr. Tena Golding, and dean of the College of Arts, Humanities, and Social Sciences, Dr. Karen Fontenot. We were fortunate to have the cheerful assistance of the staff of the Center for Southeast Louisiana Studies/Archives in all phases of the project. Lauren Guillory, Ashley Tarleton, Max Hopcraft, and Brooklyn Sherrod not only assisted with all aspects of the project, but they also worked tirelessly under strict time constraints to construct the exhibit that accompanied the project.

We were fortunate to include Governor John Bel Edwards as a participant and to afford him the opportunity to speak about a most meaningful initiative he completed while serving as the leader of our state. Shauna Sanford, Lauren Leist, and Katie Justice facilitated scheduling and all planning with the governor's office. The prompt attention to detail provided by each, and their patience with my frequent last-minute calls with yet another critical need, helped navigate some complicated arrangements.

The symposium and book could not have been possible without the generous support of some sustained center/archives benefactors. Always at the front of the line when we are in need of funds to underwrite a project promoting understanding of regional history, the Young Sanders Center, Leon Ford family, and Edward Livingston Historical Association, along with Ann Reilly Jones, Clark and Barbara Forrest, and Tom and Donna Gay Anderson, provided critical support. Their generosity is most appreciated.

The University Press of Mississippi has proven no less than delightful to work with. Their organization and efficiency turned what is frequently a burden into a much more pleasurable experience. Special thanks are due to Craig Gill, Emily Bandy, Camille Hale, Katie Turner, Laura Strong, Amy Atwood, Joey Brown, Pete Halverson, Cassie Winship, and Michael Martella.

As always, the critical commentary provided by friends and colleagues proved essential to the successful completion of this book. Keith Finley offered helpful research advice and worked with all aspects of the project planning. Brian Juban provided critical commentary of sections of the manuscript, especially regarding legal and potentially controversial issues. My wife, Sarah, as always, gave freely of her time to critique significant portions of each draft. To each of them, I am most grateful.

Finally, a word of thanks to my children, Clay, Andrews, Sammie, and Sophie, whose patience as their father obsessed over yet another project is always a source of inspiration and support. Watching them grow into the thoughtful, caring individuals that they are makes me hopeful for the future of Louisiana!

Cover images courtesy of the Center for Southeast Louisiana Studies and Archives, Southeastern Louisiana University. Image 1: Piney Woods People Photo Collection, Pix #C272, T1900s. Four girls standing around deceased baby sibling. Image 2: The *Daily Star* Photo Collection, Local, Pix L#82. Lightning over Lake Pontchartrain. Image 3: La Verna R. and Edwin A. Davis Photo Collection, Picture Number 1309, August 25, 1866. Picture from *Harpers Weekly,* riot in New Orleans. Image 4: La Verna R. and Edwin A. Davis Photo Collection, Picture Number 1319, 1875. Cypress swamp, with hunter. Image 5: La Verna R. and Edwin A. Davis Photo Collection, Picture Number 1428. Decaying Belle Grove plantation house. Image 6: Morrison Photo Collection, Picture Number 311. May 18, 1933. Farmers union rally, late 1930s.

BAYOU DILEMMA

SECTION ONE

Inequality

Chapter One

1896–2022

THE PARDON OF HOMER PLESSY AND ITS IMPACT ON RACIAL JUSTICE

GOVERNOR JOHN BEL EDWARDS

One hundred twenty-six years ago, a man named Homer Plessy walked into a train station and bought a ticket. That simple act led to a Supreme Court decision that remains a dark stain on American history. Plessy's bold decision to test the limits of de facto segregation in the South made his name a byword for racial segregation in the annals of the struggle for social justice in America.

Most Americans are well versed in the implications of the *Plessy v. Ferguson* decision. Though many likewise are aware that *Plessy* was famously overturned in the landmark 1954 *Brown v. Topeka Board of Education* decision, fewer realize that despite the ruling in *Brown*, Homer Plessy's conviction remained intact. Exercising the power afforded the governor of Louisiana, in January 2022, I signed a pardon for Homer Plessy. The opportunity to correct an historical injustice not only served as a point of personal pride for me, but it also allowed for insight into a curious aspect of the story that, though central to understanding the Supreme Court's decision, remains largely unrealized. This study is about not only the pardon, but also the multigenerational impact of the *Plessy v. Ferguson* decision and the singularly curious motives of the lone justice who stood up to injustice. Let me begin by explaining the individual aspects of my background that contributed to making this issue of uniquely specific significance to me.

One of the most positive influences on my life was my father, who was known as a relatively progressive man when first elected sheriff in 1968. Under my father's supervision, a new rule allowed, for the first time in Tangipahoa Parish history, an African American deputy to investigate a crime that happened to a white person or a white business. As a child, I remained completely unaware of the significance of the new rule. It represented an unprecedented shift in procedure that for the time proved profound both substantively and politically. There have actually been four consecutive generations of sheriffs in my family, going back to my great grandfather and extending currently to my brother, Daniel. My great-grandfather became sheriff in 1899. He secured appointment from Governor Murphy James Foster, quite frankly, because nobody wanted to serve. It was not a great job to have if a person wanted any life expectancy at all in what was then known as "Bloody Tangipahoa." At the time of his appointment, the parish tottered on the brink of judicial and political chaos amid some of the highest rural homicide rates recorded in American history. Dr. Samuel Hyde reveals the extent of the regional turbulence in his book *Pistols and Politics*.[1]

When I got out of the army and went to law school, I knew I was ready to run for office. I wanted to carry on the tradition of public service in my family. But the best job was already taken by my brother, who was already serving as sheriff. Instead, I decided to run for the second-best job, and I have had it now for seven years. It has been my pleasure to serve as governor. While we have certainly come a long way, there is still so much that we have to overcome. All one has to do is look at the history of my home region, Louisiana's Florida parishes.

Southeastern Louisiana, where the Florida parishes are located, was not immune to the social and political turbulence that characterized many regions of the nation in the aftermath of World War I. In Washington Parish, 1919 witnessed tremendous labor unrest among Black workers at the Great Southern Lumber Company in Bogalusa, which operated as the world's largest sawmill at the time. The Bogalusa trouble climaxed later that year when "special deputies," hired by the mill management, shot and killed four white union men who sought to protect one Black union organizer. The killings effectively crushed the strike and exacerbated racial suspicions among the laborers. Racial relations suffered further in the region following the 1935 lynching of Jerome Wilson, who was convicted of killing a white deputy despite an unfair, rushed trial. The state Supreme Court ordered a new trial, but it never occurred. Prior to the trial date, a mob broke into the jail and killed him. That horrific crime offers a great segue into the Plessy case and the pardon. Race and miscegenation played a huge role in the Supreme Court case of *Plessy v. Ferguson*, which in turn inspired the Louisiana 1898 Constitutional Convention and its pursuit

Figure 1.1. Justice John Harlan. Though from a former slaveholding family in Kentucky, Harlan issued a memorable dissent in the landmark *Plessy v. Ferguson* decision. (Public Domain, Wikipedia)

of white supremacy. This cycle of events set the stage for racial strife all over the state of Louisiana and extended to the entire country.[2]

Though I have worn many hats over the years, I am by profession a lawyer. Most realize that attorneys are required to know a lot about case history, especially concerning precedent-setting cases that contribute to defining our national identity. The *Plessy v. Ferguson* case is one that everyone should know. And the details surrounding the case are important for proper understanding of the decision. The relevant law secured passage by the Louisiana legislature in 1890. A Democrat and former prewar Whig named Francis T. Nichols served as governor. He had been an officer in the Confederate army during the Civil War. The era of Reconstruction concluded more than a decade earlier, and both the legislature and the governor's office were back in the hands of the Democrats. With the Republican Party effectively neutralized in the state, the legislature passed the 1890 Separation Act, which required all railway companies carrying passengers in their coaches in the state to provide equal but separate accommodations for them. It added that no person or persons shall be permitted to occupy seats in coaches other than the ones assigned to them on account of the race to which they belonged. The act required the conductors and the railroad employees to enforce the law. If they told someone to move, and the person refused, they could have that person arrested, and, if convicted, the person could receive a twenty-five-dollar fine and spend twenty days in jail.

The Citizens Committee, a civil rights organization in New Orleans, was looking for an opportunity to test recently enacted racial segregation laws, but in particular, the Separate Car Act. The leader of the Citizens Committee was Louis A. Martinet, a prominent French Creole figure in New Orleans and the editor of the *New Orleans Crusader*. Among their many various members, the Citizens Committee also included a white lawyer, Albion W. Tourgée, who absolutely believed in the equality of races. The first thing they did was try to figure out who would be positioned best to challenge the law. Ultimately, they recruited Homer Plessy, a shoe repairman from New Orleans. He was seven-eighths white and one-eighth Black. But under the law, he was Black even though he appeared white. This was a purposeful decision. They wanted to be able to demonstrate just how arbitrarily the law could be applied.

On June 7, 1892, Homer Plessy bought a first-class passage from the East Louisiana Railroad Company to travel from New Orleans to Covington, Louisiana, a short trip across Lake Pontchartrain. The origin and destination of Plessy's brief trip were specifically selected to conform to the plan. The courts had already ruled that such statutes could not govern railroads in the manner they operated interstate travel. An intrastate trip proved necessary to challenge the law. Plessy refused to sit in the "colored car." The conductor told him to move, and he again refused. The conductor accordingly had him arrested. Now, one might ask if he looked white, why did the conductor proceed with the arrest? Because, unbeknownst to most, the railroad was in on it too. The law required them to buy and maintain more railroad cars than were necessary for them to transport their passengers. It was an unwelcome, unnecessary expense that understandably made the railroad an opponent of the law as well. The whole performance was staged, but it achieved the desired result. Plessy was arrested, and the Citizens Committee was free to challenge the law. The case went to Division A of the criminal court in New Orleans, and Judge John Ferguson found that the law represented a valid exercise of regulation of intrastate railroads. He also found Plessy guilty, and the Louisiana Supreme Court affirmed, but granted Plessy a writ of error, effectively making Plessy the petitioner and the judge, John Ferguson, the respondent. The ruling led to the title of the case, *Plessy v. Ferguson*, which was heard and decided in 1896. The holding proved relatively straightforward. The court claimed that the laws did not violate the equal protection clause of the Fourteenth Amendment, where accommodations are separate and equal, and that the Fourteenth Amendment protects and addresses political and legal equality, not social equality. To the majority of the court, where one sat on the train was a matter of social implications—not one's legal rights, civil rights, or political rights.

The lone dissenter proved to be Justice John Marshall Harlan of Kentucky, who—as is well documented—once enslaved people of color and, unfortunately, initially opposed emancipation. His views of race, equality, and civil rights, however, did change, and his dissent showcased the reasons why *Plessy v. Ferguson* was incorrectly decided, accurately predicted the damage it would do to our country, and inspired *Brown v. Board of Education* six decades later. Further, Justice Harlan's dissent powerfully demonstrates that justice and decency dictate the absolute necessity of the posthumous pardon so that the last chapter in this saga exonerates Homer Plessy and celebrates his cause as right and just. In his dissent, Justice Harlan predicted that in time *Plessy* would prove every bit as "pernicious" as *Dred Scott*—the 1857 Supreme Court case universally condemned as the worst decision ever by that court, in that it held that the US Constitution did not extend citizenship to people of African descent—free or enslaved. A war was soon fought over the issue, and the Thirteenth and Fourteenth Amendments were added to the Constitution to affect change. "Pernicious" is not a word I commonly use. I concede that Justice Harlan's command of the English language was superior to mine. The word perfectly fits: "pernicious" means evil, fatal, ruinous, wicked. I think I will use the word a few more times.

Some passages from Justice Harlan's eloquent and courageous dissent reflect his reasoning:

> But in view of the Constitution, in the eye of the law, there is in this country no superior, dominant, ruling class of citizens. There is no caste here. Our Constitution is color-blind and neither knows nor tolerates classes among citizens. In respect of civil rights, all citizens are equal before the law ... It is therefore to be regretted that this high tribunal, the final expositor of the fundamental law of the land, has reached the conclusion that it is competent for a State to regulate the enjoyment by citizens of their civil rights solely upon the basis of race.
>
> The destinies of the two races, in this country, are indissolubly linked together, and the interests of both require that the common government

of all shall not permit the seeds of race hate to be planted under the sanction of law. What can more certainly arouse race hate, what more certainly create and perpetuate a feeling of distrust between these races, than state enactments, which, in fact, proceed on the ground that colored citizens are so inferior and degraded that they cannot be allowed to sit in public coaches occupied by white citizens? That, as all will admit, is the real meaning of such legislation as was enacted in Louisiana.

Harlan was right. The Supreme Court majority embraced racism and white supremacy as if the Thirteenth and Fourteenth Amendments to the US Constitution were mere ornaments without real meaning. Very sadly, it is not lost on me that one of the seven associate justices who joined in the majority opinion was Louisiana's own—Justice Edward Douglas White.[3]

The cause of the pardon, unfortunately, is not limited to righting a historical wrong. The pernicious effects of *Plessy* linger still. In terms of race relations, equality, and justice, we are not where we should be—and where we would have been—had Plessy been correctly decided. The first six decades of the twentieth century should have been filled with infinitely more promise and progress in race relations and would have been had slavery given way to equality and freedom. Instead, the Plessy majority ignored the plain meaning and purpose of the Thirteenth and Fourteenth Amendments and wrongly enshrined segregation into the law for the explicit purpose of declaring and promoting white supremacy—as immoral and factually erroneous as that was and is to this very day. The fictitious notion of "separate but equal" remained with us until the Supreme Court revisited the issue in 1954 in the context of public education and implicitly overruled *Plessy*. And in Montgomery, Alabama, in 1955, Rosa Parks—in another very similar courageous act of protest—refused to leave a bus seat reserved for white passengers. This was sixty-three years *after* Homer Plessy did the same thing right here in Louisiana on a train bound from New Orleans to Covington. Six decades later, not much had changed—because the *Plessy* majority said it did not have to change.

Plessy and its progeny also emboldened state legislatures and constitutional conventions to expressly promote white supremacy in a multitude of truly pernicious ways, including the 1898 Louisiana Constitutional Convention, which sought, among other things, to negate the impact of Black jurors by allowing criminal convictions with just nine of twelve jurors finding the defendant guilty. This wrong remained in force until 2018 by the adoption of a constitutional amendment requiring unanimous juries for criminal convictions in Louisiana. That the convention delegates were motivated by their zealous desire to perpetuate white supremacy is not debatable. Their writings and speech were memorialized in the official records. After *Plessy*, they had no reason to even pretend otherwise. Pernicious![4]

Before I add just a bit more about the pardon, I want to add a little more color to it. The pardon was required because after the Supreme Court decision, Plessy returned to Division A of the criminal court of Orleans Parish. He pled guilty on January 11, 1897, and he was fined twenty-five dollars. He died in 1925, still convicted of that crime. More than 181 years later, in 2006, the Louisiana legislature passed a bill authored by State Senator Edmund Murray of New Orleans. It is called the Avery Alexander Act, and it allows for pardons for people convicted of violating a state law, or municipal ordinances, whose purpose was to maintain or enforce racial separation or discrimination. In 2022, descendants of Homer Plessy applied for a pardon. They were joined in that effort by Phoebe Ferguson and John Howard Ferguson, descendants of Judge Ferguson, as well as descendants of Justice Harlan. That pardon application came to me, and I was able to convene a ceremony on January 5, 2022, exactly 125 years after the conviction and 97 years after Plessy's death. The ceremony was held at the New Orleans Center for Creative Arts, which occupies the very spot of ground where the train station was located, where he bought the ticket, got on the train, and was arrested. That was one of the best days that I have enjoyed in service as governor. I know that historically, it is not much more than a footnote because of the enormous importance of the case, but it carried profound personal meaning for me.

Since then, I have read even more about the case. I found some interesting things that I think illuminate why Justice Harlan acted as he did. John Marshall Harlan secured appointment to the Supreme Court by President Rutherford B. Hayes. He served from 1877 to 1911, when he died at the age of seventy-eight. In his thirty-four years of service, he came to be known as one of the best associate justices in the annals of the Supreme Court. He remained ahead of his time, which was particularly true in civil rights cases. He was actually named after perhaps the best chief justice of all time—John Marshall, who wrote the *Marbury v. Madison* decision, which established judicial review by the Supreme Court over congressional and legislative acts enacted by the states to determine whether they were constitutional. Until Marshall penned that decision, nobody really knew how the branches of government would operate in that regard and what the role of the federal government and the judiciary would be relative to the states. John Marshall Harlan was not an obvious choice to dissent in the Plessy case. He was from Danville, Kentucky, and he came from a slave-holding family. He actually opposed the Emancipation Proclamation. He believed in slavery with few limitations and restrictions. He thought emancipation was a matter for the states, not the federal government. And even though he fought as a colonel in the Union army, he was very upset by the Emancipation Proclamation. But first and foremost, he had a strong desire to preserve the Union. And in this regard, he was like his hero, another famous Kentuckian, Henry Clay. He shared other characteristics with Clay, including being a party switcher. He began his political career as a Whig. Then he became an opposition party member in the Constitutional Union Party before becoming a Unionist, and finally a Republican. Now, why did this man come to be the one person on the Supreme Court who wrote the dissent? Though we may never know that for sure; perhaps, as a Supreme Court justice, it was his fidelity to the law.

But the evidence suggests there may be another reason, specifically related to his family. Within Harlan's family, there was an individual named Robert James Harlan, who was sixteen years older than John and was a light skinned Black man. He was a fixture in John's childhood and home. John's father, James, made sure that Robert was educated. He also gave him his name, and when Robert James Harlan was thirty-two, he gave him his emancipation. I have no doubt that Robert was John's half-brother. And I think this had a profound impact on John Marshall Harlan. Kate Dillingham, his great-great granddaughter, and I had a long conversation after the New Orleans ceremony, and I asked, "How do you account for what happened?" And she replied, "It's very simple." By way of explanation, she sent me the 2021 book *The Great Dissenter: The Story of John Marshall Harlan, America's Judicial Hero* by Peter S. Canellos.[5] It provides moving detail on the impact his relationship with Robert had on his brother John. It was a relationship that undoubtedly affected Justice Harlan's thinking many years later.

In 1963, Avery Alexander staged a sit-in protest at the segregated cafeteria in the basement of the New Orleans City Hall. He said he would sit there until he was either served or arrested. His determination provoked the authorities, leading to his immediate arrest. Once detained, the arresting officers violently dragged him down the stairs. Every time they proceeded down one more step, his head would hit the stairs. Alexander is the man for whom the pardon act is named. He was an ordained Baptist preacher in New Orleans, a civil rights leader, and a state representative from 1975 to 1999. Homer Plessy's pardon was the first under the new law. There are many people who have been arrested and convicted for these crimes, but the vast majority view their conviction as a badge of honor, and they do not want to pursue a pardon. The family of Homer Plessy did, and I was very happy to be able to be a part of it.

But this is not ancient history, and it is not all history. We still have a long way to go. Until we passed a constitutional amendment in 2018, nonunanimous juries were still on the books in Louisiana. The Supreme Court had taken a case and said all those convictions were wrong, but it did not apply the decision retroactively. *Plessy v. Ferguson* did not single-handily cause white supremacy, but it certainly helped it fester as long as it did, and has. Again, the word "pernicious" fits. And remember John Marshall Harlan said it would come one day to be regarded as every bit as pernicious as Dred Scott itself. I am beyond grateful that I had a small part in ensuring that Homer Plessy's legacy will be defined by the rightness of his convictions and undefiled by an unjust criminal conviction.

NOTES

1. Samuel C. Hyde Jr., *Pistols and Politics: Feuds, Factions, and the Struggle for Order in Louisiana's Florida Parishes, 1810–1935* (Baton Rouge: Louisiana State University Press, 2018).

2. New Orleans *Picayune*, November 22, 23, 25, 1919; Hyde, *Pistols and Politics*, 337–38; Amy Quick, "The History of Bogalusa: The Magic City of Louisiana," *Louisiana Historical Quarterly* 29 (1946): 133–36; Adam Fairclough, *Race and Democracy: The Civil Rights Struggle in Louisiana, 1915–1972* (Athens: University of Georgia Press, 1995), 26–29; *New Orleans Item*, January 11, 1935.

3. Molly Townes O'Brien, "Justice John Marshall Harlan as Prophet: The Plessy Dissenter's Color Blind Constitution," *William and Mary Bill of Rights Journal* 6, no. 3 (1998): 753–75; Charles Thompson, "*Plessy vs. Ferguson*: Harlan's Great Dissent," *Kentucky Humanities* 1 (1996): 28–42.

4. "Message of E. B. Kruttschnitt, President of the Convention," *Constitution of the State of Louisiana Adopted in Convention at the City of New Orleans, May 12, 1898* (New Orleans: Convention Publisher, 1898) 9–10; Hyde, *Pistols and Politics*, 264–65.

5. Peter S. Canellos, *The Great Dissenter: The Story of John Marshall Harlan, America's Judicial Hero* (New York: Simon & Schuster, 2021).

Chapter Two

DEFENDERS OF TRADITION, CHAMPIONS OF REFORM

LOUISIANA'S FAITH COMMUNITIES CONFRONT CIVIL RIGHTS CHANGE

KEITH M. FINLEY

An analysis of long-term trends regarding the relationship between the American people and religion reveals the steady erosion of popular identification with organized faith communities. Although a sizable percentage of Americans believe in "God," far fewer attend religious observations, and as the twenty-first century progresses, even belief in a higher power erodes. Waves of church abuse scandals and the spread of a homogenizing secular culture made possible by social media figure prominently in the diminished fidelity to once-revered religious institutions. Despite this trend, there are communities, states, and regions where this decline is less evident. Not surprising, more conservative locations in America, such as the South, boast higher church attendance numbers than those outside of the so-called Bible Belt. Louisiana, like its southern neighbors, is no different. In the Pelican State, 46 percent of Louisiana adults attend religious observations at least once per week (22 percent is the national average), and another 33 percent attend once or twice a month or at least a few times per year. Taken together, nearly 80 percent of the state's adult population retains some connection to organized religion, a point that underscores the continued relevance of "faith communities" in the lives of the overwhelming majority of Louisiana citizens.[1] Faith matters in Louisiana. It always has. Any effort to understand Louisiana's history that does not account for the centrality of faith fails to engage one of the most important prisms through which people of the state

Figure 2.1. T. J. Jemison, prominent civil rights organizer and leader of the 1953 Baton Rouge bus boycott. (Courtesy of the Center for Southeast Louisiana Studies)

have viewed the world around them. In the tumultuous decades of the 1950s and 1960s, as Louisiana and the nation confronted efforts to dismantle Jim Crow segregation, churches on both sides of the racial divide sprang into action. Louisiana's major denominations confronted the question of race in an eclectic pattern dictated by the institutional apparatus that governed the state's respective faith communities. How they responded profoundly shaped the contours of the civil rights fight in Louisiana.

Historians of the civil rights movement have long recognized the importance of faith in driving the push for racial change. Indeed, the most well-known figures of the twentieth-century civil rights struggle worked within the preexisting institutional structures provided by their local churches when organizing and maintaining protest efforts. It is not coincidental that when Dr. Martin Luther King Jr. forged a regional coalition for change to keep alive the spirit of community exhibited during the famous 1956 Montgomery bus boycott, he selected the name "Southern Christian Leadership Conference." The religious impetus behind the drive to end Jim Crow was everywhere apparent and has been the subject of an avalanche of scholarship.[2] Academic interest in white resistance as expressed within segregated faith communities has likewise grown in recent years, although the depth of attention given to the oppressors in the fight continues to lag. Several recent studies, including the work of Elaine Lechtreck, explore the efforts of white southern ministers who supported racial change.[3] History proves, however, that such courageous voices were few, far between, and accomplished little in terms of impacting the situation on the ground. Others analyze how specific faith communities in either individual states or the South in general confronted the drive for racial change. In the literature devoted to the response of white religious communities to integration emerges the preponderant presence of so-called southern moderates, who preferred to sit on the sidelines as the battle over Jim Crow was fought, often violently, in their backyards. It is this group that earned the scorn of Dr. King for their failure to stand against injustice.[4] Missing in most studies that tackle the issue of faith and segregation is a thorough treatment of how the institutional apparatus that governed the actions of local congregations shaped area responses to civil rights issues. Louisianans confronted the end of Jim Crow as they did all of the crises in their lives through a faith window. This study reveals how the state's faith communities served as forces for positive social change, while equally highlighting how they sometimes served as a hindrance to reform utilizing a case study approach that captures the lived experience of the majority of adult Louisianans who identified as "Christian" in the state. Central to understanding how faith communities worked then, as today, is awareness of the importance of institutional structures. The Catholic Church, for example, is hierarchal in nature. Action on the diocesan level is often mitigated by the dictates of the larger system. Despite the assertions of scholars, such Justin Poché, who stress the need for Catholic histories that privilege the perspective of people in the pews, the story of the church's final triumph over segregation is best understood utilizing a top-down approach.[5] In contrast, the state's Baptist denominations, both Black and white, embraced a decentralized governing apparatus. Baptist governing conventions offered very broad guidelines and mandates but allowed local institutions to tackle the problems unique to their congregations in their own fashion. This decentralization, in turn, accounted for much of the controversy in this period as local ministers took it upon themselves to advance conflicting aims to either promote change or buttress the status quo.

In 1949, thirty-year-old Reverend Theodore Judson T. J. Jemison left his Selma, Alabama, home to assume pastorship of the Mount Zion First Baptist Church in Baton Rouge, Louisiana. There he would be at the epicenter of the 1953 Baton Rouge bus boycott, which served as the model for Dr. Martin Luther King's more famous Montgomery bus boycott several years later. Jemison was not just the pastor of a church; he was a crusader for the African American community that formed the basis of his congregation. If trouble threatened his people, Reverend Jemison was there. Stories abound of Jemison's presence in the community, fighting to uplift his congregants and improve the quality of life for everyone in the surrounding area. He used his pulpit to inspire and the collection plate as a tool to spread his message.[6] Mount Zion fell under the auspices of the National Baptist Convention (NBC), which represented the country's African American practitioners of the faith. The constitution of the NBC narrowly defined its interests as "independent and sovereign in its sphere, but does not claim and will never attempt to exercise any authority over any other Baptist body, whether church, association or convention."[7] On the national level, the organization broadly committed itself to furthering the fight for racial justice. The Women's Auxiliary gathering at the 1953 NBC, for example, noted "Negroes must learn that people who do not help themselves are not worth helping. Negroes can and must do more to help themselves in the causes of Christian education and general social welfare."[8] It was in the context of a national faith governing body committed to local autonomy and African American advancement that Reverend Jemison operated. When a critical issue central to his community arose, Jemison responded with the confidence of someone comfortable exercising power and one who did not need to wait for orders from above to take action.

For many poor African Americans in Reverend Jemison's congregation, the Baton Rouge Bus Company (BRBC) was the only reliable source of transportation to and from their jobs and to complete routine tasks. Like all southern bus companies in the early 1950s, the one in Baton Rouge maintained a segregated seating arrangement in which the first ten seats on the bus were reserved for whites and the back ten to twelve for Blacks. Owing to the disproportionate number of Black riders on the bus, many African Americas, despite paying their fare, were forced to stand due to a lack of sufficient Black seating. When the BRBC chose to raise its fare from ten to fifteen cents while offering no additional seating for Black riders by way of City Council Ordinance 213 in February 1953, discontent boiled over.[9] In an interview, Reverend Jemison described watching bus after bus pass on East Boulevard outside of his Mount Zion Church crowded with Black riders, some of whom were forced to stand despite lots of empty Jim Crow seats in the front. Furthermore, the predominantly Black population in the south Baton Rouge community where those busses operated suggested that few white riders would be picked up that or any day. Indeed, the seats at the front of the bus in Jemison's neighborhood usually remained vacant, while Black riders scrambled for the few seats allotted to them in the back. The grave injustice, according to Jemison, was not the system of segregation per se (although he detested it too), but the increased fare brought about without a provision for additional seating. According to the minister, "I thought it was terrible that they [African Americans] could work all day for white folks and couldn't sit down on a bus."[10] Jemison demanded the city council address the injustice. With little fanfare, the council, in March 1953, handed Jemison Ordinance 222, which passed without dissent. The ordinance called for Blacks to fill seats from the back to the front and whites from the front to the back on a first-come, first-served basis. Thrilled with the newly secured right, Jemison utilized his church apparatus to get the word out to the community regarding the council's decision. Copies of the ordinance were widely distributed, while Black radio programs further spread the good news. For a brief period, a calm settled over the city as Black riders took advantage of the new seating opportunities available to them. It was only a matter of time, however, before the defenders of Jim Crow struck back.[11]

    Each passing day brought with it the possibility of an incident as word spread that Baton Rouge buses were running in contravention to long-held customs associated with segregated seating on public transportation systems. As African American riders inched toward the front seats of buses formerly reserved for whites, all it took was for one bus operator in the all-white driver fleet to raise a commotion for an unsavory incident to emerge. On June 13, 1953, that incident unfolded as Martha White, an African American woman, refused to abandon her seat at the front of the bus at the request of the white driver. In turn, the driver halted the bus and vowed not to move until White relinquished her place. Seemingly unaware of the newly approved city ordinance, police descended on the scene and threatened to arrest White for violating the BRBC's seating requirements, which did not officially change despite City Council Ordinance 222. In a sign of solidarity with White, others on the bus spoke up, demanding that they, too, be arrested if White was detained. At this point, Reverend Jemison drove by in his new black Buick Road Master. He slammed on the brakes and jumped out to ascertain the cause of the commotion. As the reverend saw it, this was his community, and the people involved in the incident were members of his congregation. Once he established the cause of the furor, he boarded the bus and told White and the other passengers to remain where they were. Naturally, law enforcement turned on Jemison, inquiring who he was and why he had gotten involved. Jemison alerted the officers of the recently approved city ordinance, which superseded the old bus custom being enforced by the cops. Jemison went on to note that, although he was not a passenger on the bus, the people onboard it were his congregants and, therefore, his responsibility. One of the officers radioed back to the police station that he intended to arrest Jemison for his part in obstructing the investigation, which prompted a quick order not to bring the pastor to the command center. Law enforcement leaders knew Jemison and therefore understood that his detainment would send shock waves through the city's Black community, touching off far more trouble than his arrest could possibly be worth. With justice, the law, and his reputation on his side, Jemison exhibited no fear as he stood up to the police and the white driver. As indecision and recrimination rang out around the stalled bus, the manager of the bus company, Flynn Cauthern, arrived on the scene, was apprised by Jemison of Ordinance 222, and ordered the driver to continue his route. The white driver refused the command, prompting Cauthern to suspend him for not doing his job.[12] Such incidents were common as the citizens of Baton Rouge grappled with the legal ramifications of the city council's decision. Jemison recalled another incident in which a different city driver, similarly unaware of city ordinances, threatened to remove a group of Black women seated at the front of the bus. When Jemison hopped onboard and occupied a seat in the white section, the driver took the bus to the local police station and demanded they sort out the situation exacerbated by the preacher's impromptu sit-in. Law enforcement officials were eager to defuse the situation without further incident. Again, Jemison stood down law enforcement threats, and again, a city ordinance shielded him from imprisonment despite the belief in some quarters that the preacher was out of line. If nothing else, his bold actions unabashedly challenged white rule in the city. As word spread of Jemison's nascent bus protest, white agitation grew.[13]

Drivers for the BRBC responded to what they considered the shoddy treatment of one of their own in the Martha White episode by organizing a strike, bringing the city's busses to a standstill from June 15 through June 19, 1953. Picketers, however, were not just concerned with the mistreatment of one driver; they quickly turned the discussion into a racial matter and stressed the need for reinstatement of Jim Crow seating arrangements to protect white riders. At the same time, Reverend Jemison and local African American leaders sought a mechanism whereby they could assist their community members in getting to work or wherever else they needed to go with their main mode of transportation—the buses—temporarily grounded. A "free-car-lift" program that served as the foundation of the later boycott began taking shape, organized primarily through local church communities. With the bus company losing thousands of dollars while stranding countless daily riders, the desire for a resolution mounted. Many forces drove the discussion. Safeguarding white supremacy was foremost in the minds of drivers as their strike was tied exclusively to maintaining the former race-based seating arrangement. Bus company leaders, however, saw the business hemorrhaging money and sought a quick resolution to the matter regardless of the implications for Jim Crow. City council leaders considered the strike a threat to future electoral success and therefore sought any resolution that did not cast them in a negative light. They, too, wanted a rapid resolution to the conflict that left them free from opprobrium. Louisiana Attorney General Fred S. LeBlanc, after allegedly considering evidence from all sides, moved to invalidate the objectionable ordinance and return matters to their prior position in which the bus company held responsibility for seating determinations. Ostensibly, Attorney General LeBlanc argued that City Ordinance 222 ran counter to state segregation statutes requiring racially separated facilities and was therefore invalid. With a favorable ruling sewed up on June 18, expectations for a normal morning on the June 19 commute took hold. Most of the white leaders associated with the affair, including city mayor-president Jesse Webb Jr., declared victory and apologized for the lapse in judgment surrounding Ordinance 222 as well as for the resulting chaos.[14]

On the evening of June 18, as white city leaders celebrated the end of the driver strike, Reverend Jemison, acting as president of the United Defense League (UDL), an African American civic organization in Baton Rouge, urged Black residents to stay off of the busses starting immediately until the demands of the community concerning seating issues were addressed. The African American boycott began on June 19, the same day striking workers resumed their routes. The boycott represented the continuation of the free-car-lift program Jemison and others organized when the bus drivers went on strike. People needed to get to work. With the strike ended and a carpool system already in place, Reverend Jemison and the UDL sought to continue the fight until they received some measure of justice from city authorities. Using radio, newspapers, and leaflets to get the word out to area Blacks not to take the city buses, the UDL worked within the city's faith communities, drafting plans, organizing rides, and urging residents to join and sustain the boycott. Likewise, daily meetings were held before a standing-room-only crowd in Jemison's church with the pastor "speaking" not "preaching" to those in attendance, "letting them know the importance of standing together in this boycott."[15] One of Jemison's congregants recalled that her pastor "went about getting the community together behind the movement. It was a twenty-four hour a day job, seven days a week and nobody relented."[16] Jemison, ever careful to avoid transgressing the law, ensured his "fair lift" program functioned smoothly and safely. Designated ride pick-up locations were established and operated between the hours of 5:00 a.m. and midnight. At its peak, an estimated 125 vehicles were pressed into service to see the protest through. To keep the rides going, money was needed for fuel and sundry repairs. Jemison worked his contacts for assistance, urging local Black-owned gas stations to sell their product at wholesale prices to protestors while schooling his community on the dynamics of the situation. To ride-share drivers, he urged scrupulous adherence to all traffic laws.[17] Drivers were warned not to accept any payment for their proffered services, lest local law enforcement dub the effort an illegal taxi ring. Likewise, organizers requested local bar owners, who served the Black community, to cease operations during the boycott to further ensure that no incidents would occur that would alter the direction of the well-functioning protest. Jemison did not want any peripheral issues derailing his efforts. Throughout, he expressed admiration for the community, and on one occasion, he observed that the city's Black citizens "were together as they have never have been before."[18]

Mayor-President Webb, the city council, and Baton Rouge civic leaders wanted the situation resolved as soon as possible, especially following the economic fallout from the earlier driver strike. At a June 24 special session, the city council approved an agreement that satisfied the white leaders present and that they hoped would prove amenable to the Black community. The resulting Ordinance 251 effectively doubled the number of seats available to Black riders, leaving the first two side-facing seats immediately adjacent to the driver for whites, setting aside the large back seat exclusively for Black riders, and opening the remainder of the seats on a first come, first served, basis.[19] The council proposal had its detractors in the Black community. Many, including prominent leaders of the UDL, such as Johnnie Jones and his law partner, Bruce Bell, considered the ordinance too great a concession and a retrogression considering that at one point the very same Council had granted the Black community access to all seats on the bus. Likewise, protestors lamented what they considered the unnecessary concessions to racist white bus drivers, who spearheaded the efforts to dismantle the more favorable Ordinance 222. Reverend Jemison, however, was prepared to pull the plug on the protest. Before a massive crowd approaching eight thousand at Memorial Stadium on June 25, Jemison announced the end of the rideshare program. The often-angry response of the crowd, which demanded a continuation of the fight against the city, highlighted that not everyone was happy with Jemison's decision. More certainly could have been achieved. Although he led the fight, Jemison did not seek to topple the white power structure in the city. He merely wanted African Americans to get a seat at the table that they paid for, nothing more. Once that objective was met, he scrapped the protest effort. Jemison was certainly no fan of segregation; however, he believed the time was not right for an aggressive salvo against Jim Crow. Johnnie Jones, who provided legal counsel for the boycott, remembered Jemison wanting to keep litigation tied to the Baton Rouge boycott out of federal courts, therefore ensuring that the matter would be adjudicated before a prejudiced Louisiana judge. As Jones recalled, Jemison claimed, "We want to let the white people know we still believe that they want to do right. And we still trust them. . . . They are a Christian people. And since they are all Christian people, Christians want to do right."[20] Time, of course, proved Jemison wrong in that white authority, including many of the leaders of its faith communities, refused to approach the notion of equality with anything other than defiance. Jemison's faith galvanized his leadership during the boycott, just as it led him to assume the best from his adversaries, even when circumstances on the ground indicated his trust would be abused. Why did Jemison relinquish the boycott on the threshold of success? His faith guided him there, underscoring a critical lesson in the importance of viewing Louisiana history through the religious lens that so often shaped it.

Despite the criticism Jemison received at the time, his legacy as a pioneering figure in the struggle for racial justice in America lives on. He directly influenced and counseled young Martin Luther King Jr. as he prepared his own boycott of the segregated bus system in Montgomery, Alabama. The template established by Jemison became the blueprint for one of the most prominent episodes in the civil rights struggle in the midtwentieth century. Following Montgomery, King coordinated the formation of the Southern Christian Leadership Conference and turned to Reverend Jemison to become one of its founding members. As Reverend Jemison remembered it, "Dr. King came to Baton Rouge and got the pattern. See, ours was the first and of course, you leave the pattern of what you do. And so Montgomery patterned itself right after us."[21] Separating faith communities from civil rights activism is an impossible task as they are inherently linked. Reverend Jemison was able to act unilaterally and for the good of his congregation without larger concerns that a state or national church apparatus would impede his actions. He did what he thought was right when the situation arose. Nationally, the National Baptist Convention preached justice and sought equality. Jemison moved freely within these strictures to accomplish his objective. His congregation wanted opportunity, and

Jemison, as a vehicle of the church community, used his influence to stir his followers and work with local secular leaders to get things done. In this instance, the decentralized autonomy of the Baptist Church, coupled with an activist congregation, inspired the remarkable sequence of events and positive change that took place that summer in Baton Rouge.

The Southern Baptist Convention (SBC) operated in a similar fashion to the National Baptist Convention in that it was intensely decentralized; however, unlike many Black Baptist congregations, the white ones that comprised the SBC typically were not activists for social change, but rather preservers of the status quo. The Louisiana Baptist Convention (LBC) served as the state contingent of the SBC and represented Louisiana's largest Protestant denomination after midcentury. As such, it tacitly endorsed segregation and barred Black church membership. In grand design, the LBC, like the SBC, had no authority to impose policy on its members and their churches. The national convention's annual meeting of messengers elected by church members voted to adopt resolutions and reports made by agencies and committees; however, these reports were not binding. Before the landmark *Brown v. Board* case, the LBC's weekly newspaper, the *Baptist Message*, ignored race relations. However, in June 1954, the SBC, at its annual gathering, received a report from its Christian Life Commission (CLC) titled, "Don't Blame the Supreme Court" that urged members to recognize the need for racial change, especially considering the global prominence of the United States following WWII. The commission further stressed the deleterious consequences of racial segregation on Baptist overseas missionary endeavors in Asia and Africa. Summarizing its perspective, the CLC noted, "Every man is embraced in the love of God; every man has value in the sight of God; and every man is included in the plan of God. The attitude and practice of every individual in this whole matter of race relationships should be appraised in the light of these truths." Wrapping up this section of the commission's report, which fell between discussions of abstinence from alcohol and juvenile delinquency, came the shocking request: "It is time for Baptists and the other citizens of our country to restore to our 13,000,000 Negro people their rights and privileges as guaranteed to them by our constitution."[22] In succeeding years, the Southern Baptist Convention featured additional efforts from its CLC to elevate the race issue to its constituent churches, but with zero authority to force compliance—local opinion ruled.[23] Most commission pronouncements centered on the inevitability of change, the negative impact segregationists had on the church's missionary activities, and the need to approach the whole issue with Christian charity rather than hate. The commission certainly did not directly call for racial justice and the end of segregation, but it definitely advocated for moderation. Owing to the decentralized nature of the organization, local communities faced these issues on their own terms.

Finley Tinnin, sixty-six-year-old segregationist editor of the *Baptist Message*, labeled both the SBC's actions and the *Brown* verdict "ill advised" before noting that there were few instances in Louisiana where African Americans faced serious discrimination. By patterning his remarks in such a manner, he followed the standard rhetoric utilized by segregationists that emphasized the tranquil nature of southern race relations. Like Tinnin, Louisiana's US senator Allen Ellender regularly noted that "99.9 percent" of the white and Black population in the state preferred segregation. Similarly, fellow Louisiana senator Russell Long, in a comment that mirrored those raised by Tinnin, asserted, "Negroes actually have less opportunity to get ahead in most Northern States than in the South." In short, segregationist forces lampooned the idea that inequality and a lack of opportunity existed in their states.[24] The LBC ignored the integration issue at its November 1954 annual meeting and proceeded to do so for the next several years. The Louisiana Baptist Student Union did address the segregation issue at its 1954 Lake Charles gathering, where its integrated membership, which included Black delegates from Southern and Leland Baptist College in Baker, supported the *Brown* verdict and favored the continuation of integrated conventions. For his part, Finley Tinnin reported the gathering's proceedings in the pages of the *Baptist Message* without editorializing beyond mentioning that the students were entitled to express their own convictions, thereby establishing a pattern he would uphold throughout his tenure with the publication. The white Louisiana Baptist response to the *Brown* verdict proved insightful. The faith's state organ clearly touted the necessity of maintaining the racial status quo, but as the actions of the messengers of the Baptist Student Union illustrate, fidelity to segregation was not as strong as many assumed. Likewise, Tinnin, despite his support for Jim Crow, remained willing to oversee coverage of a variety of racial perspectives in the *Baptist Message* without vilifying those who disagreed with him. A monolithic white response in the wake of the gravest crisis faced by Jim Crow failed to materialize in Louisiana's Protestant communities.[25]

In 1956, racial tensions in Louisiana intensified. Judge Skelly Wright's warning to New Orleans schools to prepare for integration touched off an array of efforts by state legislators to block this eventuality, which, although successful in the short term, proved useless in the long run. The Citizen's Council movement, which promoted a South-wide effort to fight integration, emerged and quickly garnered the support of thousands as it rallied the faithful with cries of "massive resistance."[26] As violence increased, faith leaders found themselves drawn into the discussion. In the August 8 edition of the

Baptist Message, Finley Tinnin devoted his editor's column to defending the actions of the deacons of the First Baptist Church of Mansfield, whose protest of the SBC's CLC's pamphlet titled "Integration" garnered significant local attention. Like the Mansfield deacons, Tinnin stressed his disdain for the controversial CLC, which expressed opinions "far removed from the thinking of the great majority of our people." To wit, he suggested the SBC should disband the commission, which he argued did "more harm than good."[27] Tinnin's editorial promptly garnered the attention of segregationist leaders, including Louisiana State Senator Willie Rainach, who also spearheaded resistance efforts in the state legislature. Rainach praised the Louisiana Baptist Convention, and by extension Tinnin, for being the first faith community in Louisiana to willingly take on integrationists among its denominational leaders. Despite his strong opposition to the CLC, Tinnin, as he had in the past, demonstrated a degree of restraint that was not always evident in this period. A few months prior to his editorial supporting the Mansfield deacons, he penned a controversial column questioning the verbiage employed by Dallas First Baptist Church minister Wallie Amos Criswell at a South Carolina evangelism conference, which although inflammatory, was not uncommon in the region at that time. In one memorable line, Criswell observed regarding segregation that it protected his daughter from "people that are iniquitous and vile and dirty and low down" before returning to his condemnation of outsiders "trying to force upon us a situation and a thing that is a denial of all that we believe in."[28] His divisive commentary and use of racial slurs struck some, such as Tinnin, as going too far. Despite his support for segregation, Tinnin grew concerned with the growing racial unrest in his home state caused by inflammatory rhetoric such as that utilized by Criswell, state leaders, and the increasingly popular Citizens' Council movement. In the March 1956 editions of the *Baptist Message*, Tinnin urged segregationists to keep the discourse civil as the best way to advance their case, while implying that inflammatory rhetoric would only alienate the region and bring unwanted attention from the federal government. At the same time, the editor printed an array of letters from state pastors that reflected the diversity of opinion in Louisiana on the nature of the Criswell speech, Tinnin's commentary on it, and the future of the segregated South. Although the majority of the letters supported Criswell, some indicated an appreciation of Tinnin's perspective and fewer still challenged the intolerance of Louisiana's Baptist leaders.[29]

George Avery Lee, pastor of Ruston's First Baptist Church, wrote in support of Tinnin's call for a tempered discourse on race while denouncing the editor's support for segregation. Unlike many segregationists, including Criswell, who would later recant their views on race, Lee was ahead of his times. He strayed not from his basic belief "in the Bible as the Word of God; in it is our authoritative summons to practice justice towards all people of all races."[30] Likewise, he shared with his congregation, "The Negro is a creature of God, the same as I am. He has a soul, the same as I do. In the eyes of God there is no difference between us. . . . [T]he same salvation Jesus brought to me, he brought to the Negro."[31] As word of Lee's apostacy spread, local leaders threatened to cut off resources to his faith community. To the credit of Lee's congregation, they stood down such threats, arguing that they might not always like what Lee said, but they supported his right to say it.[32] Important to consider is the fact that this episode took place in north Louisiana, where resistance to integration proved far stauncher than in south Louisiana. Most of Lee's congregants did not agree with their pastor, but they did not consider his stance on this issue a deal breaker. Instead, they rallied behind their beleaguered pastor as word of his unorthodox sermons leaked to the community at large. Rather than being steamrolled out of town, Lee remained in Ruston until 1961, when he assumed the pastorship of St. Charles Avenue Baptist Church in New Orleans. While in Ruston, his outreach efforts extended to Grambling State University, a historically Black institution of higher education that existed on the periphery of the Louisiana community. Lee dedicated himself to bringing the white and Black faith communities in Ruston together. None of Lee's actions were undertaken in secret, and all of his work occurred in full view of his congregation and the community at large. Despite Lee's message that segregation ran counter to God's laws, Lee also made clear that he thought southerners, not outsiders, should oversee any reconciliation between the races. If integration was to come, Lee emphasized it should come at the hands of a homegrown effort, thereby reassuring his white congregants that they would never be compelled to love their neighbor—although they should certainly think about it. In this sense, his states' rights approach to faith no doubt marked him as a step above those who shouted for outside intervention due to the recalcitrance of the white majority. Lee wanted change to be sure, but he desired the region's white and Black citizens to forge their own future free of outside pressure.[33]

Lee remained a popular preacher despite his attitude on race, and his insights were regularly printed in the letter to the editor section of the *Baptist Message*. Despite Tinnin's clear segregationist sympathies, his publication continued handling the civil rights issue engulfing the South in the late 1950s in a reasonably balanced manner. Indeed, the *Baptist Message* often ran columns composed by preachers similar to Lee, who espoused a message devoted to accepting racial change. In the October 3, 1957 edition of the *Baptist Message*, for example, guest columnist and CLC member T. B. Maston wrote, "It would be tragic for the South, for our nation, for Baptists, for the missionary enterprise around the world, and for the cause of Christ in general for Christians to defend the segregation pattern as the final word in the area of race relations. It would be double tragic if we attempt to place the stamp of divine approval on it."[34] Maston's sternly worded warning to the Baptist faithful stressed the necessity of keeping an open mind regarding institutions such as Jim Crow while warning them to avoid attaching divinity to such man-made constructs. The next issue of the *Baptist Message* featured an article by Pastor H. T. Sullivan from Oakdale, Louisiana, which argued, "God considered segregation to be wise and best from the very beginning of time. It was never His will that the races should become so mixed and confused as they are today."[35] What Tinnin's paper revealed and, in many ways, celebrated was the variety of ideas within the Baptist community concerning the need for either racial change or the maintenance of the status quo. During his tenure, Tinnin gave voice to many perspectives and ran his paper in a loose manner, keeping with the decentralized spirit of the Southern Baptist Convention. Louisiana Baptist pastors were given a voice in Tinnin's paper even if their message ran counter to the views of the editorial board. At the same time, the *Baptist Message* addressed the civil rights issue frequently in its pages, but the topic never dominated the publication. An article here and there in the approximately twelve-page weekly publication proved all the space devoted to it. Many editions contained no reference at all to segregation, civil rights, or the growing discord on the subject taking place in the state. Race was but one of a pantheon of issues that mattered to Louisiana Baptists. Equal attention was given to concerns such as alcohol abuse, pornography, and missionary efforts. It is easy for contemporary readers to assume that white southerners were consumed with the race issue, but a careful perusal of widely circulated publications such as the *Baptist Message* points to the limited importance the issue held in most faith communities. Race certainly mattered to Louisiana's white faith communities, but it was not an all-consuming passion.

As the weight of the civil rights movement began pressing down on the South, many Louisianans quietly began losing heart as they witnessed defeat followed by defeat of efforts designed to thwart racial change. State politicians certainly did not want any discourse to take place that suggested white resolve was weakening even as evidence of it mounted. As the integration fight reached its crescendo in the early 1960s with the token desegregation of several New Orleans schools, the organs of the Baptist church fell silent, suggesting the façade of white southern unanimity on matters of race did not exist. Finley Tinnin served as editor of the *Baptist Message* until his late 1957 retirement. The editorship next fell to James Cole, who steered the publication in a different direction. The changes that took place under Cole proved dramatic. At the start of 1958, the *Baptist Message* began running its paper with a colored banner, and the columns contained in it became more regular. By contrast, the publication under Tinnin proved erratic, with features frequently shifting and the layout inconsistent. Along with the increased professionalism of the publication came the steady erosion of discussion of the race issue. By the summer of 1963, the *Baptist Message* abandoned the newspaper style it exhibited under Tinnin in exchange for a magazine-like appearance. Increasingly, articles inside the publication stressed the need to safeguard the family and especially one's children, from the ill effects of the "god-less" modern world. Segregation was fast becoming an afterthought. The passage of the Civil Rights Act of 1964 and the Voting Rights Act of 1965 served to punctuate the failed efforts of the massive resistance crowd. Indeed, by the end of 1965, the head of the New Orleans Area Citizens' Council, CK Vetter, wrote, "White people have about given up."[36] White Louisianans gave up the Jim Crow ghost when confronted with a steady stream of demoralizing defeats. By the mid-1960s, the fight was largely over.

Despite the demise of the massive resistance fight in Louisiana, the day of reckoning for the state's white Baptist leaders was still a good way off. It was not until 1995 that the SBC officially apologized for its role in the perpetuation of the institutions of slavery and segregation. The SBC was a product of its time and place. It represented a region that favored both slavery and Jim Crow. Naturally, a decentralized faith tradition would support the status quo as its individual congregants expected. As seen throughout the South in the age of Jim Crow, white community leaders and that broad amorphous group defined as racial moderates sat back and allowed the worst spirits to dictate resistance efforts. The presence of G. Avery Lee serves as a powerful reminder that even at the height of Jim Crow, there remained individuals willing to challenge the prejudices of the age. Despite the SBC's formal 1995 apology, the leadership of the organization by the 1970s had already come to embrace the need for racial reconciliation. Rank-and-file church members might not have liked what had taken place, but once integration became the law of the land, the white Baptist community slowly moved to accept the newly imposed status quo. The healing, much like the fight that preceded it, took place slowly on the congregational level.[37]

The NBC broadly pushed for reform while allowing local communities to dictate the size, scope, and nature of their efforts in support of change; whereas the SBC, utilizing identical institutional strictures, presented a decentralized and disorderly front that, in most instances, buttressed the status quo and, in a smaller number of situations, advanced a more conciliatory approach to race relations. The Roman Catholic Church that flourished in south Louisiana handled the integration question in a different manner. Its hierarchal structure certainly slowed its response to civil rights, while its parishioners, who occupied communities rife with racial prejudice, proved unwilling to accept substantive change without compulsion. The wheels of the Catholic Church moved far slower than they did in Baptist denominations, but move they did. When the Church proved ready to strike, it steamrolled change on its parishioners regardless of protests from the pew. How the Catholic Church handled the civil rights fight is a study in contrast with both the white and Black Baptist handling of the issue. Fueled initially by a crusading archbishop, the Catholic Church ultimately pushed for the integration of all of its Louisiana institutions utilizing the might of an authoritarian prelate who marshaled the full institutional weight of the church to compel compliance.

Born in Germany in 1876 before coming to the United States at age six, Joseph Rummel rose through the ecclesiastical ranks of the Catholic Church before becoming the ninth archbishop of New Orleans, serving from 1935 to 1964.[38] In Louisiana, Rummel did much to improve the financial health of his archbishopric, which experienced considerable growing pains as the area's Catholic population boomed. Rummel's reforms brought the archdiocese into the twentieth century. It did not take long before he also encountered the moral weight of the civil rights crusade. Most place the time of his civil rights awakening to the period following WWII when he and others of like mind began to question not only the immorality of segregation but also its financial cost. In a state always starved for resources, it did not make sense to divide the already scarce education dollars into two separate school systems. In 1948, Rummel admitted two African American students into Notre Dame Seminary, and three years later, he ordered the removal of offensive church signage denoting "white" and "colored" sections.[39] Slowly but surely, Rummel was bringing change. True, it happened at a slow pace, yet the cautious and deliberate speed appeared to ruffle few feathers. Naturally, there was grumbling, but overall, the changes took place with little fanfare. Then Rummel got more aggressive. In the spring of 1953, he ordered his pastoral letter titled "Blessed Are the Peacemakers" read before all of the congregations in his archdiocese. Its contents no doubt shocked many of the Catholic faithful in the pews that Sunday coming as it did before the widespread paranoia regarding segregation that hit the following year with the *Brown* verdict. As far as the churches under his command went, Rummel ordered full integration. In a paragraph that no doubt caused segregationists to bristle, Rummel noted, "Ever mindful . . . of the basic truth that our colored Catholic brethren share with us the same spiritual life and destiny . . . let there be no further discrimination or segregation in the pews, at the communion rail, at the confessional, and in parish meetings, just as there will be no segregation in the kingdom of heaven."[40] As in the past, Rummel was laying the foundation for something larger to come. He started with a heartfelt call to change in the one jurisdiction over which he had total control—the institution of the church itself. To those willing to read between the lines, however, it did not take long to notice that the archbishop's letter suggested that his activism extended beyond the church proper.

As segregationist leaders such as Willie Rainach led Louisiana in an all-out effort to block the integration of the state's public schools, Rummel prepared his own rejoinder to the cries of massive resistance emanating from segregationists.[41] If Rummel's 1953 message caught the faithful by surprise, then his 1956 letter titled "The Morality of Racial Segregation" left them in absolute shock. Not only did Rummel continue the theme of purifying God's house against the evil of racial separation, but he went so far as to list a series of reasons why "racial segregation is morally wrong and sinful." For those in attendance that Sunday, the archbishop spoke directly to the faithful's own departure from scripture by their tacit or open support for segregation. As Rummel argued, segregation denied "the unity and solidarity of the human race, it denied the unity and universality of redemption," and it violated "the dictates of justice and the mandate of love" all espoused by the teaching of Jesus Christ. In the tightly organized letter, Rummel categorically attacked everything for which segregationists stood. There was, according to Rummel, no room for hate in God's kingdom both here on earth and in the afterlife. Louisiana citizens needed to come to terms with the inherent immorality of the institution they so blindly accepted. In a nod to the exigency of history, Rummel noted that the archdiocese made peace with segregation of the races following the Civil War after recognizing the volatile state of race relations that followed emancipation. According to Rummel, segregation as it emerged after Reconstruction "was never meant to be a permanent thing," that once the passions of the Civil War cooled, the church needed to destroy Jim Crow as it existed in the institution and to call for change outside of its boundaries. Whatever temporary purpose segregation once held in the Catholic Church was at an end, Rummel opined.[42]

Lots of questions remained unanswered. True, the archbishop called for the integration of Catholic churches under his control, while publicly condemning segregation as sinful.[43] At the same time, however, he said nothing regarding the Catholic school system, which served a sizable student population along segregated lines. In his initial public letters, Rummel powerfully expressed his desire to eradicate segregation. However, when attention fell on the Catholic school system, especially in the wake of Judge Skelly Wright's

Figure 2.2. Leander Perez, arch-segregationist and acknowledged "boss" of Plaquemines Parish in south Louisiana. Perez threatened to have any civil rights agitators arrested and incarcerated in remote Fort St. Philip along the lower Mississippi River. (Courtesy of the Center for Southeast Louisiana Studies)

1956 warning of the future integration of New Orleans public schools, the archbishop proved far more pragmatic than his sermons suggested. Rather than call for the immediate integration of all schools in the Archdiocese, Rummel stressed in the summer of 1956 that, although the church supported integration, it was not yet prepared to desegregate. Rummel's initial inclination to integrate schools as soon as possible was almost universally panned by diocesan school boards. More time was needed for reflection and to convince wayward parents and board members that the proposed changes would take place gradually, not all at once. Despite delayed integration plans, Rummel's summer message made clear that integration was at hand—there would be no massive resistance crusade within the Catholic Church. Throughout the integration process, Rummel assured parents that they would know what was coming and when it would happen. Integration would start in elementary school, one grade level at a time, and it would take place under "moderate conditions." He closed his remarks by reiterating his commitment "to carry out the principles of Christian Charity and justice towards all and to bring about unity in the Mystical Body of Christ."[44] In short, the archdiocese was committed to integration yet not prepared to act on it.[45]

Spiritual imperatives no doubt guided Rummel's beliefs regarding segregation. However, equally apparent were the financial forces that shaped the multiyear delay in ultimately implementing the plan. Despite assurances in his July 1956 pastoral letter that September 1957 was the targeted date to start integration, New Orleans area Catholic schools would not begin integration until the 1962 fall term.[46] Archbishop Philip Hannan, who succeeded Rummel, argued that his predecessor was profoundly worried that his actions would split the church and thus tried to avoid overplaying his hand.[47] Support for segregation was deeply entrenched in south Louisiana. There was no telling how far parishioners would go if the cleric continued to push social reform that ran counter to the desires of the majority of his congregation. Added to this concern was trepidation that the state, which was busy bolstering segregation with an array of statutes, might withhold critical funding to area Catholic schools, which relied on free textbooks, reduced lunches, and free buses provided by Pelican State tax dollars. If he moved too quickly, the very real threat of a church schism might ensue along with a catastrophic drop in enrollment in Catholic schools that would force their closure. Rummel blinked as he confronted the possible implications of his actions. Rather than press the issue in the 1950s, Rummel waited and routinely reminded the faithful that integration was still something the church supported and would eventually bring to parochial schools. But wait, he did. Confidantes of the archbishop note that he personally believed in integration but harbored deep concerns that his actions might undermine the spiritual sanctity of his congregations. He wanted to keep the community together while hoping that events and his message would warm church members to the idea of integration. Critics of the archbishop's ideas were not hard to find. On a regular basis, the cleric faced protesters outside of his official residence, calling his leadership into question and challenging his grasp of God's intent for his belief in integration.[48]

Although many raged against the archbishop, Plaquemines Parish boss Leander Perez, owing to his status as a public figure, held disproportionate sway over his fellow Louisianans, many of whom relied on him for employment. According to Perez, who was a practicing Roman Catholic, segregation was consistent with the Bible before questioning whether or not more sinister forces were at work. Perez had long suggested that "Zionist Jews" were behind a Communist conspiracy to topple the United States by fomenting unrest under the guise of racial equality. Not surprisingly, Perez, like many of his southern peers, implicated civil rights organizations such as the NAACP as participants in the plot. Once Rummel got involved, the judge pivoted to include the Catholic Church as an unwitting participant in advancing the Zionist agenda.[49] Despite segregationist efforts, Judge Skelly Wright in 1960 issued a temporary restraining order on segregationist efforts to block federal mandates, prompting the integration of the New Orleans schools McDonogh 19 and William Frantz.[50] Massive public protests met the integration efforts that were capped off with speeches by segregationist dignitaries such as Perez, who urged New Orleanians to send their children to the segregated schools in nearby St. Bernard Parish before launching into a race-fueled tirade against the powers that brought the city to the brink of anarchy. In a horrific display of segregationist sentiments, Perez railed, "Don't wait for your daughters to be raped by these Congolese. Don't wait until the burr-heads are forced into your schools. Do something about it now."[51] Perez fanned the flames of discord, resulting in episodes of racial violence in the coming days as angry mobs set upon passing Blacks. Lawlessness reigned, and Perez was at its epicenter.

Despite obstruction efforts and a myriad of Perez-authored and Rainach-championed state laws aimed at blocking integration, federal efforts proceeded apace. The area Citizens' Council protested further integration efforts only to fall by the wayside as integration, despite their efforts, took place. New Orleans was clearly lost, its city schools gradually experiencing token integration. Increasingly white New Orleanians looked to alternative forms of education, such as a private school system funded, in part, by state tuition grants. Meanwhile, Archbishop Rummel's health began failing, especially following a 1960 fall in which he broke an arm and a leg and nearly died of pneumonia while convalescing. In response, the Vatican appointed John P. Cody as coadjutor archbishop in August 1961, ostensibly to render Rummel assistance in those trying times.[52] Cody provided just what the aging Rummel needed. As much as Rummel desired to integrate parochial schools, his advancing age left him unwilling to engage in a potentially divisive church schism to bring it about. Cody had no such reservations. To observers, he ruled with an iron fist, running his office with all of the tact of a "General George Patton." He fueled Rummel with the conviction to forge ahead with integration plans and he expected the parishioners, as well as the diocesan priests, to toe the line. There would be no dissembling under Cody's watch.[53]

With the critical stimulus provided by Cody, Archbishop Rummel's long-delayed plan for integration was finally prepared. On March 27, 1962, Rummel and Cody called for the integration of New Orleans Catholic schools for the 1962–63 school year. The moment of truth had arrived. Not to be outdone, Perez, who long asserted he ceased contributing to the Catholic Church once Rummel championed integration in the 1950s, reiterated his hostility to the archbishop's policies and urged his followers to do the same. Perez reckoned that economic retribution would be the most effective plan since his sway over the Catholic school system was negligible. On this occasion, he could not use his political clout to alter the church's direction by employing his traditional bullying techniques. In the furor over the prelate's orders, a renewed round of protests erupted outside of Rummel's residence.[54] By the summer of 1962, Cody was appointed apostolic administrator, which ostensibly meant that he handled most of the day-to-day affairs of the archdiocese. It would be he, not Rummel, who would enforce the integration edict and who ultimately pushed Rummel to take the step the aged cleric wanted to avoid.

Excommunication for Catholics represents the gravest punishment reserved for the church. It strips a person of his or her ability to be in spiritual communion with the church, denying one access to communion and all other sacraments. Left to his own devices, it is doubtful Rummel would have acted as assuredly as he did on the issue of excommunication without Cody by his side. Rummel established the grand vision, and Cody became the enforcer of Rummel's and, by extension, the church's will. Once the 1962 Catholic school integration decree was announced, Perez and others immediately ramped up the intensity of their attacks. True to form, Perez advanced his customary anti-Semitic remarks while urging his followers to stop giving money to the church. As Perez noted, "Shut their water off, and you'll see them turn about-face." As a result of his repeated efforts to undermine the will of the Catholic Church, Perez soon found his actions questioned as never before by the faith community he once embraced. Rather than rashly move against the segregationists, Archbishop Rummel sent letters in the form of a "paternal admonition" on March 31 to the most vocal critics of integration among his congregants, urging them to reconcile with the church's planned actions or face severe punishment. Who actually received the letters is a matter of debate. When pressed by the media regarding the letters, Rummel admitted they originated from his desk, but he refused to list the recipients since he considered it a private matter. Segregationists such as Perez claimed they never received communication from the archbishop and jokingly indicated they would refuse receipt of such a letter if it arrived.[55] Despite Rummel's efforts to bring his straying flock back in line, further recalcitrance met church efforts. With the archbishop's olive branch spurned, a more direct approach was needed. The decision to excommunicate Perez and his accomplices Jackson Ricau and B. J. Gaillot was pushed by Cody, as was its timing, the start of Holy Week on April 16, the most sacred time in the church's liturgical calendar. Cody wanted to send a message. The church was finished backing down and feared not who might oppose it. Proof of this is provided by the excommunication message itself, which stressed Perez's persistent refusal to obey the mandates of the church. This emphasis on obedience to the church could only have come from Cody's pen. Interesting too is the fact that the excommunication message was issued not because of racism—which the church condemned, however, it was not an excommunication-type offense—but for thwarting the intentions of the Archdiocese of New Orleans.[56] Recipients of the excommunication message believed, quite rightly as it turned out, that the kind Rummel could not have possibly been behind the deed. Several years after his excommunication, Perez seethed to an interviewer inquiring about his relationship with the Catholic church and could not bring himself to mention Cody by name, referring to him instead as "the archbishop who came down from Kansas City and Saint Louis." Recognizing fully who was to blame for his misfortune, Perez argued that Cody "was acting as a hatchet man there to enforce integration on parochial schools which was resisted, and he threatened the whole community with being disbarred from the Catholic Church."[57] Despite their indignation, little recourse was available to Perez and his compatriots as the Vatican had stood behind Rummel in previous disputes regarding matters of race and formally opposed the ideas that informed the dissent.

Nothing could stop the integration process once initiated. As parents began pulling their kids out of New Orleans area parochial schools, Cody's formidable will was on clear display. Catholic schools remained open throughout the school year despite sagging enrollment and repeated threats. Cody would not be intimidated. Despite Perez's use of all of the political and economic leverage he possessed to force parents to keep their children from enrolling in the now integrated Catholic schools, the educational apparatus of the church continued without interruption. Once the initial furor abated, enrollment in succeeding years gradually climbed back to normal, and token integration became the norm.[58]

Archbishop Rummel died in 1964 and was succeeded by John Cody. Cody's tenure was exceedingly short. He had accomplished his mission in New Orleans by bringing integration to the archdiocese. By June of 1965, his successor Philip Hannan took command of the archdiocese, and Cody assumed an appointment as archbishop of Chicago before being promoted to Cardinal in 1967. Before long, Cody ran into a slew of scandals involving financial impropriety and even accusations of sexual misconduct as he allegedly had taken a mistress. As for Leander Perez, he at first mocked his excommunication, claiming that Rummel was being duped by Communists. At one point, he joked he was going to form a new faith, the "Perez-byterians." Archbishop Hannan recalls that in 1967, Leander Perez's son Chalin, at his dying mother's urging, went to the archbishop to see how the excommunication order could be lifted. Hannan made clear Perez needed to publicly disavow what he had done and assert that he now followed "the dictates of the church." Hannan recalled that church officials eventually reached out to Perez himself to ascertain his willingness to return to the faith. Shortly thereafter, in 1968, Perez delivered a speech to a small group at the dedication of an incinerator plant at Fort Jackson in Plaquemines. Hannan dispatched a priest to witness the event based on a promise made by Perez to address his faith. The priest reported back that Perez made some nice comments about the parochial school system and about the archbishop, which was sufficient for Hannan to lift the excommunication decree. Perez died of a massive heart attack in March 1969 and received a full Catholic funeral service.[59]

The Catholic Church in New Orleans provides a perfect window into the functioning of a highly centralized faith community working its way through a social crisis. Power in the Catholic tradition cascaded downhill. In the New Orleans area, the archbishop exerted his will on individual diocesan church communities within the parameters of the teachings established by the global Catholic faith community, and when he faltered, strength from an even higher authority arrived. The Vatican, using the institutional apparatus afforded to it, exerted its will aggressively on the local level with little concern for the consequences on the ground. It took longer to affect change to be sure, but once joined, there existed no wiggle room for congregants after the wheels of the church were set in motion. One either went along, no matter how grudgingly, or one went somewhere else. The church had spoken, and its faithful were expected to obey.[60]

As the statistics noted at the top of this chapter affirm, faith still matters in Louisiana, just as it did in the 1950s and 1960s during the height of the civil rights battle. Louisiana's faith communities adopted a variety of approaches as they confronted the gravest social crisis of the previous century. The highly centralized Catholic Church initially proved cumbersome, before moving with deliberate speed to integrate all of its holdings. The state's Black Baptist congregations were not restricted by rigid institutional guidelines. Its local pastors, such as T. J. Jemison, could champion reform from the pulpit at their discretion whenever their congregants encountered injustice. By contrast, the state's white Baptists utilized the diffuse institutional apparatus of their faith to generally become a force either dedicated to preserving the status quo or to sitting on the sidelines as others decided the fate of Jim Crow. Unlike African American Baptist churches, which pushed for equality and greater opportunity, their white counterparts more often than not obstructed or at least turned a blind eye to meaningful change. Louisiana's other faith communities, including Methodists and Episcopalians, fell out along the same lines, with the institutional structures of their churches falling somewhere between the authoritarian Catholic and the congregational Baptist traditions. In all instances, institutional structure dictated how local faith communities confronted the change brought by the civil rights fight. In the present, Louisiana's faith communities remain integral to how the problems of the twenty-first century are confronted by the state's voters. Despite the mistakes of the past, these communities still serve, still influence how people vote, and still guide how their congregants view the world. Woe to the historian who fails to grapple with the importance of Louisiana's faith communities in studying the state's colorful past and to the politician who neglects the powerful anchor religion provides Pelican State denizens.

NOTES

1. PEW Research Center, Religious Landscape Study, November 18, 2022, https://www.pewresearch.org/religion/religious-landscape-study/state/louisiana/.

2. Sarah Azaransky, *This Worldwide Struggle: Religion and the International Roots of the Civil Rights Movement* (New York: Oxford University Press, 2017); Taylor Branch, *Parting the Waters: America in the King Years, 1954–1963* (New York: Simon and Schuster, 1988); Bettye Collier-Thompson, *Jesus, Jobs, and Justice: African American Women and Religion* (New York: Alfred A. Knopf, 2010); Gary J. Dorrien, *Breaking White Supremacy: Martin Luther King Jr. and the Black Social Gospel* (New Haven: Yale University Press, 2018); Michael O. Emerson and Christian Smith, *Divided by Faith: Evangelical Religion and the Problem of Race in America* (New York: Oxford University Press, 2000); Adam Fairclough, *To Redeem the Soul of America: The Southern Christian Leadership Conference and Martin Luther King, Jr.* (Athens: University of Georgia Press, 1987); David J. Garrow, *Bearing the Cross: Martin Luther King Jr. and the Southern Christian Leadership Conference* (New York: William Marrow, 1986); Stephen R. Haynes *The Last Segregated Hour: The Memphis Kneel-Ins and the Campaign for Southern Church Desegregation* (New York: Oxford University Press, 2013); George M. Marsden, *Fundamentalism and American Culture* (New York: Oxford University Press, 1980); Charles Marsh, *God's Long Summer: Stories of Faith and Civil Rights* (Princeton: Princeton University Press, 1997); Jonathan Rieder, *Gospel of Freedom: Martin Luther King Jr.'s "Letter from Birmingham Jail" and the Struggle That Changed a Nation* (New York: Bloomsbury, 2013); James M. Washington, *Frustrated Fellowship: The Black Baptist Quest for Social Power* (Macon: Mercer University Press, 1986).

3. Elaine Allen Lechtreck, *Southern White Ministers and the Civil Rights Movement* (Jackson: University Press of Mississippi, 2018); William G. McAtee, *Transformed: A*

White Mississippi Pastor's Journey into Civil Rights and Beyond (Jackson: University Press of Mississippi, 2011).

4. Joel L. Alvis Jr., *Religion and Race: Southern Presbyterians, 1946–1983* (Tuscaloosa: University of Alabama Press, 2002); R. Bentley Anderson, *Black, White, and Catholic: New Orleans Interracialism, 1947–1956* (Nashville: Vanderbilt University Press, 2005); David L. Chappell, *A Stone of Hope: Prophetic Religion and the Death of Jim Crow* (Chapel Hill: University of North Carolina Press, 2004); Donald Collins, *When the Church Bell Rang Racist: The Methodist Church and the Civil Rights Movement in Alabama* (Macon: Mercer University Press, 1998); Jane Dailey, "Sex, Segregation, and the Sacred after *Brown*," *Journal of American History* 91 (June 2004): 119–44; Carolyn R. DuPont, *Mississippi Praying: Southern White Evangelicals and the Civil Rights Movement, 1945–1975* (New York: New York University Press, 2013); Amy Koehlinger, *The New Nuns: Racial Justice and Religious Reform in the 1960s* (Cambridge: Harvard University Press, 2007); Carter Dalton Lyons, *Sanctuaries of Segregation: The Story of the Jackson Church Visit Campaign* (Jackson: University Press of Mississippi, 2017); Bill J. Leonard, *God's Last and Only Hope: The Fragmentation of the Southern Baptist Convention* (Grand Rapids: William B. Eerdmans, 1990); Mark Newman, *Getting Right with God: Southern Baptists and Desegregation, 1945–1995* (Tuscaloosa: University of Alabama Press, 2001); Newman, *Desegregating Dixie: The Catholic Church in the South and Desegregation, 1945–1992* (Jackson: University Press of Mississippi, 2018); Gardiner H. Shattuck, *Episcopalians and Race: Civil War to Civil Rights* (Lexington: University Press of Kentucky, 2000); Douglas E. Thompson, *Richmond's Priests and Prophets : Race, Religion, and Social Change in the Civil Rights Era* (Tuscaloosa: University of Alabama Press, 2017).

5. Justin Poché, "The Desegregation of Louisiana Catholicism, 1938–1962," *Louisiana beyond Black and White: New Interpretations of Twentieth-Century Race and Race Relations* (Lafayette: University of Louisiana at Lafayette Press, 2011), 35–56.

6. For examples of Jemison's work in the community, see transcript, Earline Cary-Williams, interview by Rose Jourbert-Thompson, June 21, 1997, Tape 1252, T. Harry Williams Oral History Center for Oral History (THWCOH), 8–9.

7. T. J. Jemison, *The T. J. Jemison Story* (Nashville: Sunday School Publishing Board, 1994), 19–23; Records of the 1953 NBC meeting, 5.

8. Minutes, the Women's Convention Auxiliary to the National Baptist Convention, September 1953, *NBC Annual*, 326.

9. City Record Book, Baton Rouge, Louisiana Book S, 59–62, Book U, 44–45; *Baton Rouge Morning Advocate*, February 12, 1953, 1A; *Morning Advocate*, March 12, 1963, 6A; Adam Fairclough, *Race and Democracy: The Civil Rights Struggle in Louisiana 1915–1972* (Athens: University of Georgia Press, 1995), 159.

10. Transcript, T. J. Jemison, interview by Roderick Jones, Derek Vaugh, and Michelle Johnson, June 15, 1995, THWOHC, 3.

11. Baton Rouge, Ordinance 222, Baton Rouge City Code of 1951, section 118, title, 10, chapter 2 (1953); *New Orleans Times-Picayune*, June 21, 1953, section 6, 8; Fairclough, *Race and Democracy*, 158–59; Jamahl Fields, et al., *The Baton Rouge Bus Boycott of 1953* (McKinley High School Summer Oral History Project, 1998).

12. *Baton Rouge State Times*, June 15, 1951, 1A; *Morning Advocate*, June 17, 1953, 1A, 8A.

13. Jemison interview, THWCOH, 5–7; Shannon Frystak, *Our Minds on Freedom: Women and the Struggle for Black Equality in Louisiana, 1924–1967* (Baton Rouge: Louisiana State University Press, 2009), 64–68.

14. *Morning Advocate*, June 16, 1953, 1A, 6A; *New York Times*, June 16, 1953, 15; *Morning Advocate*, June 16, 1953, 6A; *State Times*, June 16, 1953, 1A, 8A; *State Times*, June 17 1953, 1A; *Morning Advocate*, June 18, 1953, 1A; *State Times*, June 18, 1953, 1A; *Morning Advocate*, June 19, 1953, 1A; *Morning Advocate*, June 20, 1953, 2A.

15. Transcript, Johnnie Jones interview by Mary Hebert, November 13, 1993, session 4, THWCOH, 5; *Rockford Crusader*, July 3, 1953, 1. Due to the large numbers seeking access to boycott planning meetings, future discussions were held in larger venues such as McKinley High School or the even larger BREC Memorial Stadium. Fields, *The Baton Rouge Bus Boycott of 1953*.

16. Cary-Williams interview, THWCOH, 7.

17. Jemison interview, THWCOH, 13–14; see also transcript, Reverend Mary Moody interview by Amy Horn, April 17, 2002, Tape 3029, THWCOH, 9–10, 13–14.

18. *New Orleans Times-Picayune*, June 21, 1953, section 6, 8; Fairclough, *Race and Democracy*, 160.

19. *New Orleans Times-Picayune*, June 26, 1953, 10.

20. Jones interview, THWCOH, 4, 26; Dean Sinclair, "Equal in All Places: The Civil Rights Struggle in Baton Rouge, 1953–1963," *Louisiana History* 39 (July 1998): 348–56; *New Orleans States*, June 26, 1953, 10; *New Orleans Times-Picayune*, September 23, 1953, 18.

21. Jemison interview, THWCOH, 11; see also Fairclough, *Race and Democracy*, 162; Christina Melton, "'We'll Keep Walking!': The Baton Rouge Civil Rights Boycott of 1953," *Louisiana Endowment for the Humanities* (Spring 2007): 62–71; Joshua Dyer, *Deceptively Important: The Baton Rouge Bus Boycott* (Southeastern Louisiana University: unpublished thesis, 2008), 102–14.

22. *SBC Annual*, 1954, 404.

23. *SBC Annual*, 1956, 332; *SBC Annual*, 1957, 366; *SBC Annual*, 1958, 391.

24. *Baptist Message*, June 3, 1954, 3; *Baptist Message*, December 2, 1954; Newman, *Getting Right with God*, 112, 133. Allen Ellender to Reuben T. Douglas, June 3, 1953, box 668, "Legislation-Civil Rights-1954," Allen Ellender Collection, Ellender Library, Nicholls State University; Russell Long's "Washington Newsletter," May 20, 1060, box 596, folder 27, Russell Long Collection, Hill Memorial Library, Louisiana State University.

25. Mark Newman, "The Louisiana Baptist Convention and Desegregation, 1954–1980," *Louisiana History* 42 (August 2001): 389–419.

26. Numan V. Bartley, *The Rise of Massive Resistance: Race and Politics in the South during the 1950's* (Baton Rouge: Louisiana State University Press, 1999); David L. Chappell, *A Stone of Hope: Prophetic Religion and the Death of Jim Crow* (Chapel Hill: University of North Carolina Press, 2004); Pete Daniel, *Lost Revolutions: The South in the 1950s* (Chapel Hill: University of North Carolina Press, 2000); Brian J. Daugherity and Charles C. Bolton, *With All Deliberate Speed Implementing Brown v. Board of Education* (Fayetteville: University of Arkansas Press, 2011); John Kyle Day, *The Southern Manifesto: Massive Resistance and the Fight to Preserve Segregation* (Jackson: University of Mississippi Press, 2014); Keith M. Finley, *Delaying the Dream: Southern Senators and the Fight against Civil Rights, 1938–1965*

(Baton Rouge: Louisiana State University Press, 2008); Matthew D. Lassiter and Andrew B. Lewis, *The Moderates' Dilemma: Massive Resistance to School Desegregation in Virginia* (Charlottesville: University Press of Virginia, 1998); Neil R. McMillen, *The Citizens' Council: Organized Resistance to the Second Reconstruction* (Urbana: University of Illinois Press, 1971); Elizabeth Gillespie McRae, *Mothers of Massive Resistance: White Women and the Politics of White Supremacy* (New York: Oxford University Press, 2020).

27. *New Orleans Times-Picayune*, August 20, 1956, 7; *New Orleans Times-Picayune*, August 21, 1956, 49.

28. "An Address by Dr. W. A. Criswell, Pastor, First Baptist Church, Dallas, Texas, to the Joint Assembly," Wednesday, February 22, 1956.

29. *Baptist Message* (*BM*), March 1, 1956, 1; *BM*, March 15, 1956, 2; *BM*, March 29, 1956, 3. Andrew Michael Manis *Southern Civil Religions in Conflict: Black and White Baptists and Civil Rights 1947–1957* (Athens: University of Georgia Press 1987), 95.

30. G. Avery Lee, *Messages from the Second Annual Conference on Human Relations* (Raleigh, NC: Forest Hills Baptist Church, March 5–6, 1963), 7.

31. Lee, *Messages from the Second Annual Conference*, 3; G. Avery Lee, *Some Quiet Thoughts on a Turbulent Issue* (Nashville: Christian Life Commission, 1956).

32. David Stricklin, *A Genealogy of Dissent: Southern Baptist Protest in the Twentieth Century* (Louisville: University of Kentucky Press, 1999), 67; Lee, *Some Quiet Thoughts*.

33. G. Avery Lee, "Confessions of an Ex-Southern Liberal . . . Who Is Still Both," in *Baptists See Black*, ed. Wayne Dehoney (Waco: Word Books, 1969), 32–34, 39.

34. *BM*, October 3, 1957, 6.

35. *BM*, October 10, 1957, 1, 4.

36. C. E. Vetter to John Rarick, December 17, 1965, box 99, folder 420, John Rarick Collection, Center for Southeast Louisiana Studies, Southeastern Louisiana University.

37. Newman, "The Louisiana Baptist Convention," 417–18.

38. *New Orleans States*, March 11, 1935, 1.

39. Stephen J. Ochs, *Desegregating the Altar: The Josephites and the Struggle for Black Priests, 1871–1961* (Baton Rouge: Louisiana State University Press, 1990), 404.

40. Joseph Rummel to Clergy, Religious, and Laity, March 15, 1953, pastoral letter, Archives of the Archdiocese of New Orleans. *New Orleans States*, February 20, 1956, 3.

41. In response to the integration crisis, Rainach helped to form as well as chaired the Joint Legislative Committee to Maintain Segregation, which cast a wide net in its search for loopholes to defy integration efforts. For an example of his work, see Minutes of Meeting of Joint Legislative Committee, September 15, 1956, box 1, folder 14, Southeastern Louisiana University-Court Cases, Center for Southeast Louisiana Studies; Glen Jeansonne, *Race, Religion and Politics: The Louisiana Gubernatorial Elections of 1959–60* (Lafayette: Center for Louisiana Studies, 1977); Michael L. Kurtz and Morgan D. Peoples, *Earl K. Long: The Saga of Uncle Earl and Louisiana Politics* (Baton Rouge: Louisiana State University Press, 1990); Paul Quin, "The Dominance of the Shadow in Southern Race Relations," *Louisiana History: The Journal of the Louisiana Historical Association* 36, no. 1 (1995): 5–30.

42. Joseph Rummel to Clergy, Religious, and Laity, February 11, 1956, pastoral letter, Archives of the Archdiocese of New Orleans. Rummel's assessment of the role of the Catholic Church in fostering Jim Crow is challenged by recent scholarship. See James

B. Bennett, *Religion and the Rise of Jim Crow in New Orleans* (Princeton: Princeton University Press, 2005).

43. *New Orleans States*, January 23, 1956, 5; *New Orleans States*, January 24, 1956, 7.

44. Joseph Rummel to Clergy, Religious, and Laity, July 31, 1956, pastoral letter, Archives of the Archdiocese of New Orleans.

45. *New Orleans Times-Picayune*, May 27, 1956, 1; Catholic Committee of the South, New Orleans, LA Commission on Human Rights, "Handbook on Catholic School Integration," 1956. Leaders of the Catholic Church in the South took the opportunity afforded by the *Brown* decision to make recommendations concerning how Catholic educators could make the transition to integration as smooth as possible. The impact of the publication on Rummel's planned gradual/token integration efforts is clear. See pages 56–60 of "Segregation and the Catholic Schools: A Study," by the Catholic Committee of the South, box 2, folder 6, Rodd Lincoln-Plaquemines Parish Collection, Center for Southeast Louisiana Studies, Southeastern Louisiana University.

46. *New Orleans States*, August 6, 1956, 4; *New Orleans Times-Picayune*, August 6, 1956, 1.

47. Philip Hannan, *The Archbishop Wore Combat Boots: Memoir of an Extraordinary Life* (Huntington: Our Sunday Visitor Publishing Division, 2010), 291–92; Newman, *Desegregating Dixie*, 53–54.

48. Fairclough, *Race and Democracy*, 200–201; Ochs, *Desegregating the Alter*, 426; Newman, *Desegregating Dixie*, 150.

49. James Conaway, *Judge: The Life and Times of Leander Perez* (New York: Random House, 1973); Glen Jeansonne, *Leander Perez: Boss of the Delta*, 2nd ed. (Jackson: University Press of Mississippi, 1995); Robert Sherrill, *Gothic Politics in the Deep South: Stars of the New Confederacy* (New York: Ballantine Books, 1969), 5–38; *Time Magazine*, December 12, 1960, 21.

50. *New Orleans Times-Picayune*, November 15, 1960, 8; *New Orleans Times-Picayune*, November 19, 1960, 8; Justin D. Poché, "The Catholic Citizens' Council: Religion and White Resistance in Post-War Louisiana," *US Catholic Historian* 24 (2006): 47–68; Liva Baker, *The Second Battle of New Orleans: The Hundred Year Struggle to Integrate the Schools* (New York: Harper and Row, 1996); Alan Weider, "The New Orleans School Crisis of 1960: Causes and Consequences," *Phylon* 2 (1987): 122–31.

51. *New Orleans Times-Picayune*, September 24, 1967, section 3, 17; *New Orleans Times-Picayune*, November 16, 1960, 1, 2.

52. *Times Picayune*, August 15, 1961, 1, 3; *Dixie Roto Magazine*, November 5, 1961, 10–11.

53. Hannan, *The Archbishop Wore Combat Boots*, 292–93; *Time Magazine*, May 20, 1966, 96; Newman, *Desegregating Dixie*, 153.

54. David J. Endes, "Judge Leander Perez and the Franciscans of Our Lady of Good Harbor: A School Integration Battle in Buras, Louisiana, 1962–1965, *Catholic Southwest* 27 (2016): 17–25.

55. *New Orleans Times-Picayune*, April 3, 1962, 5; Hannan, *The Archbishop Wore Combat Boots*, 293.

56. *New Orleans Times-Picayune*, April 17, 1962, 1, 10; *New Orleans Times-Picayune*, April 18, 1962, 16; Jason Berry, *City of a Million Dreams: A History of New Orleans at Year 300* (Chapel Hill: University of North Carolina Press, 2018), 284.

57. Transcript, Leander H. Perez, interview by John F. Stewart, May 22, 1967, John F. Kennedy Presidential Library, 9.

58. Hannan, *The Archbishop Wore Combat Boots*, 295–96; Jeansonne, *Leander Perez*, 201–3; *New Orleans Times-Picayune*, December 27, 1962, 15; Newman, *Desegregating Dixie*, 158.

59. Hannan, *The Archbishop Wore Combat Boots*, 293–95; Jeansonne, *Leander Perez*, 200, 263–64; Endes, "Judge Leander Perez," 19.

60. Despite its actions, the Roman Catholic Church still had a long way to go in terms of addressing the racism that existed in the archdiocese of New Orleans. The act of compelling integration from the top down did not necessarily lead to immediate acceptance of it in the pews. Catholic communities throughout south Louisiana struggled with matters of race long after Perez's excommunication. See Michael Paquier, "White Catholics Have to Talk about Race and to Admit Their Racism," *America: The Jesuit Review*, July 27, 2016.

Chapter Three

A SOLDIER'S STORY

THE FIGHT FOR EQUAL RIGHTS AND SOCIAL JUSTICE IN POST–WORLD WAR II LOUISIANA

MARCUS S. COX

The "good war" thesis was first introduced in 1984 by Studs Terkel in his groundbreaking monograph, *The Good War: An Oral History of World War II*.[1] This extraordinary narrative of World War II presents the personal stories and memories of men and women who experienced every facet of the war whether through combat or contributions on the home front. It was an account that displayed the pure emotions and fear of war and a nation unprepared for a global conflict. *The Good War* was also a subliminal critique of the Vietnam War and other conflicts of the twentieth century. In retrospect, in the 1980s, Americans saw no real value in World War I. It was a conflict that held no substantial benefits for the nation and in fact led to civil liberty abuses and ended social advances of the Progressive Era. The Korean War is most often referenced as the "forgotten war." It was another conflict that America reluctantly entered that did not galvanize the attention or support of the nation. To date, it is the least known and understood American conflict with few tangible benefits for ordinary Americans. The Vietnam War reflects a period of domestic upheaval and social chaos of a deeply divided nation that arguably cements the conflict as America's nightmare of foreign policy failure and first military defeat. Hence, in comparison to other conflicts, World War II was a "good war."

War is never good because its ultimate goal is to create death and destruction in order to subdue your enemy. World War II was no exception. In fact, World War II is the most deadly and destructive conflict in global history.

More than 70 million individuals perished during the conflict, with the majority coming from the civilian population. Moreover, tens of millions of individuals died in racial and ethnic genocides through mass extermination, starvation, and disease. Even though the United States was safeguarded from the level of death and destruction experienced by much of Europe and Asia, more than four hundred thousand Americans lost their lives during World War II.[2] World War II was also a period of fear and anxiety for racial and ethnic minorities throughout the nation. For African Americans, Japanese Americans, and Mexican Americans, the period also reflects the rigidity of the color line in America. Racial discrimination in the war industry was common throughout the 1940s, in addition to racial violence and the spread of white supremacy as a result of the migration of millions of African Americans to the Midwest and West Coast. Race riots occurred in Detroit, Michigan (1943), Harlem, New York (1943), Los Angeles, California (1943), Beaumont, Texas (1943), and other cities. At the same time, African American soldiers and sailors clashed with white officers and soldiers over a number of racial indignities and abuse on military installations and bases in America and overseas. Additional race riots and conflicts occurred in Townsville, Australia (1942), Camp Claiborne, Louisiana (1942), Port Chicago, California (1944), Agana, Guam (1944), and on military bases in North Carolina, New Jersey, Virginia, Nebraska, Florida, and Alabama.[3] For many Americans, there was plenty of bad news from the good war.

However, millions of Americans improved their lives in unprecedented ways during World War II. The war is credited with ending the Great Depression, the worst economic calamity in US history. During the 1930s, more than twenty thousand businesses went bankrupt and closed, industrial production decreased by nearly 50 percent, and 25 percent of America's labor force was out of work. Poverty and homelessness created a level of despair that was never seen before. Beginning in 1941, war mobilization and industrial production increased the nation's productive output substantially. At the height of the war, the unemployment rate was a minuscule 1.2 percent. World War II created the biggest boon in American economic history.[4] Millions of American citizens selflessly joined the armed forces to serve their country to defeat Nazism and Fascism and defend American principles of freedom, equality, and democracy. Young men and women served in the armed forces, sought employment opportunities in the defense industry, and traveled far from home for the first time in their lives.

World War II is also responsible for igniting many of the social revolutions of the 1950s and '60s. The modern civil rights movement, women's liberation movement, and gay rights movement were all heavily influenced by World War II. The transformation of wartime mobilization, economic opportunity, and enhanced standard of living changed America in every conceivable way. It also prompted marginalized Americans to demand more politically and continue the fight for freedom and equality at home. Women were motivated to demand equal treatment and opportunity after serving in the armed forces and providing the necessary labor for the arsenal of democracy. Gay Americans found strength and motivation to change their lives while living in urban communities that were established through wartime migration.[5] African Americans and veterans in particular, returned home with a newfound worldview and sense of consciousness that inspired them to lead local civil rights organizations and defend their communities against domestic terrorists while demanding the benefits and virtues of first-class citizenship and social justice.[6]

Though the commencement of World War II brought optimism and hope for a brighter future, most African Americans were guarded in their expectations because of tragic events in the aftermath of World War I. Jim Crow laws and the lynching of African American men and women continued to serve as constant reminders of Black subordination and oppression despite President Franklin Roosevelt's impassioned call to arms to fight for the Four Freedoms (freedom of speech and expression, freedom to worship God, freedom from want, and freedom from fear). But World War II was different from previous conflicts and national crises. The Great Migration of African Americans to northern cities during the early twentieth century reshaped the national political map of 1939. Even Eleanor Roosevelt, the first lady, cautioned her husband not to ignore African American demands for the integration of the armed forces and a federal antilynching bill. She wrote, "There is a growing feeling among the colored people [that] they should be allowed to participate in any training that is going on in the aviation, army or navy. This is going to be very bad politically besides being intrinsically wrong and I think you should ask that a meeting be held [with Negro leaders]."[7]

Military service and wartime support have a long-standing relationship with the civil rights movement throughout American history. In a democratic society the ability to wage war is grounded upon the commitment of its population to serve in the armed forces. This commitment can be achieved through the extension of citizenship as compensation. Such an understanding arose in colonial America among free Blacks and ethnic minorities. During the Revolutionary War, the connection between freedom, citizenship, and military service was forever solidified in the minds of bondsmen and colonists alike. In an effort to incite rebellion among slaves and undermine the local economy, Virginia's royal governor, John Murray proclaimed, "I do hereby further declare all indentured servants, Negroes, and others free, that are able and willing to bear arms, they joining His Majesty's Troops, as soon as may be, for the more speedily reducing the Colony to a proper sense of their duty." As a result, the Continental army duplicated the British efforts to trade military service for freedom, and by 1777, New England state governments aggressively recruited African Americans in addition to offering equal bounty with white soldiers.[8]

To confirm their social and political legitimacy, minorities sought active roles in local militias to demonstrate their respectability and citizenship in the community. Moreover, citizen-soldiers enjoyed the rights and privileges of full citizenship. Military service was indeed an indication of citizenship status.[9] Consequently, African American civil rights struggles were historically associated with the ability to serve in the armed forces as defenders of America's democratic institutions and support the nation in times of war.[10] The World War II *Double V* campaign, victory at home and abroad, reflects a historic political strategy of civil rights leaders during the 1940s. The goal of the campaign was to encourage Black support for the United States during the war while continuing the struggle for political and social rights. The campaign was so significant to civil rights activism during the World War II era that it is rare for scholars or historians to approach the period without at least vague reference to the slogan and its importance.[11]

Though African American soldiers during World War II experienced racial discrimination, violence, oppression, and social injustices that racial minorities experienced in the US military throughout American history, World War II was distinctive. The 1940s reflect political and social change in the armed forces in several significant ways. For the first time since the American Revolution, the navy and marine corps began recruiting African American soldiers to serve in leadership and combat roles. The navy also assembled two entire African American crews on a naval destroyer (USS *Mason*) and a submarine chaser (USS PC-1264) with Black junior officers. In 1942 the marine corps began enlisting the first group of African Americans at Montford Point, Camp Lejeune, in North Carolina with Black drill instructors. Many of these individuals went on to serve in combat roles in the Pacific theater even though it was not the original intention of the War Department.[12] The most recognized African American combat unit of the war were the famed Tuskegee Airmen composed of the 332nd Fighter Group and 477th Medium Bombardment Group of the US Army Air Force. Despite becoming a highly decorated combat unit with nearly 100 Distinguished Flying Cross medals for *heroism and extraordinary* service, "White America derisively dubbed the Tuskegee Airmen Eleanor's [n----rs]."[13]

Undeniably, experiences of African American soldiers during World War II were both negative and positive and everything in between. Very similar to attitudes about the war in the Black community, African Americans supported the conflict for a host of good reasons, while others objected to any involvement as a logical response to social discrimination and second-class citizenship. Everyone chose to serve or were involuntarily conscripted and embraced or rejected the experience for a list of personal and collective reasons. African Americans who served during the war, such as Amzie Moore, Walter Greene, David Carson, and Dorie Miller, represent a small sample of individuals who struggled to navigate through systemic racism in the military while searching for ways to improve their lives and the well-being of their families.

Although Dorie Miller became a national hero for courage and exemplary service during the attack on Pearl Harbor in 1941, he reflects the experience of the average African American serviceman in World War II. He was an improbable hero from a rural community with parents who were farmers and grandparents who were former slaves, much like many others. He joined the navy to help support his family financially and searched for a way to escape poverty, racism, and the disenfranchisement experienced by African Americans in central Texas and throughout the South. Miller was not well educated and had few options in the navy besides to serve in a racially subservient role as a messman charged with making beds and shining shoes for white sailors and officers.

Because Dorie Miller was by nature a quiet and shy individual, his newfound celebrity became a source of anxiety and a burden for him for the remainder of his short life. A little more than a year after Miller was thrust on the national scene, while on a national war bond tour in the United States, Miller broke off his engagement with his girlfriend saying that he did not want to leave a war widow and became increasingly depressed and prophetic about his chances to live a prosperous life after the war. He reportedly told his brother, "This is my last roundup. I will not be back. If the Japanese don't get me, some jealous shipmate will."[14] He added, "Since receiving the Navy Cross (medal) my life is a holy hell. The white folks never did like me because I'm colored. Now the colored guys aboard ship do not like me because they say I think I'm somebody special."[15] Miller convinced himself that when he returned to active duty after the war bond tour, his next assignment would be a "suicide mission." According to his longtime friend and classmate Pauline Adams, Miller openly wept at a nightclub in Waco, Texas, and was visibly shaken. Unfortunately, when he returned for duty after that emotionally charged evening, two years to the day on December 7, 1943, his parents were notified by the War Department that his ship was sunk by a Japanese submarine, and he was "missing in action" but presumed dead.[16]

The war also produced a new generation of civil rights activists and leaders that were energized and motivated by their experiences in the military at home and overseas. Very similar to the Reconstruction era and the decade after World War I, when Black America's most militant and tenacious African American leaders were former soldiers and officers who challenged white supremacy and terrorism in the South, thousands of Black veterans of World War II and the Korean War led local and state civil rights struggles throughout the South and in many cases became staunch supporters of armed resistance and self-defense activism.[17] Many of these men and women returned home to fight another war: a war for democracy in a familiar place called home. This was reminiscent of French veterans of the American Revolution who returned home to lead their compatriots in the revolution to form a new government in France. African American veterans were hypersensitive to political conditions and were eager to correct social inequality in the South.[18] As former soldiers, they had already experienced a basic level of equality with white men in the military. This condition empowered them and created a source of pride and confidence that many white southerners found threatening.[19]

For instance, World War II veteran Amzie Moore, who upon returning to Mississippi after the war led voter registration drives. In South Carolina, William Saunders, a Korean War veteran became a well-known community activist and one of the chief organizers in the 1969 Hospital Strike in Charleston, South Carolina. Georgia native Hosea Williams served in Patton's Third Army during World War II, and in 1965 he was appointed by the Southern Christian Leadership Conference (SCLC) to organize the now famous Selma to Montgomery march in Alabama.[20] World War II veteran Walter Greene returned to Detroit, Michigan, after the war filled with an energy and passion to fight for social equality after fighting for his life in the Pacific and against racism and discrimination within his unit. Greene explains why Black soldiers were often at the forefront of the civil rights struggle when he remarked, "The Negro soldier is going to be militant because he is looking for something—he expects something better than the status quo when he gets home, or the public will have a severe problem on its hands."[21]

Military service during World War II and racial integration in the armed forces had a direct impact on African American attitudes toward military service as well as heightened expectations for social progress in general society. In Louisiana, Black men and women returned from World War II with more than a sense of entitlement to the benefits of first-class citizenship; in many cases, it included a new determination to lead their communities in the quest for civil and equal rights. Two of the more noteworthy civil rights leaders from Louisiana were World War II veterans Johnnie A. Jones from Laurel

Hill, Louisiana, and Earnest "Chilly Willy" Thomas from Bogalusa, Louisiana, who served in the air force as a radio operator during the Korean War.

Johnnie A. Jones was a native of West Feliciana Parish. He majored in industrial education at Southern University and was drafted in 1942. His army unit was all Black with white officers stationed at Camp Claiborne in Rapides, Louisiana. Jones was an exceptional soldier with a high IQ that allowed him to work in administration even though he did not know how to type. He was quickly promoted by the inspector general because of his knowledge of protocol and his organizational skills. During the 1940s, it was rare for an African American enlisted soldier to be recommended for Officer Candidate School, and despite that fact, Jones declined the invitation much to the dismay of his superior, Major Bagert, who labeled him a "Huey Long Boy and NAACPer." Shortly thereafter, he was assigned to a recruiting station in New Orleans and quickly received the support of his commander, who suggested that he apply for Warrant Officer School. Although everyone who worked with him at the recruiting station expected him to fail the qualifying test, Jones passed and became one of nation's first African American warrant officers during the war. He was stationed in Glasgow, Scotland, where he trained to take part in Operation Overlord, the Normandy Invasion of Europe, on Omaha Beach as a member of the 5th Engineer Special Brigade, 494th Quartermaster Port Battalion. While in Europe, Jones worked on special assignment out of the headquarters of the supreme commander of Allied forces, General Dwight Eisenhower and routinely engaged General George Patton. Jones also participated in the Battle of the Bulge, where he was wounded, and the Red Ball Express, the famed truck convoy system that supplied Allied forces in their push to Berlin.[22]

Like many World War II veterans, Jones later remarked that his military service motivated him to stand up for his rights upon returning home to Baton Rouge. He stated that his family never accepted slavery and were never sharecroppers. He was always willing to speak up for what was right and at a young age aspired to be either a preacher or lawyer. Jones was a member of the NAACP youth chapter in his high school and later helped establish the NAACP chapter at Southern University.[23] After the war, Jones enrolled in Law School at Southern University. Two weeks after graduation in June 1953, he was invited by Reverend T. J. Jemison, a founding member of the Southern Christian Leadership Conference, to represent organizers of the Baton Rouge Bus Boycott. In 1953, Baton Rouge became the central battleground of the civil rights movement that gained the attention of Martin Luther King, Ralph Abernathy, E. D. Nixon, and other national leaders focused on challenging white supremacy and social injustice in their local communities. The Baton

Rouge bus boycott became the model for subsequent direct-action tactics including the Montgomery bus boycott of 1955.

Jim Crow laws necessitated the development of a thriving cohesive Black community in Baton Rouge that witnessed dozens of Black-owned businesses, restaurants, barber shops, drug stores, beauty parlors, funeral homes, medical practices, service stations, churches, and a hotel. Many African American entrepreneurs and church pastors understandably became some of the community's most vocal Black leaders on the subject of racism and discrimination because their livelihood was not dependent on white patronage or support. Though Southern University employed a predominate workforce of African American administrators, professors, academic and auxiliary staff, the most low-paying jobs, and unskilled menial labor were also occupied by African Americans. Not surprisingly, a large disparity existed between white and Black public education, public facilities, and economic opportunities. As second-class citizens in a staunchly segregated society, African Americans were constantly reminded of their inferior position in society.[24]

The Baton Rouge boycott began in response to a bus driver walkout that was initiated in response to a new city council ordinance that provided that "Negroes seat from the rear and white passengers from the front." However, it added that "bus drivers can request members of either race to move forward or backwards in the bus to prevent having aisle standees and empty seats."[25] The bus driver's union wanted to revert back to the old system that reserved ten seats in the front for white customers and ten seats in the back for African Americans. All seats in between those twenty seats were open on a first-come-first-serve basis.

At the beginning of the strike, the city council reminded the BRBC and bus driver's union that in 1949, at the insistence of the BRBC, the city council passed a city ordinance immediately removing from operation over sixty African American independent buses and giving exclusive rights of operation to the BRBC if the company agreed to "provide fair and adequate transportation to all segments of the population." This exclusive franchise also came with a wage increase for the bus drivers which were mitigated by the increase in business. The city council charged that for many prior months "because of the preexisting seating arrangements, the buses were operating only partially loaded buses on three main bus lines and at the same time passing up numerous negro passengers."[26]

In an effort to solicit public sympathy and support, scores of bus drivers' wives and children marched to the parish courthouse to apply pressure on city council members in an attempt to have them rescind their vote. The women stated that "they and their children were suffering because of the strike and urged the council to overturn the seating ordinance which played a central role in the work stoppage."[27] On the next day, the fifth day of the strike, the Louisiana attorney general reported that the new seating ordinance was in direct conflict with state segregation laws requiring separation of the races. At the close of business that day, the strike was to end, and the old seating system renewed. In response, Raymond Scott, secretary of the United Defense League urged African Americans not to ride city buses until a new system could be agreed upon by all parties. Scott added that transportation would be provided to all former bus riders, free of charge.[28] Later that evening, Scott, and president of the United Defense League, Reverend T. J. Jemison, held a mass meeting at Hebron Baptist Church with several hundred African American organizers and supporters in attendance. When Jemison was asked whether the Black community was boycotting the BRBC, knowing that Louisiana state law prohibited boycotts, Jemison remarked, "It's illegal to boycott, we're just not riding."[29]

The Baton Rouge bus boycott enjoyed the full support of the Black community. In addition to well-attended mass meetings, participation of 150 cars and drivers, and the cooperation of Black bus riders, African American gas station owners sold fuel to carpool drivers at cost. Even the BRBC called the effort "100 percent effective." Actually, it did not take long for the BRBC to feel the negative impact of the boycott. A bus company spokesman reported that although the company had not fired any drivers as a result of the lack of customers, the number of bus lines was decreased in order to reduce company expenses.[30] In Baton Rouge, nearly 80 percent of the bus riders were African American.

On the third day of the protest, while the BRBC was losing $1,600 per day, the United Defense League raised over $4,000. The "love offering," as Reverend Jemison put it, was growing larger, and the number of Black attendees to the community meetings was also. More than four thousand individuals participated in a meeting held at Capitol High School on June 22, and there, Reverend Jemison told the audience, "We have $260,000 waiting on the side for a franchise if they don't do what good people ought to do, and Christian people should do."[31] Reverend Jemison was not making idle threats concerning his ability to raise the capital to purchase a franchise. On the contrary, he was one of the few Black men in Louisiana who could acquire large amounts of money without the permission or support of white politicians. Before the meeting at Capitol High School concluded, Jemison remarked, "When this is over, we're not going to stop. We're going to vote. You're going to vote, you're going to register and if you can't read or write, we'll teach you."[32]

After the city council voted to implement a new bus seating ordinance, Reverend Jemison addressed more than seven thousand African Americans at a mass gathering at Memorial Stadium the following evening. Jemison told the enthusiastic crowd that although the seven-day bus boycott was officially over, he understood if individuals in the community decided not to ride the buses. It was clear by the crowd shouts of, "Stay off. Stay off!" that many individuals had chosen to maintain the protest on a personal basis. According to Reverend Jemison, the Baton Rouge bus boycott was a sign of things to come for African Americans and Baton Rouge at large. Jemison proclaimed, "Little by little, round by round, we are going to make Baton Rouge the Utopia of the South. You cannot change traditions and customs overnight; it takes patience, prayer and downright, rock-bottom common sense. Justice is on our side . . . and brother, its on the way."[33]

Though the general mood and reaction of the Black community was of gratification and fulfillment, several leaders such as Johnnie Jones believed that Jemison settled with white power brokers for personal and political reasons. According to Jones, "Jemison was receiving death threats from the Ku Klux Klan and was hesitant to offend the white power structure in Baton Rouge. He like many older Black leaders wanted to avoid direct confrontation with whites." Jones remarked, "The older generation was used to asking permission from whites."[34] He believed that African Americans should demand change. Death threats and violence did not faze him because he had experienced traumatic violence during World War II at Omaha Beach on D-Day and during the Battle of the Bulge.[35]

The success of the Baton Rouge bus boycott was made possible for at least two reasons. First, Reverend Jemison and the United Defense League were well organized, received the cooperation and support of the Black community, and were able to raise thousands of dollars fairly easily. Aldon Morris believes that the protest demonstration could have lasted much longer if necessary. Second, and probably most important, the bus drivers received very little support from the BRBC, local white politicians, and business leaders. Therefore, the effort of the bus drivers was not sustainable.[36] Nevertheless, the Baton Rouge bus boycott reflected significant progress in the struggle for social equality and equal rights in the postwar period. In a few short years later, Black leaders throughout the South would use those same tactics to challenge segregation laws in their local communities.

By the late 1950s, as the American South became the national arena for civil rights struggles, Black college campuses became a focal point of youth participation and activism. Though Southern University president, F. G. Clark attempted to refocus student attention on educational pursuits, Black college students were taking a deep interest in the world around them and effecting social change in their communities. In December 1955, a chapter of the NAACP Youth Council was formed at Southern University by twenty-six students with the support of the dean of students, Martin L. Harvey. Felton G. Clark was already a member of the organization and he encouraged others to join as well.[37] By 1960, the NAACP Youth Council had already, participated in several protest demonstrations in the Baton Rouge area. Not surprisingly, the first president of the chapter selected to lead the organization was ROTC cadet officer Donald Delandro. Delandro graduated from Southern University in 1956 and ultimately retired from the US Army as a brigadier general.[38]

As African American military veterans returned home from the battle grounds of Europe, Asia, North Africa, and the South Pacific during the 1940s and '50s, many of them joined the historic movement of Black resistance and self-defense activism to white supremacy that dates back to the colonial period in American history. According to Charles E. Cobb, "In every decade of the nation's history, brave and determined black men and women picked up guns to defend themselves and their communities." Though many individuals attempt to describe civil rights activists as antithetical to the nonviolent movement, the tradition of armed self-defense activism cannot be disconnected from the success of what today is called the "nonviolent civil rights struggle." Much of the popular history of the civil rights era that is embraced and taught in schools today rests on the perception that the movement achieved its goals through nonviolent direct action and the support of white liberals.[39] African Americans defending themselves and protecting their families and communities in no way contradicts the nonviolent struggle that most individuals believe was the dominant tactic of Black leaders throughout history. In fact, the nonviolent strategy was supported and protected in many ways by gunfire and the threat of gunfire of African American men and women who knew that one could not be achieved without the other.[40] "Simply put, because nonviolence worked so well as a tactic for effecting change and was demonstrably improving the lives of African Americans, many military veterans chose to use their leadership experience, combat training, organizational skills, and weapons to defend the nonviolent freedom movement to ensure its success."[41]

In Bogalusa, Louisiana, in the 1960s, the local police force was composed of white officers and a small contingent of African Americans. The Black policemen were able to curtail incidents of white police brutality in addition to discouraging Ku Klux Klan caravans from committing terrorist acts in the Black community. In early 1964, two organizers operating out of the Congress on Racial Equality's (CORE) regional office in Monroe, Louisiana, began regularly visiting Jonesboro, Louisiana, to assist the Voters League. One of the organizers,

Mike Lesser, was northern, white, and inexperienced. The other was Ronnie Moore, a Black native of New Orleans; in 1962 he had been expelled from Southern University for protesting segregation in Baton Rouge.[42] By the time he made his first visit to Jonesboro, Moore had already been jailed eighteen times. In Louisiana, CORE promoted nonviolent direct action against segregation and began testing the newly passed Civil Rights Act. Jonesboro student protestors regularly targeted the public library and the municipal swimming pool.

But as welcoming as CORE's reception from the Jonesboro's Black community was, CORE organizers found themselves the target of white terrorism almost as soon as they arrived. Although they suffered minimal police harassment, the Ku Klux Klan brazenly threatened them and often fired shots at them through the windows of their headquarters, the Freedom House. But Jonesboro's Black community wanted the CORE activists in their town and had no intention of letting the Klansmen run them off. A few men like Ernest "Chilly Willy" Thomas, then twenty-nine years old, who served in the air force as a radio operator during the Korean War, began to quietly guard the Freedom House and its occupants. Thomas wanted to work with the CORE organizers, but he could not commit to nonviolence. And for their part, CORE activists were reluctant to compromise their commitment to nonviolence.[43] But the two groups were not as incompatible as they might seem. Thomas and his guardians simply found a way to assist the CORE activists. Though at first Thomas and his guardians provided unarmed protection, before long they were watching over the CORE workers with concealed weapons. Thomas and his group of military veterans of local defenders did not join the CORE activists in nonviolent direct action. The discipline was impossible for them to accept. If they were spat upon or physically attacked in any way, they were not going to turn the other cheek, and they understood that their response would cause problems for CORE. Yet they had no problem with standing on the sidelines and stepping in if someone threatened to harm the nonviolent activists. In response, Earnest Thomas established the Deacons for Defense and Justice, an armed self-defense organization. According to Lance Hill, "The name reflected the group's desire to identify with traditionally respected symbols of authority, peace, and moral order in the black community. The Deacons were attempting to wed two contradictory symbols: Christian pacifism and violence. They hoped to identify with Christianity while defying its pacifist teachings."[44] By 1965, the Deacons for Defense and Justice became so popular that chapters were started in Texas and Arkansas, and plans were implemented to organize additional ones in Florida, Georgia, and North Carolina. The Deacons for Defense became a major deterrent to white terrorism in the South and Klan activity in the

Black community. Chapters also provided security and protection for local civil rights leaders and marchers. During the Meredith March against Fear in Mississippi in 1966, the Deacons gained national attention.[45]

To truly understand the modern civil rights movement, one must appreciate the vital role of African American military veterans and the value of military service in the pursuit of equal citizenship and social justice. Many of Black America's most courageous civil rights leaders were wartime veterans who organized and provided the leadership of formidable grassroots movements throughout the South in the post–World War II era. Christopher Parker asks us to "imagine the movement without Hosea Williams leading the 'Bloody Sunday' march over the Edmund Pettus bridge between Selma and Montgomery, Alabama; without Aaron Henry's leadership of both the Mississippi Freedom Democratic Party and the NAACP of Mississippi; consider the Student Nonviolent Coordinating Committee (SNCC) without the leadership of James Forman; and how can we forget the bravery and selfless actions of James Meredith and other black military veterans?"[46] Though many students of the civil rights movement may be vaguely familiar with the exploits of the iconic leaders previously mentioned, it is less known that scores of student activists and leaders on Black college campuses during the same period were ROTC cadets, who felt it was their duty to spearhead local demonstrations to effect social change. That is why civil rights activism is important to understanding attitudes toward military service at Southern University and Black colleges and universities in general.

In 1960, students at Southern University actively led protests for social and political change in Louisiana. Student leaders at Southern University organized sit-in demonstrations and marches demanding equal rights and justice. Following the efforts of four North Carolina Agricultural & Technical College students in Greensboro, North Carolina, in February 1960, students at Southern decided to voice their dissatisfaction with racial inequality in Louisiana. Most significantly, one of the student activists at North Carolina A&T was Joseph McNeil, an ROTC cadet. McNeil was deeply influenced by his military training and follow cadets in the areas of planning, mobilization, and execution in challenging racial inequality. He later remarked, "Our thing was unique. A&T was unique inasmuch as we had military training, ROTC [Reserve Officer Training Corps], army and air force. These guys are taught a different type of leadership. Not the type that you go out and you come up with ideas—God knows the military's not creative—but they are taught a type of leadership where you methodically do things, you have an objective, you follow. If you're ever going to lead, you have to follow. So we had all these sources available to us, and we leaned on, to a very large degree, the students in ROTC to provide the mobilization concepts and to go to the meetings and to do the negotiating."[47]

The response of students and faculty at Southern was a well-coordinated effort that reflected the general reaction of African American youth at Black colleges and universities throughout the South. Within six weeks of the initial demonstration at Woolworth's store in Greensboro, student activists enrolled at Bennett College (Greensboro, North Carolina), Alabama State University (Montgomery, Alabama), Allen University (Columbia, South Carolina), Benedict College (Columbia, South Carolina), Fisk University (Nashville, Tennessee), Tennessee A & I State University (Nashville, Tennessee), Virginia State College (Petersburg, Virginia), Texas Southern University (Houston, Texas) and many other HBCUs started sit-down demonstrations in their respective communities.[48] In an act of solidarity, students at Tuskegee Institute (Tuskegee, Alabama) and Dillard University (New Orleans, Louisiana) held student protests on their college campuses as well.[49] Weeks before the student protest at Southern, four hundred students at Tuskegee marched downtown to protest deprivation of voting rights, to call for civil equality in general, and to express sympathy with other student demonstrations throughout the country.[50]

In Louisiana and throughout the South, the NAACP, the SCLC, SNCC, and CORE were the backbone of the fight for social justice and racial equality. Arguably, CORE was the most important grass-roots organization.[51] In addition to being one of the oldest civil rights organizations, beginning in 1942, CORE was primarily responsible for the Freedom Rides of 1961 and organizing the efforts of HBCU students during the sit-in movement of the early 1960s that were led by HBCU student leaders. The national architect and director of CORE was James Farmer, a pacifist and graduate of Howard University.[52] Farmer was instrumental in CORE activities in Louisiana at the request of Southern University student leaders Major Johns and Marvin Robinson, who were deeply involved in the sit-in demonstrations at S.H. Kress Department Store and Sitman's Drug Store in downtown Baton Rouge. Major Johns and countless student activists at Southern University embraced a new militancy and moral imperative that drove their actions and commitment to change when Johns remarked, "No longer can we endure the back door of public places, the denial of equal job opportunities, the right to vote or any privilege granted to a full citizen . . . We will strike the moral conscience of the white man and not his physical body. Let the echoes of the Christian principles he taught . . . and the shocking realization that, in the words of Jefferson, all men are created equal . . . ring in his own ears."[53]

Louisiana gained the attention of CORE leaders for multiple reasons, but in particular, because many rural parishes excluded Black voters from the list of registrants even though African Americans composed the majority of the local populations. In one instance, the town of Plaquemine became the focus of national attention and interest when Spiver Gordon, a former Southern University student attempted to register to vote at the Iberville Parish courthouse and was abruptly turned away. Gordon was a native of Plaquemine and a military veteran who had recently returned from Germany, where he led protests and demonstrations to desegregate base facilities. When asked how Gordon became involved in CORE and civil rights activism, he later remarked, "When I was in the Army, in 1960 it started there because there were some facilities, some clubs and black soldiers were not allowed. And, having the experience before I went in the Army of sit-ins and all of that, we organized a boycott. We sat-in and so the company commander realized a problem because everything in the army was open in 1948. Well, we initiated the boycott, and we began to protest. And, they opened the clubs, that was the first thing that happened. But it was in the military when I was first called the N word."[54]

Gordon's efforts in March 1963 reflected a CORE strategic initiative that sent hundreds of African Americans to several Parish courthouses throughout south Louisiana with the goal of soliciting the intervention of the US Justice Department. According to August Meier and Elliott Rudwick, "In April [1963] when CORE tried to register 138 in Pointe Coupee Parish, 92 were turned down, including three schoolteachers. At Tangipahoa Parish, a black high school graduate asked the registrar if he had passed the test, and was told, You didn't flunk, you just got to come back some other time. Complaints sent to the Justice Department were ignored. Even a trip by James T. McCain, CORE Louisiana Field Secretary to personally confer with Burke Marshall, head of the Civil Rights Division in the U.S. Justice Department proved unproductive."[55] Despite the discouraging reaction and strategic setback, CORE leaders were determined to expand their voter registration efforts in the region.

Several months later, in August 1963, CORE redoubled its efforts to register voters in Plaquemine to gain African American access to municipal improvements such as paved roads, sewerage and open gutters, and better living conditions in the partitioned Black community. At the request of Ronnie Moore, New Orleans field secretary, James Farmer agreed to join the protestors for a three-day visit that culminated in a ten-day jail sentence in nearby Donaldsonville. Two days later, a group of young African Americans led a demonstration to protest racial segregation in public facilities that was immediately rebuffed by local police and state troopers on horseback armed with billy clubs and cattle prods. The level of violence and abuse inflicted on African American youth was described as gratuitous savagery and horrific.

The very next day, the events were replayed with the same outcome. State troopers charged into the crowds of women and children on horseback waving billy clubs and cattle prods screaming, "Run [n----rs], run!"[56]

Farmer and numerous protestors found refuge in Plymouth Rock Church while they sought medical attention and hid from a coordinated manhunt of police officers, sheriff's deputies, and state troopers. Troopers were canvasing the streets, kicking in doors, and yelling, "Come on out, Farmer, we know you're in there. Come on out, Farmer! We're going to get you."[57] At sunset, Farmer and dozens of individuals left the church and crawled through an adjacent grassy field to a local funeral home in an attempt to distance themselves from the pursuing manhunt. Unfortunately, it was not long before troopers found him and kicked in the outer door screaming, "Farmer, come out!" With hundreds of individuals' lives at stake, Farmer decided to surrender to the mob that disguised itself as law enforcement officials. As Farmer started to move toward the door between him and the state troopers, he later remarked, "Men around me grabbed me silently and pulled me back into the front room, whispering fiercely, We're not going to let you go out there tonight, That's a lynch mob. You go out there tonight, you won't be alive tomorrow morning."[58] As time slowly passed, Farmer's level of anxiety and fear began to heighten with nervous anticipation of the impending doom. To his surprise, his lawyers from New Orleans, Lolis Elie and Robert Collins, made their way through the dark, surrounding cemetery and pushed themselves past the traumatized crowd in the inner room with outside news of the siege. Most assumed that it was only a matter of time before state troopers charged into the funeral home and took Farmer to a location where he would be assassinated.[59]

But to Farmer's surprise, another knock at the door disturbed him once more. Farmer remarked,

> I remembered that troopers don't knock. The two men who entered were recently acquired friends from Plaquemine, and pretty rough characters in their own right: my neighbor from town, whom I shall call Fred, and Bill, a buddy of his, ex-Marines who, I knew carried several guns in their car at all times. Then Fred and Bill set forth their plan to send two hearses in opposite directions using one as a decoy and the other as a get-away vehicle. Ronnie Moore, Reverend Jetson Davis and I crawled in the back and crouched down as the ex-Marines heavily armed followed in another car to provide safe passage out of Plaquemine to New Orleans while driving on back roads under the cover of darkness.[60]

Thousands of civil rights protests and demonstrations occurred throughout the South and in Louisiana during the decades after World War II. African American military veterans with combat experience were active participants and even risked their lives to protect demonstrators in support of the philosophy of armed self-defense. If not for the courageous, cool, and calm demeanor of two ex-marines who orchestrated a plan to save the lives of James Farmer and his colleagues, Plaquemine, Louisiana, would have been known for the possible tragic end of a civil rights leader and icon in 1963.

During the early post–World War II period, America fought a war of ideas and political principles against communism, and military integration and Cold War rhetoric encouraged African Americans to make greater social and political demands on American society. The postwar period reflected significant achievements in the struggle for equality in the federal justice system, and US Armed Forces that further motivated and empowered African Americans and students at Black colleges and universities. As America moved closer to the 1960s, and a new phase of youth inspired civil rights activism, the state of Louisiana continued to be a prominent actor in the struggle for social justice and equality on the national scene. Beginning in 1960 with Ruby Bridges and the integration of the New Orleans Public School System, the Freedom Rides, Southern University student sit-in demonstrations led by SNCC, the CORE voter registration project in rural Louisiana, the killing of two Southern University students during campus demonstrations in 1972, and antipoverty programs during the 1970s that linked economic inequality and civil rights activism, these events reflected a continuum of leadership, courage, dedication, and selfless service designed to challenge an unfair and unpatriotic system of injustice and inequality. The struggle for social equality in Louisiana and throughout the South was very much a soldier's story of how military service and training motivated ordinary men and women to return home after serving their nation to fight for democracy and freedom in Louisiana.

NOTES

1. Studs Terkel, *The Good War: An Oral History of World War II* (New York: New Press, 1997).

2. *Beyond All Boundaries Film Documentary*, National World War II Museum, New Orleans, LA.

3. Rawn James Jr., *The Double V: How Wars, Protest, and Harry Truman Desegregated America's Military* (New York: Bloomsbury, 2013), 159.

4. David M. Kennedy, *Freedom from Fear: The American People in Depression and War, 1929–1945* (New York: Oxford University Press, 1999), 162–65.

5. Terry H. Anderson, *The Movement and the Sixties: Protest in America from Greensboro to Wounded Knee* (New York: Oxford University Press, 1996), 4–28.

6. Marcus S. Cox, *Segregated Soldiers: Military Training at Historically Black Colleges in the Jim Crow South* (Baton Rouge: Louisiana State University Press, 2013), 90.

7. Cox, *Segregated Soldiers*, 90–91.

8. Benjamin Quarles, *The Negro in the American Revolution* (Chapel Hill: University of North Carolina Press, 1961), 19, 53–54.

9. Mary Frances Berry, *Military Necessity and Civil Rights Policy: Black Citizenship and the Constitution, 1861–1868* (Port Washington, NY: Associated Faculty, 1977), 1; see also Rod Andrew Jr., *Long Gray Lines: The Southern Military School Tradition, 1839–1915* (Chapel Hill: University of North Carolina Press, 2001), 3; Cynthia Enloe, *Maneuvers: The International Politics of Militarizing Women's Lives* (Berkeley: University of California Press, 2000), 247.

10. Charles D. Chamberlain, *Victory at Home: Manpower and Race in the American South during World War II* (Athens: University of Georgia Press, 2003), 4–5.

11. James, *The Double V*, 18.

12. Kai Wright, *Soldiers of Freedom: An Illustrated History of African Americans in the Armed Forces* (New York, 2002), 165–68.

13. Wright, *Soldiers of Freedom*, 175.

14. Thomas W Cutrer and Michael Parish, *Doris Miller: Pearl Harbor and the Birth of the Civil Rights Movement* (College Station: Texas A&M University Press, 2018), 75.

15. Cutrer and Parish, *Doris Miller*, 76.

16. Cutrer and Parish, *Doris Miller*, 82.

17. Christopher B. Strain, *Pure Fire: Self-Defense as Activism in the Civil Rights Era* (Athens: University of Georgia Press, 2005), 55–56.

18. Ronald R. Krebs, *Fighting for Rights: Military Service and the Politics of Citizenship*. (Ithaca: Cornell University Press, 2006), 8.

19. Christopher S. Parker, *Fighting for Democracy: Black Veterans and the Struggle against White Supremacy in the Postwar South* (Princeton: Princeton University Press, 2009), 61–74.

20. Parker, *Fighting for Democracy*, 52; Felice F. Knight, "Portrait of a Community Activist: William 'Bill' Saunders and the Black Freedom Struggle in Charleston, SC, 1951–2004" (thesis, College of Charleston, 2006), 45–46.

21. Robert F. Jefferson, *Fighting for Hope: African American Troops of the 93rd Infantry Division in World War II and Postwar America* (Baltimore: Johns Hopkins University Press, 2008), 2.

22. Johnnie A. Jones, interview by Mary Hebert, tape recorded transcript, Baton Rouge, LA, T. Harry Williams Center for Oral History Collection, Louisiana State University Library, session 1—session 3, tape 451–82, September 1, 1993.

23. Jones, interview by Hebert.

24. Jones, interview by Hebert, 5–8.

25. "City Bus Strike Will Continue, Talks Planned," *Morning Advocate*, June 16, 1953, 6-A, 2.

26. "Called by Negotiators Brief Meet: City Bus Strike Still On," *Morning Advocate*. 17 June, 1953, 8-A, 4.

27. "Bus Strike Talks Continuing, Said More Favorable," *Morning Advocate*, June 18, 1953, 1-A.

28. "City Bus Strike to End at Dawn Today: Attorney General Says City Seating Law Is Invalid," *Morning Advocate* June 19, 1953, 1-A.

29. "Negroes Here Continue Bus Boycott; Company May Curtail Service," *Morning Advocate* June 20, 1953, 1-A.

30. "Negroes Here Continue," 2-A, 3.

31. "New Ordinance on Bus Seating Is Kept Secret," *Morning Advocate* June 23, 1953, 1-A.

32. New Ordinance on Bus Seating Is Kept Secret," *Morning Advocate*. 23 June, 1953: 6-A, col. 7.

33. Cox., *Segregated Soldiers*, 97.

34. Johnnie A. Jones, interview by Mary Hebert, tape recorded transcript, Baton Rouge, LA, T. Harry Williams Center for Oral History Collection, Louisiana State University Library, session 4, tape 508, September 1, 1993.

35. Johnnie A. Jones, interview by Mary Hebert, tape recorded transcript, Baton Rouge, LA, T. Harry Williams Center for Oral History Collection, Louisiana State University Library, session 5, tape 510, September 1, 1993.

36. Aldon D. Morris, *The Origins of the Civil Rights Movement: Black Communities Organizing for Change* (New York, 1984), 25.

37. E. C. Harrison, interview by Marcus S Cox, tape recorded interview, Baton Rouge, LA, March 29, 2010.

38. "NAACP Chapter Formed on Campus," *Southern University Digest* 27, no. 5, December 2, 1955, 1.

39. Lance Hill, *The Deacons for Defense: Armed Resistance and the Civil Rights Movement* (Chapel Hill: University of North Carolina Press, NC, 2004), 4.

40. Charles E. Cobb Jr., *This Nonviolent Stuff 'll Get You Killed: How Guns Made the Civil Rights Movement Possible* (Duram, NC: Duke University Press, 2016), 2.

41. Cobb, *This Nonviolent Stuff*.

42. Hill, *The Deacons for Defense*, 21.

43. Hill, *The Deacons for Defense*, 25.

44. Hill, *The Deacons for Defense*, 38–47.

45. Strain, *Pure Fire*, 111–15.

46. Parker, *Fighting for Democracy*, 196–97.

47. Joseph McNeil, interview by William Henry Chafe, William Henry Chafe Oral History Collection, Civil Rights Greensboro, Digital Archive, Duke University, 1978.

48. "Integration Action in N.C. Spreads," *Morning Advocate*, February 9, 1960, A-1; "Chanting Negroes Parade in Alabama against Segregation, *Morning Advocate*, March 2, 1960, A-1; "Negroes Continue Demonstrations for Integration," *Morning Advocate* March 4, 1960, A-1; "11 Negroes Arrested for Trespassing," *Morning Advocate*, March 8, 1960, A-1.

49. "Demonstrations by Negroes Hit Two Big Cities," *Morning Advocate*, March 9, 1960, A-1.

50. "400 Students Parade in Support of Civil Rights," *The Campus Digest*, March 1, 1960, 1.

51. August Meier and Elliott Rudwick, *CORE: A Study in the Civil Rights Movement, 1942–1968* (New York: Oxford University Press, 1975), 3.

52. Meier and Rudwick, *CORE*, 5–6.

53. Meier and Rudwick, *CORE*, 107.

54. Spiver Gordon, interview by Monty J. Thornburg, July 28, 2019, transcript, Eutaw, Alabama.

55. Gordon, interview by Thornburg, 177–78.

56. James Farmer, *Freedom—When?* (New York: Random House, 1965), 5–6.

57. Farmer, *Freedom*, 9.

58. Farmer, *Freedom*.

59. Farmer, *Freedom*, 12.

60. Farmer, *Freedom*, 13–14.

SECTION TWO

Corruption, Violence, and the Limits of Reform

Chapter Four

PUBLIC CORRUPTION IN LOUISIANA

THEN AND NOW

ADAM FAIRCLOUGH

"Half of Louisiana is under water, and the other half is under indictment." This quip, attributed to ex-congressman and Big Pharma lobbyist Billy Tauzin, summarizes a common view: When it comes to politics, the Pelican state is egregiously corrupt. Residents of other states adopt a version of the "thank God for Mississippi" line: however rotten the condition of their own politics, it will always be worse in Louisiana. As the *Chicago Tribune* put it: "For . . . infused-in-the-gumbo style public venality, Louisiana has Illinois, and the rest of America, beat." Veteran politician Bill Dodd admitted as much in his memoirs, published in 1991. "A big-time politician who failed to get rich and make his friends rich has been considered stupid," he wrote. "And Louisiana produced only a few stupid politicians."[1]

What accounts for Louisiana's high level of corruption? One theory is that the state is a "banana republic." Not literally, of course, but in the sense that its French, Spanish, and Catholic roots set it apart from the rest of the union. As political commentator John Maginnis put it, "While the American political experience derived from distrust of monarchs and centralized authority, Louisiana's political traditions grew out of European and Catholic attitudes of submission to authority and fealty to the king, or the pope, or both." Hence the state's government was "built around the banana republic principle of one strong man, accountable only to the vote of the people and unfettered by the checks and balances found in established democracies."[2]

Journalist A. J. Liebling argued that Louisiana's political culture was more Mediterranean than American. He likened the complexity of the state's politics to that of Lebanon, with Catholics, Protestants, and Blacks standing in for Maronites, Muslims, and Druze. In both countries, building a winning political coalition demanded a level of wheeler-dealing that encouraged political expediency and loose ethics. "The expression of conventional indignation [over corruption] is not so customary in Louisiana as farther north. The Louisianians, like Levantines, think it naïve."[3]

Explanations that emphasize Louisiana exceptionalism, however, are open to an obvious objection: Before the 1970s there was no metric that could enable us to rank states on a scale of least corrupt to most corrupt. Whether or not Louisiana's public officials have been more corrupt, historically, than those of other states is impossible to determine. What we do know is that corruption has been ubiquitous in American, not merely Louisianian, politics.

Three other caveats are in order. First, the words "corrupt" and "corruption" were terms of political abuse that, especially from 1865 through 1914, were thrown about with abandon. In the words of historian Mark Summers, "the cry of corruption was as widespread, as defamatory, and as indiscriminate as the charge of Communism" after 1945. During Reconstruction, for example, Democrats painted the Republican Party in the South as universally corrupt, which it clearly was not. Moreover, many instances of corruption turned out to be, to quote Summers again, examples of "negligence, incompetence, or extravagance."[4]

In the second place, as far as the nineteenth century is concerned, behavior that nowadays might send a politician to prison did not violate the law. Stealing public money was a crime, but the giving and taking of bribes, insider trading, buying votes and treating voters, and exchanging gifts for government favors were either legal or so widespread as to be practically so. Although public opinion became increasingly critical of such practices, such was the complexity of American government that "corruption wasn't just a form of aberrational behavior; it was how business got done."[5]

Finally, actions that are now regarded as unethical or corrupt were intrinsic to the development of mass democracy. Bribes and kickbacks fueled the party machines that managed the never-ending electoral cycle and imposed a semblance of order on a Rube Goldberg–like governmental structure. The spoils system enabled parties to tithe government employees and mobilize them as election workers; it also produced brilliant politicians, many of humble origin, who cultivated the loyalty of working-class voters, especially immigrants. The ward boss, often to be found in a saloon, might provide a job, a loan during hard times, a bucket of coal during a harsh winter, and help with obtaining licenses and permits. There was no welfare state then. Such assistance meant a lot. Bear in mind, too, that the mass of voters paid little in the way of direct taxation. The up-front costs of corruption were mostly paid for by the wealthy. To the poor, the costs were indirect and invisible. Faced with a choice between smiling, open-handed bosses and scowling, tight-fisted reformers, voters more often than not opted for the former.[6]

Such caveats notwithstanding, Louisiana's reputation for public corruption is longstanding and well founded. From the state's earliest days in the union, public officials set about enriching themselves with what historian Joe Tregle called "piratical exuberance." Looking at the Jacksonian era, Tregle found himself astonished at the sheer scale of malfeasance. In the space of just fifteen years, "six postmasters, a federal marshal, one naval officer, one federal attorney, one surveyor general, no fewer than ten receivers of public monies, [and] at least two collectors of customs" were exposed as thieves. Corruption during the 1850s was, according to Summers, even more pronounced.[7]

During Reconstruction, legislators openly traded their votes for cash or company stock. Parish officials stole school board funds. The state auditor was exposed as a forger and embezzler. Two Republican governors, Henry Clay Warmoth and William Pitt Kellogg, used more subtle but equally shady means of making themselves wealthy. Rival candidates for the US Senate—then elected by the state legislature—advanced their cause by bribing lawmakers. Congressional investigating committees were appalled at the ethical swamp of Louisiana politics. As Ben Butler of Massachusetts put it—and he was hardly a model of probity—"they do things differently here." When looking at the state's politics, he explained, one must constantly keep in mind "the inertia of conscience in Louisiana politicians." After seeing a parade of witnesses give evidence about the 1876 election, the *New York World* likened that conscience to a "patent duplex back-action India-rubber."[8]

It would be nice to report that the "redemption" of the state from Republican rule in 1877 marked a return to honest government. But there was no tradition of honest government to return to. Democrats gladly accepted backhanders from the Louisiana Lottery Company. State treasurer E. A. Burke exiled himself to Honduras after an audit revealed a hole in his accounts amounting to $1,267,905. There were, to be sure, public officials of integrity, and advocates of honest government were sometimes elected to the governor's office. But such men did not set the tone. By the 1880s, writes William Ivy Hair, Louisiana "had become a byword for political corruption and general lawlessness." By 1900, the Democratic Party had secured a monopoly on power through electoral fraud, violence, and the disfranchisement of Black voters. This one-party system provided a perfect climate in which corruption could flourish.[9]

Huey Long, elected governor in 1928 and US senator in 1932, gave corruption a new twist. Jacking up taxes on Standard Oil, he turned state government into a public benefactor, providing highways, toll-free bridges, free school textbooks, and improved charity hospitals. He also forged a profitable alliance with Frank Costello, allowing the New York mobster to operate illegal casinos and import thousands of equally illegal slot machines. As Maginnis put it, Long "revolutionized Louisiana politics by taking from the rich, keeping some of it for himself and his friends, and giving more to the poor than government ever had before." After Long's death, however, his followers turned Louisiana into a kleptocracy. The stealing became so rampant that the federal government, fearing that state authorities would fail to take action, stepped in. Governor Dick Leche, bagman Seymour Weiss, and Louisiana State University president James Monroe Smith all went to jail. Hundreds of other politicians, state officials, and businessmen were indicted. Four of them committed suicide.[10]

Earl Long, Huey's younger brother, who served two full terms as governor (1948–52, 1956–60), was shrewd enough not to steal from the public treasury. But his FBI file revealed Earl to be, in the words of his biographers, "a man on the take, a politician who did not hesitate to accept bribes and engage in wholesale graft." Like Huey, he profited from the gambling operations of Costello, now assisted by local crime boss Carlos Marcello.[11]

Sheriffs were vital cogs in Earl's corrupt political machine. Men like Frank "King" Clancy of Jefferson Parish and D. J. "Cat" Doucet of St. Landry Parish shared in the profits of gambling and prostitution. But the uncrowned king of corruption was undoubtedly Leander Perez, for half a century the dictator—that is not too strong a term—of Plaquemines Parish. By manipulating the lease of oil—and sulfur-rich public land, Perez siphoned off an estimated $82 million that should have gone to the parish treasury.[12]

Nevertheless, before the 1970s, the chances of a bent politician going to jail were slim. The federal prosecutions of 1939 and 1940 were exceptional. The Department of Justice (DOJ) lacked the will, and the presidential backing, to mount a systematic attack on political corruption. The FBI, under J. Edgar Hoover, was more interested in persecuting radicals and discrediting Black leaders. Prosecutions by state authorities were also rare. As Maginnis put it, "Local corrupt politicians had nothing to worry about as long as the attorney general was your Jack P. F. Gremillion-type." Gremillion (of whom Earl Long once said, "If you want to hide something from Jack Gremillion, put it in a law book") served four consecutive terms. [13]

In 1971, however, a federal court convicted Gremillion of lying to a grand jury about his dealings with the Louisiana Loan and Thrift Company. He was sentenced to a prison term of three years. The case was significant. Along with the jailing of Hugh Addonizio, a former mayor of Newark, New Jersey, and the bribery investigation that forced Vice President Spiro Agnew to resign, it showed that the federal government was beginning to take political corruption seriously. Indeed, after the Watergate scandal of 1972–74, public opinion demanded a housecleaning. In 1976, the DOJ created a Public Integrity Section in order to strengthen and coordinate "efforts against official corruption at all levels of government." Armed with federal anticorruption laws, which had been strengthened by the Racketeer Influenced and Corrupt Organizations (RICO) Act of 1970, the DOJ went on the attack. US attorneys received their marching orders. The FBI, eager to restore its tarnished reputation after the abuses of the Hoover years had come to light, employed aggressive techniques, including undercover and "sting" operations, to snare crooked politicians and public officials.

The results were startling, as this ten-yearly snapshot of federal convictions for public corruption reveals.

Table 4.1. Federal Prosecutions by US Attorneys' Offices of Corrupt Public Officials

	1970	1980	1990	2000	2010	2020
Federal	9	131	583	422	397	207
State	7	51	79	91	108	30
Local	161	168	225	183	280	110
Other	12	252	197	242	251	122
Total	44	552	1084	938	1036	469

Source: Department of Justice, Public Integrity Section, Report to Congress for 1978 (Washington, 1979), 1–2; Report to Congress for 1980 (Washington, 1981), 24; Report to Congress for 2000 (Washington, 2001), 36; Report to Congress for 2020 (Washington, 2021), 22–24.

Between 1976 and 2019, federal courts convicted hundreds of Louisiana officials of public corruption—697 in the Eastern Judicial District alone. They included some of the biggest fish in the political pond:

- US Representative Rick Tonry (1977)
- State Senator Gaston Gerald (1979)
- Commissioner of Agriculture Gil Dozier (1980)
- Commissioner of Administration Charles Roemer (1981)
- President of the State Senate Michael O'Keefe (1983, 1999)

- Commissioner of Insurance Doug Green (1991)
- Commissioner of Insurance Sherman Bernard (1993)
- State Senator Larry Bankston (1997)
- Commissioner of Insurance Jim Brown (2000)
- Commissioner of Elections Jerry Fowler (2000)
- Four-time governor Edwin W. Edwards (2000)

Among those prosecuted but not convicted were New Orleans district attorney Harry Connick, East Baton Rouge Parish district attorney Ossie Brown, state senator Gregory Tarver, agriculture commissioner Bob Odom, and US Representative Claude "Buddy" Leach.

Louisiana's sheriffs, many of whom had a well-earned reputation for brutality and corruption, lost the informal immunity they had long enjoyed. That they often stayed in office for decades, used their authority to appoint deputies as a form of political patronage, and were courted by governors and would-be governors, had magnified their impunity. But the freewheeling days of "King" Clancy and "Cat" Doucet ended. As the following list indicates, sheriffs now faced the real possibility of being prosecuted by state and federal authorities and of appearing before juries that were prepared to convict them.

Convicted sheriffs in Louisiana, 1985–2021[14]

- Johnny Lee Bridges (Sheriff of East Carroll Parish, ?–1983). Convicted 1985. Attempted murder.[15]
- Eugene Holland (Sheriff of St. Helena Parish, 1985–97). Convicted 1987. Misuse of government funds, using prison inmates for personal labor.
- Billy Tardo (Sheriff of Lafourche Parish, 1971–75). Convicted 1989. Attempted murder.
- Duffy Breaux (Sheriff of Lafourche Parish, 1975–92). Convicted 1993. Fraud.
- Dallas Cormier (Sheriff of Jefferson Davis Parish, 1980–92). Convicted 1993. Obstruction of justice.
- Dale Rinicker (Sheriff of East Carroll Parish, 1983–97). Convicted 1997. Mail fraud, conspiring to launder money, money laundering.
- Chaney Phillips (Sheriff of St. Helena Parish, 1997–98). Convicted 1998. Conspiracy, mail fraud, theft, money laundering.
- Jeff Britt (Sheriff of Tensas Parish, 1991–98). Convicted 1999. Malfeasance.

- Ronald Ficklin (Sheriff of St. Helena Parish, 1998–2005).
  Convicted 2005. Illegal use of prison labor in illegal business.
- Irwin "Jiff" Hingle Sheriff of (Plaquemines Parish, 1992–2011).
  Convicted 2011. Bribery, conspiracy to commit mail fraud.
- Royce Toney (Sheriff of Ouachita Parish, 2007–11).
  Convicted 2012. Conspiracy, computer fraud, identity theft, obstruction.
- Jack Strain (Sheriff of St. Tammany Parish, 1995–2015).
  Convicted 2021. Sex crimes, conspiracy to solicit bribes, conspiracy to commit wire fraud.[16]

With statistics on indictments and convictions from the DOJ, we can make comparisons between states that are more than mere guesswork. And it turns out that Louisiana heads the league table, with more convictions per head than any other state, Illinois coming in second.[17]

Table 4.2. Federal Public Corruption Convictions per 100,000 Population, 1976–2018	
Louisiana	2.62
Illinois	1.66
Tennessee	1.53
New York	1.50
Pennsylvania	1.44
Virginia	1.38
Ohio	1.33
New Jersey	1.28
Georgia	1.0

Source: Dick Simpson, Thomas J. Gradel, Michael Dirksen et al., Chicago Still the Corruption Capital (Anti-Corruption Report #12: University of Chicago at Illinois, Department of Political Science, February 17, 2020), 5, Corruption.Rpt_12.Complete.pdf (uic.edu). It might be objected that Louisiana's high ranking resulted from the zeal of federal prosecutors there, and the comparative laxity of US attorneys elsewhere. But careful study suggests otherwise: that the figures approximate the actual incidence of public corruption.

The civil rights movement, despite its democratic idealism, led to no cleansing of Louisiana's Augean stables. The new class of Black professional politicians played by the existing rules. That was hardly surprising: Having grown up seeing white politicians use public office for private gain, many naturally wanted in on the action. Lacking experience, however, the dishonest ones were less skilled at covering their tracks. Robert F. Collins, the first African American to be appointed to the federal bench in the South, was jailed for taking bribes from a marijuana smuggler. William Jefferson, the first Black congressman from Louisiana since Reconstruction, received a thirteen-year sentence for soliciting bribes from companies seeking to do business in Africa. (It turned out that corruption was a Jefferson family business: a brother, two sisters, and a niece were also convicted.) In 2003, the *Times-Picayune* drew hope from the election of Ray Nagin, who vowed "to restore integrity to city government." The irony of that statement only became apparent ten years later.[18]

The federal government's prosecutions, which in the mid-1980s put Edwin Edwards twice in the dock (he was twice acquitted), contributed to one of those periodic bouts of reform that have interrupted business-as-usual politics. In 1988, after defeating Edwards, Charles E. "Buddy" Roemer created the Office of State Inspector General (OIG). He appointed Bill Lynch, a muckraking journalist, to head it. Lynch installed a fraud hotline and was promptly inundated with tips. In short order, his office investigated Southern University in New Orleans, Nicholls State University, Delgado College in New Orleans, Lafayette's University Medical Center, the state racing board, and the state real estate commission. They found what might be expected: "political patronage, general mismanagement, payroll abuse," and the misappropriation of public funds for private use. Resignations and dismissals followed.[19]

It was no surprise that a good number of politicians hated Bill Lynch. William Jefferson complained that he was "harassing and intimidating state employees" and introduced a bill, which the state Senate approved, to weaken his independence. The bill failed to become law, but Edwards, running for a fourth term in 1991, vowed to abolish the office. However, after defeating Roemer in the primary and facing David Duke in the run-off, he needed the outgoing governor's endorsement. Roemer gave it on condition that, if elected, Edwards retain Lynch. The governor-elect announced his U-turn through gritted teeth—Lynch had been savaging him in print since 1971. After taking office, he barred the inspector general from investigating colleges, universities, and most statewide elected officials. [20]

If Edwards clipped Lynch's wings, the inspector general could still bite, or at least nip. In report after report, many of them dealing with the various state boards and commissions, his office detailed waste, profligacy, nepotism, and sweetheart deals that cost the state untold millions. A fairly typical example was a report on the Louisiana Board of Massage Therapy. It found that the agency's executive director, Kayla Aymond, not only received a full-time salary but also an additional $28,000 under a contract to investigate and inspect massage therapists. But she failed to document these inspections. Many that she claimed to have done she never carried out. Aymond also persuaded the board to hire her husband, children, and sister, despite a state law against nepotism. The records of the agency were in total disarray. The OIG recommended her dismissal.[21]

Small beer, perhaps, but indicative of the absence of oversight and the predatory attitude that characterized some of these boards and commissions. Numbering in the hundreds, they thrived on favoritism, nepotism, and contracts awarded on the basis of political connections rather than fair and open competition. For many of their members and officers, an appointment from the governor was not so much an opportunity for public service as a chance to make money. For example, the president of the Orleans Levee board was entitled by law to receive a per diem of $75 a day for a maximum of 36 days a year. But in 2006 he awarded himself $91,000, representing $1,000 a month for the past several years. The board also spent—again, contrary to state law—$3.2 million on outside lawyers. This in the space of just two years, and despite the fact that the commission had its own full-time attorney.[22]

The profligacy and rule-breaking uncovered by the OIG often fell short of criminal behavior. Nevertheless, the sums wasted on dubious expenses were eye-watering. A report on the Lake Charles Port Commission noted that in 2002 the commissioners spent $350,000 on travel and entertainment, including $26,000 on alcohol "over and above dinner drinks." Eleven commissioners attended the annual Mardi Gras Ball in Washington DC under the guise of promoting "economic development." They claimed $11,000 for the food and drink dispensed at their hotel hospitality suite. The port's director of maintenance claimed a more modest $658 for attending a "German Beer Night" in Dulles, Virginia. A conference in Kansas City on food aid, sponsored by the federal government, induced seven commissioners to claim $47,000 in expenses. Of that sum, $38,000 went on a reception at which 900 lamb chops and 1,200 alcoholic drinks were consumed. A "legislative briefing" in Baton Rouge soaked up $10,000, nearly all of it for food and alcohol. At a "customer Christmas party," 435 guests guzzled their way through $4,000-worth of booze. Three commissioners took their wives on a seventeen-day tour of the northwest in a Port of Lake Charles van and put in a claim for $14,000. What any of this expenditure had to do with the Port of Lake Charles was anyone's guess.[23]

The work of the inspector general was valuable in exposing waste and mismanagement, but the agency's limited terms of reference and restricted powers hampered its effectiveness. Although the boards and commissions were low-hanging fruit, they could, and often did, refuse to cooperate with the OIG's investigators. Nor were they required to act upon the OIG's recommendations. The Board of Massage Therapy, for example, refused to dismiss Kayla Aymond, who continued her free-spending inefficiency for twelve more years. When the OIG investigated the board for a second time, in 2010, it found that Aymond had awarded herself $113,000 in undocumented expenses on top of her annual salary of $98,000. Despite the 1998 report, her record keeping remained chaotic to nonexistent: An auditor found her office in "unbelievable disarray." Small wonder that elected officials treated the inspector general as a minor nuisance, and assumed that the public would soon tire of reform, as it always had in the past.[24]

The DOJ, however, did not let up. Under the leadership of, successively, John Volz, Harry Rosenberg, Eddie Jordan, and Jim Letten, the US attorney's office for the Eastern District (which covers New Orleans) prosecuted a string of high-profile politicians, whose trials kept the corruption issue front and center. The new millennium began with the convictions of former governor Edwin Edwards, insurance commissioner Jim Brown, and elections commissioner Jerry Fowler.

The FBI also probed the New Orleans Police Department, widely regarded as the most corrupt and brutal in the nation. It discovered that officers in the Fifth District routinely shook down drug dealers and, in return for bribes, protected the drug suppliers. It recorded one officer, Len Davis, ordering the murder of a woman who had filed a complaint against him. Between 1994 and 2004 dozens of other policemen were prosecuted for crimes that included money laundering, drug distribution, extortion, rape, bribery, auto theft, and murder.[25]

The public was also exposed to the unedifying spectacle of wholesale corruption at the Orleans Parish School Board. The extent of the rot was staggering:

> Corruption was so rampant that the FBI opened an office within the district's administrative building. A payroll clerk, indicted for stealing over $250,000, had been employed despite a previous indictment for stealing from a bank. $70 million the district had received in federal grants could not be accounted for . . . Graft was ubiquitous from bus drivers all the way up to the [school board]. Employees regularly pilfered computers, band equipment, even air conditioners, as well as funds raised by students, with "missing" property totaling in the tens of millions of dollars. Bus drivers used their district-issued credit cards to sell fuel to truck drivers. Each year, payroll sent out hundreds of thousands of dollars in checks for unearned wages and benefits to terminated or deceased employees.

Officials who handled insurance contracts took bribes of over $300,000. The president of the school board, elected as a self-styled corruption fighter, accepted $140,000 from a computer software company.[26]

In the past, voters had tolerated crooked politicians and public officials on the grounds that the corruption did not really affect them. Office holders may have been on the take, but they were taking from corporations and casinos. Most voters had paid little in the way of state taxes; the costs of corruption were invisible. But times had changed. Oil revenues were down, and state taxes were up. Worse, citizens were getting less for their taxes because public services provided by the state were being cut. The school board scandal laid to rest the myth of the politician as Robin Hood—stealing from the rich, keeping some for themselves, and giving generously to the poor. These officials were stealing from the poorest school system in the nation that served some of the poorest and most disadvantaged children.[27]

A single example: in January 2000, a freak hailstorm damaged the roofs of a dozen New Orleans schools. The board awarded multimillion-dollar contracts to repair them with no competitive bidding, no supervision, and no inspection of the work done. After school board officials, contractors, and subcontractors had taken their respective cuts, precious little money was left over for actual repairs, especially when roofers were ostensibly earning $81 an hour. Two companies received $532,000 to fix one roof, but supplied just $35,000 worth of work. Two dozen former employees of the Orleans Parish School Board pleaded guilty to federal corruption charges.[28]

Meanwhile, in neighboring Jefferson Parish, the FBI carried out "Operation Wrinkled Robe." It snared two elected judges and sent them to jail. In Caddo Parish, in the northwestern corner of the state, "Operation Broken Gavel" led to the conviction of two more elected judges.[29]

And then came the theft of recovery funds after Hurricane Katrina. According to the General Accounting Office, about $1 billion of the disaster relief expenditures, 16 percent of the total, went on fraudulent claims. Prison inmates, using post office boxes as addresses, received millions. A claimant who lived in West Virginia gave his address as Greenwood Cemetery. The Federal Emergency Management Agency (FEMA) gave another claimant $2,358 in rental assistance while also paying him $8,000 to stay in a hotel in Hawaii. FEMA debit cards were used to buy jewelry, Caribbean vacations, Saints season tickets, sex toys, divorce lawyer services, and a meal in Hooter's that included a bottle of Dom Perignon. GAO investigators went undercover to test the system. They had no trouble at all in securing $2,000 checks from FEMA on the basis of false identities, fake addresses, and phony disaster stories. By 2011, the Disaster Fraud Task Force had prosecuted 1,439 people.[30]

Churches large and small filed fraudulent claims. Ricky Sinclair, pastor of a Baton Rouge–area megachurch, overcharged FEMA by $81,000; after Hurricane Gustav in 2008, he falsely claimed $380,000 for operating a public shelter. The minister, wrote the state inspector general, "enriched himself by repeatedly using his church as a front to cheat public agencies of hundreds of thousands of dollars of public money." Even the Catholic Church received Katrina funds on the basis of false or misleading information. Sixteen years after the disaster, the Archdiocese of New Orleans agreed to return over a million dollars.[31]

Fraudsters also plundered reconstruction funds that came from private donors. After Katrina, renowned jazz trumpeter Irvin Mayfield presented himself as New Orleans's unofficial ambassador to the world, performing benefit concerts and meeting with Presidents Bush and Obama. But after Mayor Nagin appointed him to head the New Orleans Library Foundation, a charity devoted to rebuilding the city's devastated public libraries, Mayfield began to divert the foundation's money to himself, via the New Orleans Jazz Orchestra, which he controlled. Along with jazz drummer Ronald Markham, he depleted the funds of the Library Foundation by $1.3 million.[32]

The involvement of politicians in the frauds was sickening. Those convicted included Sheriff Irvin "Jiff" Hingle of Plaquemines Parish, Councilman Joe Impastato of St. Tammany, Jon Johnson of the New Orleans city council, and, most shocking of all, Ray Nagin, mayor of New Orleans during and after the Katrina disaster. In 2014, a federal court handed Nagin a ten-year prison sentence.[33]

For the citizens of Louisiana, the stealing of Katrina relief funds was the last straw. Political corruption was no longer a matter to be laughed at or shrugged off. In 2008, Bobby Jindal, elected on an anticorruption platform, put the OIG on a statutory basis. With an annual budget of $1.6 million and a staff of thirteen, it was granted the power to subpoena individuals. Its new head, Stephen B. Street, repurposed the office to focus on criminal investigations. The state became a full partner of the federal government, working with the US attorneys, the FBI, the Internal Revenue Service, and other agencies to investigate, indict, and prosecute malefactors. Whenever possible, the OIG had corruption cases tried in federal court, where the chances of conviction were higher and the sentences longer. Federal cases also presented the opportunity of using plea bargaining to persuade defendants to cooperate in investigations.[34]

The state-federal offensive quickly bore fruit. In 2009, investigators, including an undercover FBI agent, identified a corrupt ring in the Baton Rouge City Court that arranged for "pending criminal cases . . . to be dismissed or otherwise 'fixed'" in exchange for bribes. The DOJ indicted ten people, including an assistant prosecutor, a worker in the Clerk of Court's Office, and several police officers. All were convicted; several received prison sentences.[35]

The year 2009 also saw the exposure of a ring in Jefferson Parish involving parish attorney Tim Whitmer, chief administrator Tom Wilkinson, and parish president Aaron Broussard. Using informants, wiretaps and secret cameras, the FBI proved that the trio were lining their pockets through bribes, payroll fraud, insurance scams, and kickbacks from staffers. Another FBI investigation led to the impeachment and removal of US District Judge Walter Porteous.[36]

In 2022, Stephen Street was two years into his third six-year term. "The Inspector General business is not for the faint of heart," he confessed. His office takes on "politically toxic investigations . . . the cases that are guaranteed to infuriate the very politicians who get to decide how much money you get in your annual budget." But Street has fended off two efforts in the state legislature to defund it. In contrast to New Jersey, where the office lasted barely five years before Chris Christie abolished it, Louisiana's agency has achieved a degree of permanence and is one of the most effective in the country. Since 2012, it has secured convictions in 97 percent of the cases it brought to federal court. The money it saves the state by identifying waste and fraud pays for its budget many times over. It is testimony to Street's success that the National Association of State Inspectors General has repeatedly elected him its president.[37]

The inspector general's report for 2017 provides a useful snapshot of its work. The office received 376 complaints and began 60 investigations. Among those convicted: a woman who stole Pell Grant funds from a school she had headed; a man who raided a Community Development Grant to pay for his children's cell phones, buy concert tickets, go on cruises, and repair his private cars; the mayor of New Roads, who allowed the town's financial officer, with whom he was having an affair, to use her city credit card to buy personal items; and the town clerk of Arcadia, who embezzled $39,000 over three years.

The biggest scalp belonged to Walter Reed, district attorney for St. Tammany and Washington Parishes. Not content with his $200,000-a-year salary, Reed arranged side deals with the Causeway Commission, which paid him $52,000 a year for doing nothing; and with St. Tammany Parish Hospital, which over a period of twenty years paid him $524,000 to which he was not entitled. Reed also pillaged his campaign chest of $2.9 million dollars to give liberally to his son and to spend lavishly on meals and gifts for friends and supporters. Convicted in 2016, he entered federal prison three years later.[38]

Another powerful district attorney, Harry Morel of St. Charles Parish, was also convicted in 2016. The source of corruption in this case was not money, but sex. During his thirty-four years in office, Morel solicited sexual favors from dozens of women in exchange for helping them, or their family members, in pending court cases.[39]

Long the subject of FBI investigations, the New Orleans Police Department was subjected to a thoroughgoing reform after its lamentable performance during and after the Katrina disaster. A damning report by the DOJ led to a sweeping consent decree. Under its terms, which had the force of federal law, the NOPD agreed to implement far-reaching changes whose progress would be tracked by a federal monitoring team. After six years of federal oversight, the *Christian Science Monitor* praised the NOPD as a "model force."[40]

The promise of reform, of course, seldom matches reality. In 2021, the NOPD suspended twenty-six officers for suspected payroll fraud—double-dipping, falsifying time-sheets, and so on—in connection with "detail work" (paid private assignments). One sergeant boosted his income to $192,000 in 2020 by earning $55,000 from off-duty shifts. But he was frequently absent from both his on-duty and off-duty shifts, spending the time racing his fast car at the Motorsports Park.[41]

One might suppose that the exposure of the scam demonstrated that the NOPD's Public Integrity Bureau, the consent decree monitor, and the independent police monitor were doing their jobs. But the fraud was in fact discovered by a chemistry professor at the University of New Orleans, who spent six months doing his own, private, investigation. The very system that the DOJ had described as the "aorta" of corruption within the NOPD had survived ten years of federal oversight. As *The Advocate* acidly noted, the Washington lawyer appointed to monitor the consent decree, Jonathan Aronie, "has collected millions in fees . . . and he now admits that the city still has to rely on the volunteer sleuthing of a private citizen to keep its cops honest." Indeed, after issuing a report on detail work in 2017, Aronie had ceased to audit the system, leaving oversight to the NOPD's own Office of Police Secondary Employment. But the NOPD was incapable of keeping its own house in order. Indeed, one of the officers involved in the "double-dipping" scandal, Lt. Sabrina Richardson, had headed the department's Public Integrity Bureau.[42]

In his 2007 campaign for the governorship, Bobby Jindal had vowed to hold the state legislature to stricter ethical standards. After his election, he secured the passage of laws that forbade legislators to take state contracts, required them to disclose outside income and declare conflicts of interest, and prohibited former legislators from working as lobbyists for two years after leaving office. "Whistle-blowers" were accorded legal protection. Lobbyists were strictly limited in what they could spend when they treated legislators to meals. Candidates for office were required to report what they received in campaign contributions and how they spent the money. Jindal hailed the reforms as the "gold standard" of transparency. Outsiders were impressed.[43]

But it quickly became apparent that little had changed and that lawmakers were sidestepping the rules. Barred from lobbying the legislature for two years, ex-legislators could still earn money as "consultants," lobby state agencies, and take jobs with state agencies. Concealing outside income proved simple. In 2016, for example, state senator Danny Martiny was paid $836,000 for representing the Jefferson Parish sheriff's office. He declared only $13,000 of it because the rest was routed to him indirectly.[44]

Legislators had little to fear from the Louisiana Board of Ethics: Jindal's reforms left it as ineffective as ever. The first chairman of the reformed board, Rick Gallot, was himself the subject of seven ethics charges, but he made those complaints go away by reducing the deadline for pressing charges from two years to one. The Gallot board also relaxed the standard of proof for conviction: evidence must now be "clear and convincing" rather than "reliable and substantial."

Small wonder that legislators regard the Board of Ethics as a minor nuisance. Conflicts of interest are self-policed. Complaints against legislators proceed at snail's pace, taking an average of four years to resolve. One case, opened in 2010, was still active in 2019. Despite a doubling of its budget and an increase in its staff from twenty-three to thirty-nine, the number of charges filed by the board dropped from 140 in 2013 to 20 five years later. When ethics violations are proven, they result in fines so modest as to preclude any deterrent effect. In 2014, for example, the Board of Ethics ruled that Sheriff Mike Couvillon of Vermillion Parish had breached the ethics code by buying a house at a sheriff's sale for half its assessed value. Couvillon paid a fine of $2,500 and kept the house. Most fines simply went unpaid. In 2016, the board had collected only $57,665 of the more than $1 million in fines that it had levied; 248 political candidates had gotten away with not paying anything.[45]

In 2015 the State Integrity Project placed Louisiana forty-first in terms of anticorruption oversight and declared that the 2008 ethics reforms had turned out to be ineffectual. This is actually true of ethics oversight in most states. The reality is that public corruption is an American problem, not just a Louisiana one. International studies have placed the United States at around twenty-five in the list of least corrupt countries. For comparison, New Zealand, Singapore, and the Scandinavian countries are the least corrupt; followed by the Netherlands, Germany, Luxemburg, the UK, Iceland, Austria, Canada, and Australia.[46]

The United States will likely always have more public corruption than these countries. The enormous number of elective offices, the nonstop electioneering, and the absence of any effective limits on political spending provide more opportunities for corruption. At the same time, federalism, separation of powers, and checks-and-balances make it hard for the national government to impose reform from above. The creation of a nonpolitical, honest, and efficient civil service has been a slow process with uneven results; moreover, civil servants have never commanded the prestige they enjoy in countries like France and the UK. And despite the extension of civil service rules to most government employees, many positions remain the gift of the executive, be it the president of the United States or the governor of a state. Louisiana's Department of Education, for example, has 170 unclassified (political) employees, of whom 37 were paid annual salaries of $100,000 or more.[47]

Anticorruption efforts may have passed their peak. For one thing, convicting corrupt politicians has become more difficult. In the wake of the FBI's ABSCAM investigation of 1978 and 1980, which led to the conviction of a US senator and six US representatives, Congress successfully pressured the DOJ to adopt stricter guidelines regarding undercover "sting" operations targeting politicians. In 1987 the Supreme Court made it harder to convict officials for public corruption by narrowing the definition of what constitutes bribery. Two years later, a federal appeals court applied this precedent to reverse the 1981 convictions of Charles Roemer and Carlos Marcello. In 2016, the Supreme Court further weakened federal anticorruption law when it overturned the conviction of Robert McDonnell, a former governor of Virginia. Although he and his wife had accepted over $175,000 from a businessman in the form of gifts, cash, and loans, the Court ruled that the help McDonnell rendered in return did not constitute an "official act" and hence did not rise to the level of bribery.[48]

When it comes to democratic accountability, however, *Citizens United* is by far the Supreme Court's most damaging decision. This 2011 ruling made it impossible for Congress to rein in political donations and sparked a massive increase in campaign spending. What use is a state law that limits a lobbyist to $65 when treating a legislator to lunch if that same lobbyist can steer thousands of dollars into the legislator's campaign fund and that same politician can use his campaign war chest as a personal ATM? During one session, legislators dipped into their campaign funds to spend $1.5 million on meals; $779,000 on golf; $168,000 on gifts; $88,000 on flowers; and $24,000 on hunting lodges and shooting ranges. About a third of campaign funds are spent on things that have nothing to do with elections.[49]

Beyond using campaign funds to subsidize a lavish lifestyle, politicians naturally feel beholden to their big-dollar donors. They help these benefactors by passing or blocking legislation, awarding them state contracts, and appointing them to one of Louisiana's 478 boards and commissions. In this regard, Bobby Jindal's commitment to ethics reform rang hollow. It is not hard to explain why he vetoed a bill that would require politicians to declare campaign contributions they receive from people they hire or appoint to public office. After all, 316 of the people he appointed to state boards and commissions gave Jindal $1.8 million in campaign funds between 2009 and 2012. Of twelve such bodies over which the governor has sole discretion over appointments, 96 of Jindal's 118 choices had donated to his political war chest. Corruption? Not in the eyes of the law. And no different from the long-accepted practice of presidents awarding prominent donors with ambassadorships and other "plums."[50]

The Trump presidency lowered the ethical bar across the board. Openly promoting his own businesses and refusing to disclose his tax records, Trump flaunted his "conflicts of interest" and sought to profit from his office. Attacking the so-called Deep State, he tried to discredit the Justice Department and the FBI, and, more broadly, the ideal of a nonpartisan civil service. In pardoning the likes of Kwame Kilpatrick, convicted ex-mayor of Detroit, and Rod Blagojevich, convicted former governor of Illinois, he signaled his indifference to public corruption. In attempting to subvert the 2020 election, and deploying violence in the attempt, he showed contempt for democratic and constitutional norms. By the time Trump left office, monitors had demoted the United States from around the twenty-fifth to around the thirty-fifth least corrupt country.[51]

On paper, Louisiana has strong anticorruption laws and an impressive anticorruption apparatus that includes the Office of Inspector General, the State Board of Ethics, and the state legislative auditor. Orleans and Jefferson Parishes have inspectors general of their own; Orleans Parish has its own Ethics Review Board. All these bodies work closely with the FBI, which maintains three public corruption units, two in New Orleans and one in Baton Rouge.

To what extent have their efforts changed the state's culture of corruption since 1991, when Bill Dodd observed that "corruption is the rule rather than the exception among Louisiana's high public officials"? Not much, according to Jeffrey Sallet, who, having headed the FBI's New Orleans office, complained in 2017 that the prevalent attitude seemed to be, "Hey, I'm in an office, and I'm going to take what I can get." The 2015 bribery conviction of Ira Thomas, former president of the Orleans Parish School Board, illustrated his point. The 2010 conviction of predecessor Ellenese Brooks-Sims, also on bribery charges, apparently deterred Thomas not one whit. [52]

Greed does not necessarily lead to criminal behavior, but it does encourage officials, both elected and appointed, to take advantage of their positions in dubious ways. Michael Edmonson, superintendent of the Louisiana State Police from 2008 to 2017, saved an estimated $434,000 in rent by living at the police compound, an unauthorized "perk" that he failed to declare in his tax returns. The state's top cop also took free meals at the LSP cafeteria, had troopers run personal errands, and, during Mardi Gras, lodged friends and family members in hotel rooms paid for by the city of New Orleans to provide accommodation for LSP officers. Edmonson resigned his position shortly before the legislative auditor issued a damning report.[53]

The instinct to use elective office to help oneself rather than one's constituents is hard to shake. In 1993, the *Times-Picayune* revealed that members of the state legislature, each of whom had the right to award a scholarship to Tulane University, had been making these awards to their own children, and, in the case of one legislator, to himself. (The mayor of New Orleans, who had five such scholarships in his gift, gave one to his son.) The resulting scandal led the Board of Ethics to prohibit politicians from giving scholarships to themselves or immediate family. But lawmakers continued to favor the children of friends and political allies. District Attorney Walter Reed, for example, one of the highest paid officials in the state, secured a scholarship for his son at the instance of state representative Harold Ritchie. Illegal? No. Merely a "perfect example of the good 'ol boy network, where the connected get first crack at these perks."[54]

As any glance at the Office of Inspector General website will show, the most blatant form of corruption, theft of public funds, continues to attract the unscrupulous. In 2021 four female administrators at Bossier Parish Community College who had sent themselves false "refunds," in the name of unknowing students, to the tune of $287,000 were convicted. At Baton Rouge Community College, an administrator falsified applications for student loans and grants and diverted the proceeds to himself. After stealing close to $1.5 million, the law caught up with him in 2022.[55]

The most contemptible thefts involved "nonprofit" organizations that had contracted with the state Department of Education to disburse meals for needy children under the federally funded Summer Feeding Service Program. Instead of using the money to fill hungry young stomachs, they were stuffing it into their own pockets. As the result of a yearslong investigation that came to fruition from 2019 through 2022, seven program administrators received jail sentences for stealing roughly $3 million. The case of Lynn D. Cawthorn was typical. Cawthorn, along with his sister, had formed United Citizens and Neighbors Inc., a Shreveport-based nonprofit that received $1,015,000 between 2011 and 2014. In 2021, the pair pleaded guilty to wire fraud, having disbursed only $56,351 on children's meals. They had stolen the remaining $987,919. As he went off to prison, Cawthorn resigned his seat on the Caddo Parish Council.[56]

Students of corruption agree that the least corrupt countries are healthier, happier, better-educated, more prosperous, and more equal in terms of wealth and income. They suffer less crime and have smaller prison populations. The most corrupt nations do badly by all these metrics. The same applies to American states, including Louisiana. The ten most corrupt spend more on law enforcement and jails, less on health, education, and public welfare. They have more poverty and greater economic inequality. Despite poorer public services, state spending in the most corrupt states is, per capita, above average. State spending on wages and salaries is also higher.[57]

Nowhere is the correlation between high levels of corruption and low quality of life more evident than in Louisiana. The state has the highest incarceration rate in the United States and also the highest homicide rate. It boasts the highest rate of poverty and the worst health. In terms of food insecurity, economic hardship, income inequality, and educational attainment, Louisiana ranks second or third from the bottom. Public corruption reflects these inequalities by expressing a form of extreme individualism that militates against collective responsibility for the well-being of all the citizens of the state. It also exacerbates those inequalities by acting as a form of upward redistribution of wealth. By one calculation, corruption amounts to a tax of $1,308 on every man, woman, and child in the state.[58]

Yet the fact that malefactors are investigated, indicted, and convicted indicates that the public's tolerance of corruption is diminishing. Many, if not most, prosecutions begin when an ordinary citizen calls one of the confidential "hotlines" maintained by the OIG and the FBI. For citizens who distrust government agencies and are afraid to approach them, the Metropolitan Crime Commission (MCC), a private organization established in 1952 by the business community of New Orleans, provides an alternative. After the Katrina disaster, the MCC received an unprecedented number of complaints, which, when credible, were referred to the FBI. Between 2009 and 2021, such referrals led to eighty-eight convictions, including those of Ray Nagin and Aaron Broussard.[59]

Sections of the press also expose corruption, sometimes compelling the authorities to take action. The reporting of Bill Lynch (1929–2004), who wrote for the *Shreveport Times*, the *States-Times*, and the *Times-Picayune*, prodded the federal government to indict and prosecute Edwin Edwards in 1984. James Gill, with forty years of reporting under his belt, most of it writing for the *Times-Picayune*, continues to lambast the mendacity, greed, and incompetence of public officials. Veteran reporter Tom Aswell's web blog, *Louisiana Voice*, provides a daily commentary on the corruption and loose ethics that infect every level of government. Aswell also uses litigation and freedom-of-information requests to uncover information that public officials would rather keep hidden.

The most tenacious investigator is Lee Zurick, since 2009 a reporter for WVUE television (Fox 8) in New Orleans. In 2013, Zurick, along with Manuel Torres of the *Times-Picayune*, led a team of twenty journalists in an investigation of money in Louisiana politics. The resulting reports, under the series title "Louisiana Purchased," illustrated how "so-called 'pay to play' in public contracting has cost taxpayers tens of millions of dollars in mismanagement and overpaid services." They also detailed how politicians plundered their campaign funds for their own private benefit—one report prompting the DOJ to prosecute Walter Reed.[60]

Has the level of public corruption declined? The risk of a corrupt official in Louisiana being caught and going to jail has increased exponentially since 1976. The last four governors have restored some degree of integrity to state government. Stephen Street, who probably knows more about the state's public corruption than anyone, is convinced that the investigations, indictments, and prosecutions are having a deterrent effect.

That deterrent effect, however, is hard to demonstrate. If convictions represent the tip of the iceberg, how large is the iceberg's submerged portion? How much corruption goes undetected and unpunished is impossible to measure, but it must be, as a matter of simple logic, much greater than the corruption we know about. It is also possible that new sources of public expenditure, especially federally funded programs, provide wider opportunities for frauds and thefts. Even if we grant that public corruption is diminishing, moreover, the decline has done little to lift Louisiana's economic performance, improve the quality of its governance, or decrease the stark inequality between its richest and poorest citizens. It is one thing to crack down on corruption; instilling a sense of disinterested public service, a far more difficult proposition, is another matter.

NOTES

1. Tim Morris, "The Most Corrupt State? Louisiana Owns It," *NOLA.com*, July 25, 2019; Howard Witt, "Most Corrupt State: Louisiana Ranked Higher than Illinois," *Chicago Tribune*, March 27, 2009; William J. Dodd, *Peapatch Politics: The Earl Long Era in Louisiana Politics* (Baton Rouge: Claitor's, 1991), 5–6. Corruption is commonly defined as "the use of public office for private gain." The term "public office" embraces elected politicians, appointed officials, and people employed in state and local government, including schools and universities. For the purposes of this chapter, the term "corruption" is also applied to private citizens and private institutions that dishonestly or unethically appropriate public or charitable funds.

2. John Maginnis, *Cross to Bear: America's Most Dangerous Politics* (Baton Rouge: Darkhorse, 1992), 5; John Maginnis, *The Last Hayride* (Baton Rouge: Gris Gris, 1984), 8. For a more sophisticated version of the "banana republic" theory, see Justin Callais, "Laissez les bon temps rouler? The Persistent Effect French Civil Law Has on Corruption, Institutions, and Incomes in Louisiana," *Journal of International Economics* 17 (2021), https://www.cambridge.org/core (accessed September 19, 2022).

3. A. J. Liebling, *The Earl of Louisiana: Profile of an Eccentric* (London: W. H. Allen, 1962), 15, 87–88.

4. Mark W. Summers, *The Era of Good Stealings* (New York: Oxford University Press, 1993), x.

5. Summers, *The Era of Good Stealings*, ix–xi; Matthew Stephenson, "A History of Corruption in the United States," *Harvard Law Today*, September 23, 2020, https://hls.harvard.edu/today/a-history-of-corruption-in-the-united-states/ (accessed September 19, 2022).

6. M. Ostrogorski, *Democracy and the Organization of Political Parties* 2 vols. (New York: Macmillan, 1902), 2:378–80; Francis Fukuyama, *Political Order and Political Decay: From the Industrial Revolution to the Globalization of Democracy* (London: Profile Books, 2014), e-book, 2513–59.

7. Joseph G. Tregle, Jr., "Political Corruption in the Early Republic: Louisiana as a Case Study, 1829–1845," *Louisiana History* 31, no. 2 (Spring 1990): 125–39; Mark W. Summers, *The Plundering Generation: Corruption and the Crisis of the Union, 1849–1861* (New York: Oxford University Press, 1988), 14.

8. Adam Fairclough, *The Revolution That Failed: Reconstruction in Natchitoches* (Gainesville: University Press of Florida, 2018), 149–61; Adam Fairclough, *Bulldozed and Betrayed: Louisiana and the Stolen Elections of 1876* (Baton Rouge: Louisiana State University Press, 2021), 259.

9. William Ivy Hair, *Bourbonism and Agrarian Protest: Louisiana Politics, 1877–1900* (Baton Rouge: Louisiana State University Press, 1969), 112, 141.

10. Maginnis, *The Last Hayride*, 5; Michael L. Kurtz and Morgan D. Peoples, *Earl K. Long: The Saga of Uncle Earl and Louisiana Politics* (Baton Rouge: Louisiana State University Press, 1990), 81, 98–99; Harnet Kane, *Huey Long's Louisiana Hayride: The American Rehearsal for Dictatorship, 1928–1940* (Gretna: Pelican, 1941, 1986), passim; William Ivy Hair, *The Kingfish and His Realm: The Life and Times of Huey P. Long* (Baton Rouge: Louisiana State University Press, 1991), 295. Smith was convicted in both state and federal courts.

11. Michael L. Kurtz, "Political Corruption and Organized Crime in Louisiana: The FBI Files on Earl Long," *Louisiana History* 29, no. 3 (1988), 229–52; Morgan and Peoples, *Earl K. Long*, 180.

12. Tom Aswell, *Louisiana's Rogue Sheriffs: A Culture of Corruption* (Baton Rouge: Claitor's Law Books and Publishing Division, 2019), 1–12, 22–23; Adam Fairclough, *Race and Democracy: The Civil Rights Struggle in Louisiana, 1915–1972* (Athens: University of Georgia Press, 1995), 466.

13. Maginnis, *The Last Hayride*, 21–22; *New York Times*, May 20, September 26, 1971; January 5, 1973.

14. Aswell, *Louisiana's Rogue Sheriffs*, passim.

15. *AP News*, "Former Sheriff Gets 10 Years," April 16, 1985, https://apnews.com/article/5d5dce130b49285ed7e15886004c558f; *State v. Bridges* 480 So. 2d. (La. Ct. App. 1986).

16. *NOLA.com*, November 8, 2021; Department of Justice, Eastern Division of Louisiana, "Former St. Tammany Sheriff Jack Strain Sentenced," news release, April 6, 2022.

17. Tim Morris, "The Most Corrupt State?" *NOLA.com*, July 25, 2019; Dick Simpson, Marco R. Rossi, and Thomas J. Gradel, *Corruption Spikes in Illinois* (Chicago: University of Illinois at Chicago, February 22, 2021), 7.

18. *NOLA.com*, July 25, 2019; fbi.gov/history/famous-cases/william-jefferson (accessed September 2, 2022).

19. *Washington Post*, February 6, 1989; *New Orleans Times-Picayune*, December 20, 21, 1988; February 4, 1989.

20. *New Orleans Times-Picayune*, June 6, 1989; November 7, 1991; January 18; August 21, 24, 1992.

21. Office of the State Inspector General, *Louisiana Board of Massage Therapy* (Baton Rouge, June 18, 1998), 1–9.

22. Office of the State Inspector General, *Orleans Levee District* (Baston Rouge, April 3, 2006).

23. Office of the State Inspector General, *Lake Charles Port Commission* (Baton Rouge, February 28, 2005). Only one commissioner actually attended the proceedings of the Kansas City conference. The report also revealed that the commission had signed an unbreakable contract with private attorney Mike Dees that paid the lawyer a base salary of $189,000 a year, rising to $283,000 with benefits.

24. Office of the State Inspector General, *Louisiana Board of Massage Therapy*, 4–6.

25. FBI, "FBI New Orleans History," fbi.gov/field-office-histories/neworleans (accessed September 19, 2022); Metropolitan Crime Commission, archived case files, 1993–2004, https://metrocrime.org/archived-case-files/; NOLA.com, October 15, 2014. The FBI also recorded the police officer who ordered the hit, Len Davis, whooping with joy upon learning that the woman had been murdered; see *The FBI Files: Shattered Shield*, broadcast December 14, 1999, https://www.youtube.com/watch?v=TR4jk1A_HBM.

26. Terry Moe, *The Politics of Institutional Reform: Katrina, Education, and the Second Face of Power* (Cambridge: Cambridge University Press, 2019), 41–42.

27. Stephenson, "A History of Corruption in the United States"; Maginnis, *The Last Hayride*, 4–6, 353–53; Tyler Bridges, *Bad Bet on the Bayou: The Rise of Gambling in Louisiana and the Fall of Governor Edwin Edwards* (New York: Farrar, Straus and Giroux, 2001), 34.

28. *New Orleans Times-Picayune*, April 12, August 11, August 12, 2002; February 18, 2003; *New Orleans Times-Picayune*, August 13; October 1, 31, December 29, 2002; October 9, 2003; July 20, December 17, 2004; June 28, 2007; US Department of Education, "Federal Grand Jury Indicts Eleven in Orleans Parish Corruption Investigation," news release, December 16, 2004; NOLA.com, March 12, 2010.

29. *New Orleans Times-Picayune*, April 2, 2003; June 23, 2005; US Attorney's Office, Western District of Louisiana, new release, October 11, 2007.

30. General Accounting Office, *Hurricane Katrina and Rita Disaster Relief*, June 14, 2006, https://www.gao.gov/products/gao-06-844t (accessed September 19, 2022).

31. Office of State Inspector General, *2011 Annual Report* (Baton Rouge, January 18, 2012; Office of State Inspector General, "Inspector General releases report on Miracle Place Church, Ricky Sinclair," news release, March 11, 2011; US Department of Justice, "Archdiocese of New Orleans agrees to pay more than 1 million dollars to resolve Hurricane Katrina-related false claims and allegations," news release, November 15, 2021.

32. Mark Guarino, "In New Orleans, Scandal Tarnishes a Jazz Star and the Libraries He Was Asked to Help," *Washington Post*, July 16, 2016; Louisiana Legislative Auditor, Investigative Audit: The New Orleans Jazz Orchestra, Inc.," September 26, 2018. In 2021 Mayfield and Markham each received a jail sentence of eighteen months.

33. Department of Justice, US Attorney's Office, Eastern District of Louisiana, news release, February 12, 2014; NOLA.com, August 21, 2015.

34. *New Orleans Times-Picayune*, March 1, 19, 20, 28, 2008; Office of State Inspector General, *2009 Annual Report* (Baton Rouge, March 2, 2010), 1–2.

35. Office of State Inspector General, *2010 Annual Report* (Baton Rouge, May 4, 2011), 13–15; FBI, New Orleans Division, "Indictments in Baton Rouge, Louisiana in Operation Illegal Motion," news release, December 29, 2009; Department of Justice, Middle District of Louisiana, news release, June 14, 2012; WAFB.com, "Sentencing Day in Operation Illegal Motion," August 19, 2010.

36. *New Orleans Times-Picayune*, January 10, 2010; July 28, 2012; NOLA.com, September 12, 2012; November 15, 2020. After Broussard went to jail, Jefferson Parish followed the example of New Orleans in creating its own Office of Inspector General.

37. Office of State Inspector General, *2017 Annual Report* (Baton Rouge, March 9, 2018), 2; *2016 Annual Report* (Baton Rouge, March 21, 2017), 2–8.

38. Office of State Inspector General, *2017 Annual Report*, 8–15; NOLA.com, April 5, 2017.

39. *St. Charles Parish Herald Guide*, April 29, 2016; NOLA.com, September 21, 2016; Department of Justice, Eastern District of Louisiana, new release, August 17, 2016.

40. Interview with Stephen B. Street, September 7, 2022; Department of Justice, Civil Rights Division, "Investigation of the New Orleans Police Department," March 16, 2011, https://www.justice.gov/sites/default/files/crt/legacy/2011/03/17/nopd_report.pdf (accessed September 22, 2022; NOLA.com, October 15, 2014; *Christian Science Monitor*, February 26, 2019.

41. NOLA.com, November 18, 2021.

42. Lee Zurick, "NOPD Sergeant Appears to Be behind the Wheel of a Racecar, Instead of Patrol Car," Fox8live.com, November 16, 2021; *The Advocate*, June 1, 2022; John Simerman, "11 New Orleans Police Officers Are under Federal Investigation over Details Pay," Fox8live.com, May 26, 2022.

43. *Chicago Tribune*, March 27, 2009; *New York Times*, February 28, 2008.

44. *New Orleans Times-Picayune*, April 13, June 7, December 19, 2018.

45. *New Orleans Times-Picayune*, September 20, 2009; June 7, December 19, 2018; May 16, 2019; Louisiana Board of Ethics, "In the Matter of Mike Couvillon: Consent Order," December 16, 2006, https://ethics.la.gov/EthicsOpinion/DocView.aspx?id=362290&searchid=09597c47-6b87-42d9-a527-0b04d9e757fd&dbid=0; Tom Aswell, "What Does It Take?" *Louisiana Voice*, July 29, 2016, https://louisianavoice.com/2016/07/29/what-does-it-take-of

-248-fines-for-ethics-violations-totaling-more-1-million-only-about-less-than-58000-has-been-collected/.

46. Center for the Advancement of Public Integrity, *Oversight and Enforcement of Public Integrity, a State-by-State Study: Louisiana* (New York: Columbia University Law School, 2018), 6; Mark Ballard, "Louisiana gets F grade in 2015 State Integrity Investigation," Center for Public Integrity, November 9, 2015, https://publicintegrity.org/politics/state-politics/state-integrity-investigation/louisiana-gets-f-grade-in-2015-state-integrity-investigation/; Transparency International, "Corruption Perception Index, 2020," https://www.transparency.org/en/cpi/2020 (accessed September 20, 2022).

47. *Louisiana Voice*, May 14, 2018, https://louisianavoice.com/category/recovery-school-district/.

48. *Daily Beast*, July 11, 2017, https://www.thedailybeast.com/the-real-story-and-lesson-of-the-abscam-sting-in-american-hustle?ref=scroll; McNally v. United States, 483 U.S. 350 (1987); United States v. Marcello, 876 F.2d 1147 (1989); McDonnell v. United States, 579 U.S.(2016); Amie Ely, "What McDonnell v. U.S. means for state corruption prosecutions," *National Association of Attorneys General*, https://www.naag.org/attorney-general-journal/what-mcdonnell-v-united-states-means-for-state-corruption-prosecutors/.

49. NOLA.com, January 30, 2014.

50. NOLA.com, November 5,6, 2013.

51. Transparency International, "Corruption Perception Index, 2021," January 22, 2022, https://www.transparency.org/en/cpi/2021/media-kit (accessed September 20, 2022); World Population Review, "Most Corrupt Countries, 2022," https://worldpopulationreview.com/country-rankings/most-corrupt-countries (accessed September 20, 2022).

52. Emily Lane, "Corruption in Louisiana 'Can't Get Much Worse,' Says Outgoing New Orleans FBI Director," NOLA.com, November 3, 2017; NOLA.com, October 1, 2015. Sallet noted that the Bureau maintained *two* anticorruption squads in New Orleans—remarkable for such a relatively small city.

53. Louisiana Legislative Auditor, Investigative Audit, "Office of State Police," December 14, 2017, https://app.lla.state.la.us/publicreports.nsf/0/15e57eee0c43ce228625821f00533efd/$file/00016d74.pdf?openelement&.7773098. the State Board of Ethics refrained from taking any action over Edmonson.

54. *New Orleans Times-Picayune*, June 10, 1993; NOLA.com, October 24, 2013; *Tulane Hullabaloo*, October 30, 2013. The quotation is by Rafael Goyeneche, head of the Metropolitan Crime Commission.

55. Department of Justice, Western District of Louisiana, news releases, February 22, March 11, 2022; Department of Justice, Middle District of Louisiana, news release, March 22, 2022.

56. Department of Justice, US Attorney's Office, Middle District of Louisiana, news releases, October 8, 2021; April 29, 2022; Southern District of Mississippi, news release, November 23, 2021; Western District of Louisiana, news releases, January 16, 2020; March 16, 2022; April 29, 2022, all available at Office of State Inspector General, https://oig.louisiana.gov/index.cfm?md=newsroom&tmp=archives&catid=1&nid=20&pnid=0&startIndex=1 (accessed October 12, 2022).

57. Liu and Mikesell, "The Impact of Public Officials' Corruption on the Size and Allocation of U.S. State Spending," 353–56. At least 230 people on Louisiana's payroll earn more than $200,000 a year; at least 8,000 earn between $100,000 and $200,000.

58. The Sentencing Project: State-by-State Data, https://www.sentencingproject.org/the-facts/#rankings; World Population Review: Poverty Rate by State 2022, https://worldpopulationreview.com/state-rankings/poverty-rate-by-state; World Population Review: Murder Rate by State 2022, https://worldpopulationreview.com/state-rankings/murder-rate-by-state; U.S. News, Public Health Rankings https://www.usnews.com/news/best-states/rankings/health-care/public-health; United Health Foundation, America's Health Rankings 2021, https://www.americashealthrankings.org/explore/annual/state/LA; Liu and Mikesell, "The Impact of Public Officials' Corruption on the Size and Allocation of U.S. State Spending," 353–56.

59. Rafael Goyeneche, Metropolitan Crime Commission, interviewed on "William Wallis for America," December 20, 2021, https://www.youtube.com/watch?v=uRgadLSPBvo.

60. NOLA.com, November 5, 2013.

Chapter Five

AS LOUISIANA AS CRAWFISH PIE

ENDEMIC VIOLENCE AND THE NONUNANIMOUS JURY VERDICT

SAMUEL C. HYDE JR.

In the early months of 2018, a movement gained traction in the Louisiana legislature that rapidly became a profound cause of a transformative nature. Driven by national advocacy groups as well as local activists, and benefitting from the seemingly unanimous endorsement of state and national media, Louisiana lurched hurriedly toward a fundamental change in its legal system. Specifically, the Bayou State responded to the barrage of ferocious criticism directed at a curious wrinkle in its system of criminal justice—one that permitted nonunanimous jury verdicts in felony cases.[1]

Though capital cases, those that could result in a death sentence would require a unanimous verdict; other felony cases, including trials for murder, could be decided on a ten-to-two jury vote. Those who wished to change this curious aspect of Louisiana's legal system, along with the media, proclaimed the nonunanimous jury verdict directive as a product of Louisiana's racist past. According to opponents of the nonunanimous jury-verdict rule, it was a creation of Louisiana's indisputably racist Constitution of 1898, a document that in their view existed solely to enshrine white supremacy within the organic law of the Bayou State. The jury-verdict rule, or "Jim Crow's last stand" as some called it, was designed to facilitate enhanced incarceration of Black people, especially men, as a means of racial intimidation and to fill the ranks of chain gang workers whose practically free labor was exploited for the benefit of the state's ruling Bourbon Democrats.[2]

The Bourbons, so named because they were alleged to have never learned or forgotten anything, presided over a state where racial segregation defined all aspects of life. The Constitution of 1898 codified, in the organic law of the state, white supremacy and the mechanisms necessary to keep Black people "in their place." Among the tools the Constitution offered the Bourbons to further their nefarious goals, the nonunanimous jury verdict ranked among the most potent. It dangled the fear of harsh, extended, incarceration in front of any Black people who did not learn, and abide by their assigned place in society.

In trumpeting this aspect of the Constitution of 1898 opponents of the jury-verdict rule are irrefutably correct. Members of the convention that created the 1898 document announced at the outset that their intention was to craft a constitution that enshrined white supremacy in all aspects of state government. E. B. Kruttschnitt, president of the convention, proclaimed in his opening remarks that they were meeting for one sole purpose, "to eliminate from the electorate the mass of corrupt and illiterate voters who have during the last quarter of a century degraded our politics," an obvious reference to Black voters who remained the obstacle to absolute white political supremacy.[3]

Louisiana's troubled history of racial injustice is well-chronicled and incontrovertible. However, in proclaiming the jury-verdict rule to be exclusively a tool of white racism, opponents of the rule diminished the potential for further analysis and consideration of the sources of this judicial curiosity. Within months, Louisiana voters overwhelmingly overturned the nonunanimous jury verdict and celebrated the elimination of one more antiquated pillar of the legacy of Jim Crow. Yet questions remain. Especially those concerning where the jury-verdict rule may fit in another unpleasant certainty of life in Louisiana—historical endemic violence.[4]

The nonunanimous jury-verdict rule is both an oddity and an outlier. With the exception of Oregon, in the far northwest, no other state in the union embraced the rule. Despite the unanimity of fealty to white superiority across the South, no other southern state followed Louisiana's lead in employing the rule as a bulwark of white supremacy. Even neighboring Mississippi, whose historic commitment to white superiority at least equaled that of Louisiana, never applied the jury-verdict directive to augment white rule. Judge Soloman S. Calhoon, president of the Mississippi Constitutional Convention of 1890 declared in his opening remarks, "We all know there exists here in this state two distinct and opposite types of mankind." He noted further, "We also all know that the rule of one race means moral and economic ruin and the rule of the other race has always meant prosperity and happiness to all races."[5] Despite these extreme views, Mississippi nonetheless required unanimous felony convictions.

The rejection of nonunanimous jury verdicts as a tool to augment white dominance by every southern state except Louisiana demands consideration of other possible motives in the Bayou State. In the case of Oregon, legal scholars frequently point to a 1933 murder case as the source of the jury-verdict rule. A single juror prevented the conviction of a Jewish man accused of murdering a Protestant. The resulting public fervor led to calls for restrictions on immigrant jurors. Oddly, the case involved the murder of a man and a woman, but the trial focused only on the man. The accused, Jacob Silverman, was both a businessman and a criminal who, reports indicated remained cocky and indifferent during the trial. The lone holdout juror spared him from a life sentence despite the fact that multiple witnesses saw Silverman with the victims earlier in the day, and a car of the same model and color as his wife's was seen speeding from the crime scene. The nativist tone of media reports, especially those decrying mass immigration from southern and eastern Europe in reference to the lone juror, facilitated a racist agenda for later media and scholarly critique of the Oregon law.[6]

Despite the anti-Semitic undertones of the law, Oregon did not rush to eliminate nonunanimous verdicts as did Louisiana. The Oregon law was not tainted by the implicit racism evident in the Louisiana rule since that northern state did not share in the historical bigotry assigned to the South. The law remained on the books when on April 20, 2020, the Supreme Court ruled, in the case of *Ramos v. Louisiana*, that the sixth amendment to the Constitution requires unanimous jury verdicts for a conviction in a criminal case. Writing for the majority in a split decision, Justice Neil Gorsuch argued that nonunanimous jury verdicts were a comparatively recent invention created after the Civil War in an attempt to nullify African American jurors' votes and otherwise undermine minority participation in the judicial process. Unanimous jury verdicts, according to Gorsuch, dated back to the fourteenth century and were ever a pillar of common law.[7]

A simple reading of the sixth amendment, the constitutional basis of *Ramos*, reveals that it includes no explicit stipulation requiring unanimous jury verdicts. The text itself guarantees only "the right to a speedy and public trial, by an impartial jury." Whether Louisiana and Oregon's unorthodox, nonunanimous verdict rules nonetheless violated a constitutional right was first considered by the US Supreme Court some forty-six years before *Ramos* in the 1972 case *Apodaca v. Oregon*. There the court found that although the sixth amendment did require *federal* criminal courts to convict defendants unanimously, states remained free to apply a nonunanimous verdict rule. In 2018, *Ramos* effectively overruled *Apodaca* and extended the sixth amendment's prohibition on nonunanimous verdicts to state courts as well. It did so based on the so-called doctrine of incorporation—the legal theory whereby, through the Fourteenth Amendment, constitutional guarantees enshrined in the Bill of Rights (the first ten amendments) are deemed fully applicable to the states. Before the Civil War, the Bill of Rights limited the federal government, but it did not apply to the states. More recently, many historians and legal scholars argue that one important purpose of the Fourteenth Amendment, ratified after the Civil War, was specifically to change that limitation. Initially, the Supreme Court resisted this view, but in a series of cases in the twentieth century, it gradually held that almost every provision of the Bill of Rights is "incorporated" into the Fourteenth Amendment's guarantee of due process. In other words, the sixth amendment requirement of unanimous jury verdicts in federal criminal cases applies to the states via the Fourteenth Amendment.[8]

Through this method of interpretation, over the course of the twentieth century, supporters of unanimous jury verdicts in criminal cases ultimately triumphed. And, by highlighting the overt racism of the Louisiana Constitution of 1898, they compromised, if not neutralized, further consideration of the issue. Surprisingly absent in most media accounts of the demise of the nonunanimous jury stipulation are crucial antecedents that may offer insight into why Louisiana stood alone among the states of the South in applying this legal rule.

Critics of nonunanimous jury verdicts agree that in both Louisiana and Oregon, the rules existed for "essentially racist reasons." In Oregon, the racist motives accompanied the Silverman case, while in Louisiana they were seen as a response to the 1880 ruling in *Strauder v. West Virginia*, wherein the Supreme Court ruled that Black men could not be excluded from jury service. Critics of the *Strauder* ruling insisted that if unanimous verdicts were required, skillful defense attorneys could rely on a single juror motivated by racial, religious, or political sympathies to prevent a conviction, effectively diminishing the dispensation of justice. Despite such arguments, though every state in the South would be impacted in the same manner by the *Strauder* decision—none chose to join in Louisiana's extreme reaction, suggesting the presence of other motives in the Bayou State.[9]

Another precursory factor that likely weighed heavily on the minds of the delegates to the 1898 Louisiana constitutional convention was an obsessive fear of a loss of power and their dominant class status. They would certainly have argued that they had good reason to be concerned. Throughout the state's history, Louisiana endured a series of restrictive constitutions. The initial 1812 document was arguably second only to South Carolina in the restrictions it set for voting and office holding. As late as 1824, Louisiana remained one of only six states in which the legislature persisted in selecting presidential electors. The absence of popular participation in the selection of presidential electors led the *St. Francisville Asylum* to urge its readers to follow the policy advocated in the *Journal*, another West Feliciana Parish newspaper, and write the name of their choice for president on their congressional ballot so that "a tolerably correct idea of the public sentiment may be obtained." The legislature continued to select the governor from among the top two candidates in the general primary, and the governor continued to enjoy sweeping powers of unregulated appointment.[10]

Responding to Jacksonian-era calls for reform, in 1845, a new Constitution secured approval with overwhelming support. Nearly 80 percent of those voting cast their ballots in support of a new organic law for the state. The Constitution of 1845 provided for extensive reforms, including curbing the power of the legislature, the establishment of free public education, and protection of basic civil liberties, in addition to eliminating all property tests for voters and candidates for office.[11]

Sharing power did not sit well with the planter elite, nor with their banking and commercial allies. Barely seven years later, they engineered a countercoup with the Constitution of 1852, which rolled back many of the progressive reforms of the 1845 document. And, unlike in 1845, where a huge majority voted in favor of reform, the vote on the 1852 Constitution was very close, suggesting growing concern about the locus of power in the Bayou State.[12]

The Civil War witnessed the forcible subjugation of Louisiana by the armed might of the federal government. In the aftermath, the state was governed by a coalition of freedmen, Northern adventurers derisively known as "carpetbaggers," and their Southern allies contemptuously regarded as "scalawags" by the prewar rulers of the state. Once in power, the new masters of the Bayou State moved forthrightly to enshrine their dominance. Insisting that they were merely following the requirements of the federal Reconstruction Acts of 1867, the Radical Republicans called for a new constitution. The Radicals employed the "Ironclad Oath," which required all voters and officials to swear that they had never supported the Confederacy in any way, to effectively disenfranchise the vast majority of white voters in Louisiana. The Radical majority in Congress further institutionalized their power, in March 1867, through passage of the first Supplemental Reconstruction Act, which required an oath of past loyalty in order for any man in the South to vote.[13]

Although other factors undoubtedly contributed, the result of these measures represented a cataclysmic shift in Louisiana's voting patterns. The Constitutional Convention proposal secured approval by a vote of 75,083 to 4,006. Republicans elected ninety-six of the ninety-eight delegates. On the opening day of the 1868 Constitutional Convention, the delegates offered "that we the representatives of the loyal people of Louisiana are thankful to

Almighty God for the success of the Radical Republican party in this state." The introductory comments continued: "Rebellion is disfranchisement; we do endorse the acts of the thirty-ninth and fortieth Congress and will reconstruct Louisiana on the basis of the Reconstruction Bill. We are friendly to universal liberty, but no universal amnesty; but the continuance of disfranchisement of all Congress has and all others we may think necessary for the safety of our common country." The commander of the military district was called upon to remove all men from office disfranchised by Congress, replacing them with men of unquestioned loyalty. The governor was likewise empowered to organize a militia of one thousand men of "undoubted loyalty" to be apportioned out to the parishes.[14]

The Reconstruction Acts of 1867 specifically disfranchised any who had "voluntarily" given aid to the Confederacy. The measure extended from Confederate soldiers to postmasters and even any farmer who may have sold grain to the Confederate army. The affected men were to be denied the right to vote until January 1, 1878, to allow time for Republican rule to become ensconced. Former Union soldiers received permission to raise militias in the parishes composed exclusively of men loyal to the Union to help facilitate the transfer of power. Having ruled the state with an iron fist in the antebellum period, the prewar elite and the mass of white Louisianians were rendered powerless and placed at the mercy of Yankees, freedmen, and a handful of homegrown Unionists as a result of the Reconstruction Acts and the Louisiana Constitution of 1868. Even if the loss of power was only temporary, their dismay was matched only by their rage. It was a lesson in powerlessness they would not soon forget.[15]

As congressional Reconstruction wound down and the final Union troops departed the South, the former masters of the state called for a new constitution. The resulting Louisiana Constitution of 1879 returned circumstances as close to prewar conditions as the convention dared. The delegates declared that the Constitution of 1868 had "transferred the government of the state to the negro race. It now becomes the duty of this convention to re-transfer the government." The lesson of the war had nonetheless been well learned. Addressing the apprehension many Black Louisianians felt concerning the intentions of the convention, the delegates issued a resolution declaring: "There is no intention whatever entertained by this body of impairing or restricting the political, civil, or religious rights of any class of citizens of the state. But on the contrary the intention is to defend and perpetuate every and all rights now guaranteed them by this state and by the Constitution of the United States."[16]

The framers of the 1879 Constitution realized, of course, that the Fourteenth and Fifteenth amendments to the federal Constitution specifically prohibited them from denying the vote or curtailing the civil rights of any citizen. And, with memories of the Civil War still fresh, they were careful to avoid overt measures or language that could suggest that was indeed their purpose. It required yet another historical antecedent to produce the rhetoric and the restrictions mandated by the 1898 constitution.

In the early 1890s a powerful grassroots movement for social and political reform emerged across the nation. Originating in the Midwest but rapidly expanding into the South and West, the movement included agrarian reformers, free silver advocates, Christian conservatives, and temperance proponents, among others, all of whom coalesced in a crusade known as the Populist Revolt. Though the interests of adherents were diverse, they shared a profound challenge to the prevailing political order. In all regions, they attacked the masters of the existing social and political narratives that prevailed in the era. The captains of banking and industry who exercised immense influence over Congress were favorite targets, as were those who manipulated the money supply to further their own interests. In the South and Midwest, commercial and railroad enterprises who advanced their own schemes on the backs of long-suffering farmers remained a principal enemy. The chorus of calls for change climaxed in the hugely contested election of 1896.

The 1896 election provided a singular curiosity in the annals of American political history. Not since Bacon's Rebellion in 1676 Virginia had the oppressed similarly overcome prescribed boundaries to forge a profound coalition of Black and white, town folk and country dwellers, to challenge the prevailing political order. The implications of Bacon's Rebellion produced a seismic shift in American social and political relations. In his seminal work, *American Slavery, American Freedom*, Edmund Morgan argues that Bacon's Rebellion propelled the transformation of America from fixation on Old World class identity to New World racial identity. Nathaniel Bacon's rebel army briefly overwhelmed the colonial government of Virginia necessitating the importation of British troops to put down the rebellion. Virginia, and by association her sister colonies, had tottered on the threshold of social realignment. In the aftermath, the ruling elite moved quickly to ensure that racial divisions would serve as a bulwark against any further race-neutral class uprising that could overwhelm them by sheer force of numbers.[17]

As is frequently the case, Louisiana served as an anomaly in the context of the Populist Revolt. Since the Civil War, the Republican Party had governed the nation virtually inviolate. Their policies reflected disregard for common farmers and laborers and contempt for the values of rural America. Absolute dominance of Congress, along with their fixation on personal wealth and power, caused them to ignore the needs of the poor and, in the South, tolerate the return to power on the state level of Democrats, whose policies exacerbated the misery of the impoverished sharecropping mass of farmers. Many of these desperate farmers migrated to the Populist Party, which nominated agrarian reformers William Jennings Bryan for president and Tom Watson for vice president. Desperate to qualify the dominance of the Republicans, nationally, the Populists "fused" with the Democrats in a joint campaign to elect Bryan.[18]

In Louisiana, it was the Republicans who fused with the Populists in an effort to break the statewide dominance of the Bourbon Democrats. Horrified by the sight of agrarian reformers urging struggling Black and white farmers to join forces to change their condition in life, Louisiana Democrats engaged in a campaign of intimidation and fraud. The alignment of the remnants of the Louisiana Republican Party with the emerging coalition proved beyond comprehension for many Democrats. Poor whites and Blacks had long been held equally in contempt, but the addition of wealthy sugar planter Republicans to this "mongrel coalition" seemed incredible. Statewide Democrats remained dumbfounded that under the existing Constitution of 1879, such an alliance of voters could develop, and the strength of numbers they possessed could lead to success. As early as the legislative session of 1894, Governor Murphy Foster had insisted that the "mass of ignorance, vice and venality without any proprietary interest in the state," must be totally disfranchised.[19]

As the election drew close and increasing evidence of the Populist-Fusion tickets potential for success emerged, some Democrats began to openly call for the election to be stolen. The Shreveport *Evening Judge* forthrightly declared, "It is the religious duty of Democrats to rob Populists and Republicans of their votes whenever and wherever the opportunity presents itself. . . . rob them! You bet! What are we here for?" Despite the intimidation tactics practiced by the Democrats, across the state, the calls for courage increased, and the sheer number of voters available to them suggested the Populists were poised to win. Populist state senator Hardy Brian declared as the election neared that only a "gigantic piece of stealing" could deny the Populists victory.[20]

When election day, April 21, 1896, arrived, the Populists carried twenty-five of Louisiana's thirty-two parishes, with a white voter majority. They also carried four Black majority parishes in south Louisiana. The overwhelmingly Black Mississippi River parishes in the northern and central portions of the state served as the key to the Democrats' "fine piece of stealing." Though maintaining populations that were more than eighty percent Black, the parishes of East Carroll, Madison, and Tensas collectively reported 6,406 votes for Democrat Murphy Foster without a single vote recorded for his Populist gubernatorial challenger, John Pharr. Similarly, West Feliciana Parish, astride the Mississippi River in the Florida parishes, returned 3,093 votes for Foster, with Pharr receiving but a single vote.[21]

In the aftermath of the election, enraged mobs of Black and white Populists rose from the hill country of north central Louisiana to the sugar parishes in the south. Governor Foster dispatched state militia, replete with artillery, to quell Populist risings led by white mobs in Natchitoches and Black ones in St. John Parish. Few Democrats sought to deny the voter fraud; instead, they condemned the Populists for demanding that Blacks be allowed to cast free ballots. None other than future president Theodore Roosevelt declared that Populism must be suppressed "as the Commune in Paris was suppressed, by taking ten or a dozen of their leaders out, standing them against a wall, and shooting them dead." Despite the hysterics, the Populists clearly lacked the resources necessary to forcibly overturn the election. Instead, they demanded a legislative investigation, which, on the very day it convened, a joint session of the legislature promptly refused. In his second inaugural address a few days later, Governor Foster insisted that some action toward suffrage restriction was necessary to remove what he later called "the menace of former conditions."[22]

In the same session, the legislature enthusiastically heeded the governor's call by passing a series of complicated election and registration laws that were ultimately designed to inhibit voting among the less educated, both Black and white. Not surprisingly, the legislature also approved an administration bill that would allow the reduced electorate to approve the convening of a constitutional convention in early 1898. Ominously, the convention bill included a provision declaring that if the voters approved the call for a new constitution, the work of the convention was to be the final say in the matter. In other words, the new document would not be submitted to the voters for ratification.[23]

The election held on January 11, 1898, proved an unqualified triumph for the Bourbons. Fewer than fifty thousand voters submitted the confusing, nearly four-foot-long ballot. In the end, proconvention forces prevailed by a five-to-one margin, with only one Populist securing election. In his opening remarks, convention president E. B. Kruttschnitt boasted, "We have here none of the clash of faction . . . I am called upon to preside over what is little more than a family meeting of the Democratic party of the state of Louisiana." Kruttschnitt reminded his listeners just how "exciting" the election of 1896 had been, and he cautioned that the election of 1900 would be just as tense but for the wisdom of the people in calling this convention. He continued, "We are all aware that this convention has been called by the people of Louisiana to deal with one question. This convention has been called together by the people of the state to eliminate from the electorate the mass of corrupt and illiterate voters who have during the last quarter of a century degraded our

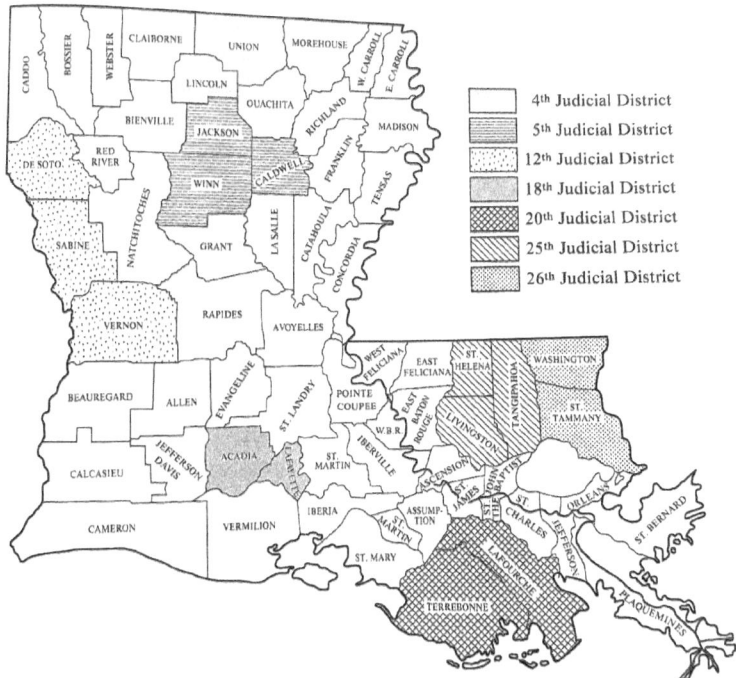

Figure 5.1. Judicial Districts of Louisiana in the Early Twentieth Century. Cartography by Mary Lee Eggart. (Courtesy Samuel C. Hyde)

politics." To loud applause, Kruttschnitt stated further, "With a unanimity unparalleled in the history of American politics, they have entrusted to the Democratic party of this state the solution of the question of the purification of the electorate. They expect the question to be solved and solved quickly."[24]

Kruttschnitt's words radiate a racial purpose. Yet coerced Black votes delivered the nearly unqualified power they now enjoyed to the Bourbons and broke the back of the Populist movement. Indeed, none other than agrarian reformer Tom Watson, Populist candidate for vice president and critic of the mistreatment of Southern Blacks—the very man who could summon mobs of white farmers to protect a Black man from being lynched—would come to regard Blacks as unreliable allies and accordingly transform into a race-baiting hate monger. Kruttschnitt plugged into the power of racial division. He lamented, to "the large class of people of Louisiana who will be disfranchised," insisting the loss of rights they would soon endure was not done in hostility, but instead for "the protection of the weaker classes, to guard them against the machinations of those who would use them to further their own base ends. We owe it to the ignorant, we owe it to the weak, to protect them just as we would protect a little child and prevent it from injuring itself with a sharp edged tool placed in its hands." Or, stated otherwise, we *must* remove the vote from impoverished whites and Blacks lest they seek to unify again and we are forced to destroy them.[25]

Just as the Constitution of 1898 functioned as a pillar of white supremacy, it similarly functioned as an instrument of political supremacy. Commanding unqualified power, the ruling party now assumed a posture of magnanimity. Calls for a free system of public education so that "no man in the future shall complain that he has been deprived of the right to vote because of the poverty of himself or his parents" were reported to be endorsed unanimously. The convention even went so far as to invite the failed Populist candidate for president, William Jennings Bryan, to address the convention.[26]

Kruttschnitt then turned his attention to an issue of profound importance to the rural parishes admitting that "the chief demand for change comes from the country." Suggesting uncertainty as to how best to proceed, he urged the convention to come together and shape a judiciary system that is "both efficient and economical." Delegations and individual delegates from various regions of the state quickly submitted a variety of suggestions for judicial reform. A memorial submitted by the citizens of Rapides Parish called for restructuring of the judiciary system "since petty cases get the same amount of attention as serious cases," and it continues to create a serious backlog. Thomas J. Semmes, chairman of the committee on the judiciary, likewise addressed the "outcry in the country parishes." Semmes noted that the demands included greater logic in indictments, reforming the jurisdiction of justices of the peace, and expanding the district courts' ability to try minor cases without a jury. He added that reformers also wanted both grand juries and the district courts to be continually in session, instead of various times during the year, so that the delays "which have so often resulted in a man being hung by a mob will disappear. And that everyone accused of a crime may receive a speedy trial, and if found guilty, receive his just punishment at the hands of the legally constituted authorities." R. L. Draughon, delegate from blood-soaked Tangipahoa Parish, pleaded for reform in the commissioning of justices of the peace to allow them to preside over all cases except those that may result in "imprisonment at hard labor or death," to improve the efficiency of the district courts.[27]

Though apparently less realized by the elites of New Orleans and the state's few other urbanized areas, the delegates from the "country parishes" well understood that sustained, endemic violence defined life in their home regions. And, in some of those regions, the ineffectiveness of the judiciary provided an accelerant to the brutality.

The scourge of lynching and other forms of racial cruelty common to the South accounted for much of the violence. However, racial violence often occurred with the tacit approval of an otherwise healthy legal system. Abundant intraracial trouble, white-on-white and Black-on-Black, often proved chronic in areas hosting a compromised legal system. In many such regions, backcountry justice often filled the void created by an ineffective legal system. To many rural Southerners, rather than a set of legal statutes, justice remained a pattern of societal norms allowing for respect of property rights, individual honor, and a maximum of personal independence. Any violation of this pattern amounted to a breach of justice requiring a specific response from the injured party. Upon learning that a youthful neighbor had approached his wife in an overly friendly manner at a public place, Robert Leard, of Tangipahoa, Louisiana, promptly tracked the young man down and killed him. Under the backcountry code of justice, anything less would have invited shame and ridicule upon the Leard family. Likewise, a bloody Mississippi feud resulted from the failure of one family to restrain its chickens from entering a neighbor's garden. Pulitzer Prize–winning author Hodding Carter recalled serving as foreman of a jury in Tangipahoa Parish in a case where a man who had been verbally insulted by two teenage boys grabbed his gun and shot them both, killing an innocent bystander in the process. When Carter expressed dismay that his was the only vote to convict the shooter, an older member of the jury advised, "Son you are a good man but you have got a lot to learn, he wouldn't have been much of a man if he hadn't shot them boys." In each case, as in countless others, the judicial system remained perfectly irrelevant. Instead, backcountry justice defined the proper response that best demonstrated individual honor and the power of independent conviction. An Alabama agrarian circular summarized the force of this creed, advising rural farmers that "if you wish to be loyal to every instinct of true manhood, if you want to maintain every principle of self-respect, and the respect of others, carry out your convictions." Much as in many of our urban centers today, in large areas of the rural South, violent resolution of disputes remained the norm, not the unusual.[28]

Regions of southwestern Mississippi, upcountry South Carolina, and hill country Arkansas, Alabama, and Tennessee all endured chronic patterns of rural violence in the late nineteenth and early twentieth centuries. Yet none matched the sustained pattern of endemic violence that characterized specific regions of Louisiana. A survey of homicides in the fifteen years following the election of 1896 reveals exceptional rates of violent crime in virtually all of Louisiana's rural judicial districts. The historically troubled Twelfth Judicial District, including Vernon, Sabine, and DeSoto Parishes, endured extraordinary levels of violence, with the Twenty-Sixth District (St. Tammany and Washington) and the Fourth District (Lincoln and Union) close behind. But it was the Twenty-Fifth District, in the heart of arguably the most chaotic region in all of the South, the piney woods region of Louisiana's Florida parishes, that led the state in rural homicides. Livingston, St. Helena, and Tangipahoa Parishes comprised the Twenty-Fifth District. Not only did these parishes lead the survey groups in the number of homicides, but, most ominously, they maintained the lowest conviction rates of all the survey parishes.[29]

Issues complicating the effective dispensation of justice in the Twenty-Fifth District sound remarkably similar to the debates occurring in many of our urban centers today. The challenges included incompetent or cowed police services, inefficient or compromised prosecutions, and juries unwilling to convict the guilty. In his biannual report to the state legislature in 1900, Louisiana attorney general M. J. Cunningham complained that "if police and sheriffs would do their duty by arresting and incarcerating all persons violating the law it would be obeyed." In a follow-up special report submitted the same year, Cunningham asserted that he had been advised by the district attorney of the then Sixteenth Judicial District (later the Twenty-Fifth) that all indictments, and records of criminal cases, in Tangipahoa Parish had been stolen.[30]

Part of the problem in perennially chaotic Tangipahoa involved the men elected to serve as chief law officer. Before he was forced from office for nonfeasance, Sheriff Pleasant P. McMichael's failure to perform the duties incumbent on his office had contributed mightily to the spiraling violence, provoking condemnation in the press and a personal rebuke from the governor. In an unusual move, a Tangipahoa Parish grand jury gently criticized McMichael, declaring him "able and efficient though at times a little too lenient with prisoners." The report continued that "through his regard for his fellow human beings," he had allowed three prisoners, all charged with murder, to escape. At least two of the three would soon commit additional murders, attracting the dismay of the New Orleans press at the dysfunction prevailing in Tangipahoa.[31]

Throughout the 1890s, the bloodiest decade in the region's history, McMichael remained completely unwilling to confront the most violent elements. When asked how a mass-murderer could so blatantly snub the legal system, a female member of one of the notorious feuding families responded curtly, "They were afraid to arrest him." Worse, McMichael seemed to resent those who possessed the aggressive nature he lacked. For months prior to the fall of 1896, merchants in the town of Hammond had been bullied by a notorious thug who was "trying to run the town with a small gang at his back." When Hammond city marshal Tom Rhodes courageously confronted the gang, a shoot-out resulted, leaving one of their number dead and Rhodes seriously

Table 5.1. Recorded Homicides in Sample Judicial Districts, 1902–1912

Judicial District	Parishes Included	District Population 1900	District Population 1910	Reported Homicides 1902–12	Percent Conviction	Percent Acquittal	Percent Nol-Prossed
Fourth	Lincoln Union	34,480	38,936	55	49%	47%	3%
Fifth	Caldwell Winn Jackson	25,684	40,768	52	59%	35%	6%
Twelfth	Vernon Sabine DeSoto	50,811	64,947	101	56%	28%	16%
Eighteenth	Acadia Lafayette	46,308	60,580	54	51%	42%	7%
Twentieth	Lafourche Terrebonne	53,346	61,431	37	64%	21%	15%
Twenty-Fifth	Tangipahoa Livingston St. Helena	34,204	48,959	131*	38%	46%	16%
Twenty-Sixth	St. Tammany Washington	22,963	37,803	53	69%	27%	4%

*Includes the ten "known murders" wherein the perpetrator had never been arrested as reported by the district attorney.

Sources: United States Census Compendium, 1900 and 1910; "Report of the Attorney General to the General Assembly of the State of Louisiana," 1900–1902, 1902–1904, 1904–1906, 1906–1908, 1908–1910, 1910–1912.

wounded. To the dismay of residents who applauded Rhodes's bravery, McMichael arrested him for creating a disturbance. The remaining gang members continued to roam free, "making threats." McMichael's predecessor and successor as sheriff, F. P. Mix, proved similarly baffling. In one instance Mix provoked outrage by simply releasing a "dangerous negro maniac" into the streets when he arrived at the state asylum in Jackson and found the facility full.[32]

A particularly grisly 1901 case reflected the public perception of the problem. After a night of hard drinking at a party, a group of white men inexplicably attacked the home of a Black farmer named Arthur Nickerson near Arcola, Louisiana. The group murdered Nickerson and his five-year-old daughter before sexually assaulting his thirteen-year-old daughter and Nickerson's wife, even as she hid their youngest child under the bedcovers. A third daughter was shot and wounded by the gang who were alleged to have boasted that they intended to kill the entire family but had run out of ammunition. A visit to New Orleans by prominent Amite City attorney and secretary of the state senate W. H. McClendon provided insight into the despair of regional residents and the contempt of the region's largest press organ. In an article titled, "Will Tangipahoa Prosecute the Nickerson Outrage?" a reporter questioned McClendon.

Picayune: "What is the sentiment in Tangipahoa over the Nickerson killings?"
McClendon: "There is outrage."
Picayune: "Will the perpetrators be prosecuted?"
McClendon: "Like all other cases have been prosecuted in Tangipahoa the past eight years."
Picayune: "You mean indifferently?"
McClendon: "The record speaks for itself."
Picayune: "Where will they be tried?"
McClendon: "Right in Amite City."
Picayune: "And you think indifferently?"
McClendon: "I think like all other cases have been prosecuted."[33]

With the close of Reconstruction, the piney woods region of the Florida parishes, which comprised the Twenty-Fifth and Twenty-Sixth judicial districts, tottered on the brink of utter chaos. Family feuds, political killings, and random bushwhackings held the residents in the grip of fear and intimidation. The meltdown of the local legal systems, almost daily killings of innocent persons, and Governor Murphy Foster's inability to control the situation despite the issuing of bounties on some of the most notorious offenders and the dispatch of state militia, provoked a statewide howl for the restoration of order in the region. The *Crowley Signal* complained that murder in Washington and Tangipahoa parishes constituted little more than a misdemeanor. The *New Orleans Daily Picayune* declared: "Law has ceased to be supreme and society in the parish of Tangipahoa has degenerated to that primitive state where each individual must look out for himself as best he can. The entire state demands that the reign of law shall be restored in Tangipahoa, no matter what the cost." The *Shreveport Times* came to a similar conclusion: "Nowhere in the state does a feeling of such dread and terror exist as in Tangipahoa. Only a determined and unflinching effort to discover and punish the assassins will redeem Tangipahoa from its Baptism of Blood." Similarly, the *Plaquemines Journal* condemned those responsible for the murders: "The soil of Tangipahoa has literally been drenched with blood of late, most of those who have lost their lives being victims of cowardly and heartless assassins. There is no coward so vile and despicable as he who strikes a fellow being from behind under the favoring shadows of the night or the protecting trees of a forest. These black hearted miscreants have made the name of that fair section of the state a byword and a reproach."[34]

Perhaps no single homicide reflected the impotence of the legal system more so than the 1899 murder of Avery Draughon. Almost from the outset, as the piney woods region of southeastern Louisiana began its descent into near anarchy, the Draughon family had worked to restore order. The deceased man was, in many senses, the very face of the regional legal system. He had been the mayor of the village of Tangipahoa for six years; he was also a police officer who was on the threshold of being elected sheriff on a law-and-order platform. When he was attacked in broad daylight, while awaiting a train, by three brothers who paraded him about the town beating him before ultimately shooting him to death and departing town laughing and waving their hats free of any fear of the system of justice, the rule of law reached a tipping point.[35]

After months of timid haggling to secure the surrender of the accused, the trial of Draughon's killers finally commenced, and the state seemed certain of convictions. Ten prosecution witnesses from a variety of professions, and locations, testified that they saw the accused attack, abuse, and ultimately murder Draughon. Seven defense witnesses, including one of the accused, another who multiple witnesses testified was not even in the parish the day of the killing, and still another, who was arrested for perjury after the trial, proclaimed it a case of self-defense. District Attorney Robert Ellis closed the prosecution with a prophetic statement to the jury: "If the state has not made out a clear case of murder against the accused it could never make out one in any case." The jury deliberated forty-five minutes before returning not guilty verdicts on all counts. Two businesses belonging to prosecution witnesses, including the post office at Tangipahoa, were burned to the ground the evening after their testimony.[36]

Limitations in police services and nonaggressive prosecutions played an important role in compromising the judicial system. Observers nonetheless noted that the ultimate problem centered on juries who "lacked the courage, or the virtue, to convict the guilty." In a scathing demand for the restoration of order, the *New Orleans Picayune* offered a list of reasons the region, and especially Tangipahoa, should be a model of progress. The list concluded, "These would seem to be highly civilizing instruments and influences, and yet cowardly assassination and savage human slaughter are as rife there as when the country was densely covered with pine forests and modern development was unknown. The question is naturally asked

Figure 5.2. Crowd gathered in Amite City, Louisiana, for the mass execution of six men for the 1921 murder of businessman Dallas Calmes. The crowd is being restrained from approaching the specially erected wooden scaffold adjacent to the parish jail by a cordon of National Guardsmen and a moat. Tangipahoa Parish endured such high rates of violence and low rates of conviction that regional delegates to the 1898 constitutional convention enthusiastically supported the nonunanimous jury verdict. (Courtesy of the Center for Southeast Louisiana Studies)

why this is so and it presses for an answer." The same paper noted that if the majority of the people were not peaceable, "it would be the duty of state authorities to go into that region with sufficient force and subdue its savage people into a condition of civilization and order. What then is the matter?" Grimly answering its own queries, the *Picayune* bemoaned the region's future: "Even if the lawless element is in the minority it is able to so terrorize the balance of the community to such a degree, that the bloody outlaws work their will while everybody submits. As to the courts apparently they punish none of the worst criminals, if indeed they ever get possession of them, but the defaults of the criminal courts are wholly chargeable to the juries."[37]

In the fifteen years following the election of 1896, despite astounding rates of homicide, the Twenty-Fifth District reported a conviction rate of 38 percent, the lowest of the rural districts statewide. Maintaining reporters at every major case in the Twenty-Fifth and Twenty-Sixth Districts, the *Picayune* denounced the prevailing condition in which juries refused to convict out of sympathy for the accused or out of fear of being killed by friends of the criminals. The *Picayune* concluded, "The burden is placed where it belongs upon the people." The same paper noted that in a fifty-year period, Washington Parish had convicted only one accused murderer amid the relentless violence. Dispatched to the region by Governor

Murphy Foster at the head of a company of state militia, the state adjutant general, Allen Jumel, held meetings and conducted interviews with parties involved on all sides of the "difficulties." Jumel concluded that the violence had spiraled out of control because the victims "could not secure juries with the moral courage to bring in verdicts against the parties charged with crimes." He added, "This was the fault of the people not the courts."[38]

The delegates attending the 1898 constitutional convention were well aware of these problems; hence the demand for judicial reform from the country parishes. They understood that in many areas of the state, defense attorneys requested lists of jurors' names in advance of a trial. The jurors were regularly intimidated or otherwise coerced into ignoring the evidence presented against the accused and merely cast their vote to acquit. Despite defense attorneys' efforts to suppress the statements, in the Draughon case alone, three prosecution witnesses testified that they had been visited by friends and family of the accused and warned not to testify. Several jurors expressed concern regarding the consequences for their families if they voted to convict. As bribing and coercing jurors increasingly assumed an implicit role in the legal process, unanimity in verdicts to secure a conviction became a threshold of unobtainable commitment.[39]

In the spring of 1921, six recent Italian immigrants to the New Orleans area received word that a bank in the small town of Independence in central Tangipahoa Parish offered "easy pickings" for a robbery. The botched robbery attempt resulted in the murder of Independence businessman Dallas Calmes, who mistakenly thought he was confronting a chicken thief when he intercepted the robbers attempting to gain access to the bank through his property. The resulting series of capital trials drew national attention to conditions prevailing in Tangipahoa and nearly provoked an international incident as multiple lynch mobs menaced the accused, who were hurried to prison in New Orleans for their own protection. The mob's threats to storm the courthouse provoked a diplomatic crisis with the Italian government and a demand that federal troops be deployed in the parish seat of Amite City.[40]

Following two trials, which both ended in convictions, and multiple appeals to the Supreme Court, the convicted men were returned to Tangipahoa Parish to face the executioner. State militia deployed around the courthouse, which was separated from the jeering crowd by a water-filled moat specially created to hold back the throngs who came to watch. The convicted men were hastily brought from the train station to the courthouse surrounded by a cordon of troops. Yet before the executed men were even in the ground, a familiar scandal added to the excitement. One juror claimed that he had voted to acquit but had been intimidated into voting guilty by the other jurors and threats from the crowd. A notorious bootlegger confessed that defense attorneys offered him $5,000 to bribe just enough jurors to throw the case. One of those jurors admitted that he had received $2,000 to vote to acquit, and a second fled the state before he could be arrested.[41]

Beginning with the close of the Civil War prosecutors in certain rural judicial districts across Louisiana, including the Fourth, Twelfth, Twenty-Fifth, and Twenty-Sixth struggled to secure convictions of seemingly obviously guilty parties. Press reports bemoaned the impotence of justice in regions where jurors were openly bribed or intimidated and where witnesses proved "willing to testify to anything in order to rescue friends from the clutches of the law." Desperate efforts to improve the reliability of the courts in the long-suffering Twenty-Fifth District led officials to appoint a so-called "talisman," whose duty was to screen and secure competent jurors. It also led them to send delegates to the 1898 Constitutional Convention with the mission of changing the law to make it more difficult for friends and family of the accused to bribe or intimidate a juror to secure the release of a guilty defendant, and ultimately contribute to the undoing of a legal system. The Tangipahoa Parish delegate to the 1898 convention was none other than R. L. Draughon, whose nephew, Avery Draughon, would be brutally murdered in plain sight only months later. His killers would be acquitted in a split decision and would never answer for the crime—the nine of twelve votes threshold to secure a conviction as mandated by the Constitution of 1898 would not become law until January 1904.[42]

The delegates to the 1898 convention approved reforms designed to assist the state judiciary in confronting the rampant violence that consumed certain areas of the state. In addition to lowering the bar to secure a conviction in felony cases, the new Constitution mandated that cases not subject to punishments of hard labor could be heard by a judge alone. In cases that could result in a sentence of hard labor, five jurors were required, and their decision had to be unanimous to convict. Felony cases, including manslaughter and second-degree murder, which became the most utilized charge due to the difficulty in securing unanimous jury verdicts, required nine of twelve jurors in agreement to convict, and capital cases continued to require a unanimous decision. Justices of the peace were empowered to hear an expanded array of cases to relieve the burden on district courts. In response to pleas from some reformers to have the district courts remain in session year-round rather than in infrequent short terms, the delegates approved a provision directing the courts to remain in session ten months of the year. They also approved consolidation of cases to reduce the backlog created by separate trials for each offense committed by multiple offenders.[43]

The Louisiana Constitution of 1898 was a document imbued with racism. But it was also driven by the countless tears of widows and orphans, by near hysterical demands from the press, and by the entreaties of soberminded citizens of certain troubled districts who understood that civilization required the rule of law sustained by a reliable, respected, legal system. Securing twelve randomly selected individuals to agree on almost anything is a challenge from the start. In regions where violent groups intimidated jurors and/or skillful defense attorneys effectively played the "he had it coming" card, it frequently proved impossible no matter what the evidence. Homicide rates in Louisiana reflect this certainty.[44]

As the demands for Louisiana to abandon the nonunanimous jury verdict played out in the press during the spring of 2018, there emerged a consistent refrain. Specifically, most media accounts included a healthy dose of dismay that it endured into the twenty-first century. Critics designated Louisiana's nation leading incarceration rate among the nefarious products of the jury-verdict law. Seldom, if ever, mentioned, was Louisiana's other dubious distinction: uncontested leader in statewide per capita homicide rates. In 1996, almost a century to the date of the 1898 convention, the Federal Bureau of Investigation (FBI) released criminal statistics revealing the United States status at the forefront of violence among industrialized nations. The South led in rates of violent crime among the various regions, contributing disproportionately to the national homicide rate of 7.4 per one hundred thousand deaths. Louisiana led the nation with a rate of 17.5 per one hundred thousand deaths, which contrasted sharply with last-place South Dakota's 1.2 per one hundred thousand. FBI statistical reports for 2012 indicated a reduction in the rates of homicide, yet confirmed Louisiana's leadership in national rates at 10.8 per one hundred thousand deaths over second-ranked South Carolina at 6.8. Not surprisingly, when broken down by parish in state reports to the FBI, the regions comprising the Twenty-Fifth and Twenty-Sixth Judicial Districts continue as leaders in rural homicide in the Bayou State. Statistical analysis included in the 2013 Louisiana Supreme Court Annual Report further demonstrates that the parishes in the former Twenty-Fifth District led the Florida parishes of southeastern Louisiana in criminal cases filed with the former Twenty-Sixth District parishes second.[45]

In February 2021, the *New York Times* published an article that asked, "Why Does Louisiana Consistently Lead the Nation in Murders?" The article listed all the contributing factors long known to scholars of the Bayou State and wider South. It listed the presence of a lingering "frontier mentality" wherein people take the law into their own hands as well as the preeminence of "honor" as a guiding cultural principle. Signs of disrespect to an individual could be perceived as affronts to one's personal or familial honor that demanded violent retribution. The consequences of one's actions proved secondary to the fear of public or private humiliation. The same study found that southerners, and especially Louisianians, are more likely than other Americans to view the system of justice as untrustworthy. People frequently do not take part in a system they do not trust, fueling cycles of retribution outside the law.[46]

The easy availability of guns is another consideration, though it remains unclear why Louisiana stands apart from other states offering easy access to firearms. Finally, cultural conditioning plays an important role. The historical tradition of violently resolving perceived grievances has long been a cultural identifier in Louisiana, so much so that it has been employed as a mitigating factor in capital death penalty appeals cases. A recent article appearing in multiple regional newspapers observed that the tradition of perceiving violence as not merely an accepted but an expected response in certain situations is becoming even more common in rural areas of the state.[47]

The comprehensive answer to the questions of why Louisiana alone among the states of the South embraces the nonunanimous jury verdict and why it endures into the twenty-first century seems obvious. The Bayou State is known for its passions: unmatched cuisine, unique cultural and ethnic diversity, prolific rates of alcohol consumption, legendary festivals and carnival celebrations, and a general laissez les bon temps rouler attitude toward life. That same passion likewise includes a very high-strung temperament and a quick tendency toward violent resolution of grievances. Passion has an outsize influence in Louisiana, and it is not always something to celebrate.

Tradition too plays a crucial role. Virtually all Louisianians can relate to, or know someone who can, enduring family memories that conclude, "Nobody messed with grandpa." The power of the culturally ensconced convention to maintain a misplaced vision of courage, one requiring forthright personal defense of one's family honor, standing your ground when confronted by a bully, challenging the scoundrel who claimed to have taken liberties with your sister, can be understood only by those who live it. And, in Louisiana, whether in the nineteenth century or the present, there are few long-time families who do not.

It takes only moments of research to identify cases wherein skillful defense attorneys employed race, religion, gender, or simply the "he had it coming defense," to play on the sympathies of certain jurors and secure acquittal of a seemingly obviously guilty defendant. The implications are as open-ended as they are grotesque. The newly acquitted defendant who boasts that he did indeed murder the victim, secure in the certainty of the legal protection offered by the no double-jeopardy rule; the juror convinced that the victim would be alive if he had not been buying drugs, so why send the perpetrator away for life; the prosecutor who believes in a second chance for an offender, who instead empowered by the knowledge that he can get away with murder, kills again—all are certainties that may very well become ever more common in the Bayou State.

In the time it took to write this article, one can only wonder how many people in Louisiana died violently and how many perpetrators will actually answer for their crimes. Yet there is a certainty connected to the question. Specifically, until social justice pioneers and judicial reform experts identify a method for curtailing violence in its infant form, the unanimous jury verdict is certain to add to the numbers of the sad club that admits only those families and friends of murder victims who never witnessed justice served upon their killers. It is not a problem unique to Louisiana, but in the state that consistently endures the highest rates of homicide in the nation, most almost certainly wish to see it diminished.

No one wants to see an innocent person incarcerated for a crime they did not commit. And, most would probably agree that if the price to ensure that does not happen includes an occasional murderer getting away with his crime, it is worth it. How many among the families of murder victims who never see justice done would agree remains a distinctively separate question. The repeal of the nonunanimous jury verdict is a restructuring delivered to Louisiana by those who ever remind us to remember the humanity of the accused while frequently seeming to fail to offer the same to the victim. Let us hope that reform of the judicial system does not stop here.

NOTES

1. *Baton Rouge Advocate*, April 1, 5, 8, 18, 24, 28; May 1, 6, 14, 15, 21; November 1, 2018; October 5, 2019; November 29, 2020; *New Orleans Times Picayune*, November 7, 2018; New York Bloomberg, November 8, 2018; Jessica Rosgaard and Wallis Watkins "The History of Louisiana's Non-Unanimous Jury Rule," WWNO, New Orleans Public Radio Report, October 22, 2018. The "Yes on Two Committee" raised $2.15 million to support repeal of the nonunanimous jury rule. Major donors included national liberal advocacy groups such as the Tides Advocacy Fund, Open Society Foundation, and the American Civil Liberties Union. No committees or donor groups supported the opposition to repeal. Ballotpedia, Louisiana Constitutional Amendment Election, November 6, 2018, amendment 2.

2. *Baton Rouge Advocate*, April 1, 5, 8, 2018; *London Guardian*, May 10, 2022; Thomas Aiello, *Jim Crow's Last Stand: Non-Unanimous Criminal Jury Verdicts in Louisiana* (Baton Rouge: Louisiana State University Press, 2015).

3. "Message of E. B. Kruttschnitt, President of the Convention," *Constitution of the State of Louisiana Adopted in Convention at the City of New Orleans, May 12, 1898* (New Orleans, 1898) 264.

4. On November 6, 2018, Louisiana voters repealed the nonunanimous jury verdict rule by a margin of 64.35 percent to 35.65 percent. See Ballotpedia, "Louisiana Constitutional Amendment Election," November 6, 2018, amendment 2.

5. *Journal of the Proceedings of the Constitutional Convention of the State of Mississippi, 1890* (Jackson, MS: E. L. Martin, 1890), 10, copy located in Mississippi Department of Archives and History, Jackson, MS.

6. *Portland Morning Oregonian*, April 23, 24; November 3, 19, 25, 1933; Robert Black, "Ramos v. Louisiana: Does the Fourteenth Amendment Require Unanimous Jury Verdicts?" *Constitution Daily* (Washington DC: National Constitution Center, 2019) 1.

7. Stephanos Bibas and Jeffrey L. Fisher, "Common Interpretation, the Sixth Amendment," *Interactive Constitution* (Washington DC: National Constitution Center, 2014) 2.

8. Bibas and Fisher, "Common Interpretation, the Sixth Amendment," 3; Black, "Ramos v. Louisiana," 2.

9. Black, "Ramos v. Louisiana," 1–2; Stephen Cresswell, "The Case of Taylor Strauder," West Virginia Archives and History, *Archiving Wheeling*, April 20, 2020.

10. *Constitution or Form of Government of the State of Louisiana* (New Orleans, 1812), art. III, sects. 9, 10, pp. 13–14, sect. 2, pp. 11–12; St. Francisville *Asylum and Feliciana Advertiser*, July 3, 1824; Emmett Asseff, *The History of the Government of Louisiana* (Baton Rouge, 1964) 53.

11. *Journal of the Convention Called for the Purpose of Re-Adopting, Amending, or Changing the Constitution of the State of Louisiana* (New Orleans, 1845); *Louisiana Constitutional Convention of 1844–45, Official Report of Constitutional Debates* (New Orleans, 1845), 342.

12. *Journal of the State Convention to Form a New Constitution for Louisiana, 1852* (New Orleans, 1852).

13. *Official Journal of the Proceedings of the Convention for Framing a Constitution for the State of Louisiana, 1868* (New Orleans, 1868); Michael Les Benedict, *A Compromise of Principle: Congressional Republicans and Reconstruction, 1863–1869* (New York: Norton, 1974); Jesse Russell and Ronald Cohn, eds., *Ironclad Oath* (New York, 2013).

14. *Official Journal of the Constitutional Convention of 1868*, 1–6, 15–23; New Orleans *Daily Picayune*, September 27, 1867.

15. *Official Journal of the Constitutional Convention of 1868*, 24, 30, 35, 59, 92; *New Orleans Daily Picayune*, April 15, 17, 1868; Thomas G. Davidson to James Taliaferro, April 25, 1868, in James G. Taliaferro Papers, Louisiana and Lower Mississippi Valley Collection, Louisiana State University (herein after referred to as LLMVC); *Amite City Times*, August 31, 1867.

16. *Official Journal of the Proceedings of the Constitutional Convention of the State of Louisiana, 1879* (New Orleans, 1879) 13, 38.

17. Edmund S. Morgan, *American Slavery, American Freedom: The Ordeal of Colonial Virginia* (New York: W. W. Norton, 1975).

18. Steven Hahn, *The Roots of Southern Populism: Yeoman Farmers and the Transformation of the Georgia Upcountry, 1850–1890* (Oxford: Oxford University Press, 1983); Lawrence Goodwyn, *The Populist Moment: A Short History of the Agrarian Revolt in America* (Oxford: Oxford University Press, 1978); William Ivy Hair, *Bourbonism and Agrarian Protest: Louisiana Politics 1877–1900* (Baton Rouge, 1969).

19. *Louisiana Senate Journal*, 1894, 28; Covington, *St. Tammany Farmer*, March 28, 1896; Hair, *Bourbonism and Agrarian Protest*, 234–67.

20. Shreveport, *Evening Judge*, December 15, 1895; Natchitoches, *Louisiana Populist*, March 20, 1896; Hair, *Bourbonism and Agrarian Protest*, 260–63;

21. *Eleventh Census of the United States, Compendium*, 1890, 782–83; *Louisiana Senate Journal*, 1896, 22; *Baton Rouge Daily Advocate*, April 26, 1896; Hair, *Bourbonism and Agrarian Protest*, 262–63.

22. *Baton Rouge Daily Advocate*, May 15, 19, 1896; *Franklinton New Era*, May 21, 1896; *Natchitoches Louisiana Populist*, July 10, 1896; "Message of Governor Murphy J. Foster," *Louisiana Senate Journal*, 1900, 18–30.

23. *Louisiana House Journal*, 1896, 393–94; Hair, *Bourbonism and Agrarian Protest*, 268–69.

24. *Proceedings of the Constitutional Convention of the State of Louisiana, 1898*, 8–9; *Baton Rouge Daily Advocate*, January 27, 1898; Hair, *Bourbonism and Agrarian Protest*, 274–76.

25. *Proceedings of the Constitutional Convention of the State of Louisiana, 1898*, 9–10; C. Vann Woodward, *Tom Watson, Agrarian Rebel* (New York, 1938), 221, 239–40, 378–79, 432–33.

26. *Proceedings of the Constitutional Convention of the State of Louisiana, 1898*, 10, 39, 97, 113–21

27. *Proceedings of the Constitutional Convention of the State of Louisiana, 1898*, 10; "Memorial by the Citizens of Rapides Parish," 76, 378, 17.

28. *New Orleans Weekly Picayune*, October 2, 1895; *Franklin Advocate* (Meadville, Miss.), July 30, 1914; "Address to the Alliance of the Second Congressional District," 1891, in Thomas Jefferson Carlisle Papers, Alabama State Archives, Montgomery; Hodding Carter, "Not Much of a Man if He Hadn't," in *Southern Legacy* (Baton Rouge: Louisiana State University Press, 1950). For examples of patterns of violence in the rural South, see Bertram Wyatt-Brown, *Southern Honor: Ethics and Behavior in the Old South* (Oxford: Oxford University Press, 1982); William Montel, *Killings: Folk Justice in the Upper South* (Lexington: University Press of Kentucky, 1986); Christopher Waldrep, *Nightriders: Defending Community in the Black Patch, 1890–1915* (Durham, NC: Duke University Press, 1993); Altina Waller, *Feud: Hatfields, McCoys, and Social Change in Appalachia, 1860–1900* (Chapel Hill: University of North Carolina Press, 1988); Samuel Hyde, *Pistols and Politics: Feuds, Factions, and the Struggle for Order in Louisiana's Florida Parishes, 1810–1935* (Baton Rouge: Louisiana State University Press, 2018).

29. Samuel Hyde, "Backcountry Justice in the Piney Woods South," in *Plain Folk of the South Revisited*, ed. Samuel Hyde (Baton Rouge: Louisiana State University Press, 1997); "Report of the Attorney General to the General Assembly of the State of Louisiana," 1900–1902, 1902–1904, 1904–1906, 1906–1908, 1908–1910, 1910–1912; Hyde, *Pistols and Politics*, 317–21.

30. "Report of the Attorney General of the State of Louisiana, 1898–1900" (New Orleans, 1900), 5–6; "Report of the Attorney General to the General Assembly of Louisiana, 1900" (New Orleans, 1902). The Sixteenth Judicial District later became the Twenty-Fifth District and is today the Twenty-First District.

31. *New Orleans Times Democrat*, December 23, 25, 1897; *New Orleans Picayune*, December 20–21, 1897; Sixteenth Judicial District Court Minute Books, nos. 5, 6, and 11, Tangipahoa Parish Clerk of Court Archives; *Kentwood Commercial*, February 17, 24, March 3, 10, 1900.

32. *New Orleans Daily Picayune*, February 7, 1889; October 31, 1896; *Weekly Picayune*, August 2, 1894; *Kentwood Commercial*, October 24, 1896; January 23, 1897.

33. New Orleans *Picayune*, February 3–7, 1901; *Baton Rouge States*, February 21, 1901.

34. *Crowly Signal* and *Baton Rouge Capital Item*, rpr. *Franklinton New Era*, December 17, 1898; *New Orleans Daily Picayune*, December 11–14, 21, 1897; *New Orleans Times Democrat*, December 11–13, 1897; *Baton Rouge Daily Advocate*, *Plaquemine Journal*, *Shreveport Times*, and *Amite City Florida Parishes*. All rpr. *New Orleans Daily Picayune*, January 4, December 21, 1897.

35. Sixteenth Judicial District Court Minute Books, no. 6, docket no. 304, State of Louisiana v. Alonzo and Gage Gill, Tangipahoa Parish Clerk of Court Archives; W. W. Draughon to Robert Reid, June 15, 1900, in Reid Papers, LLMVC; *New Orleans Picayune*, October 8–10, 1899; January 23, 1901; *St. Tammany Farmer*, October 14, 1899; *Baton Rouge Daily Advocate*, October 12, 1899, January 17, 1901.

36. *St. Tammany Farmer*, February 2, 1901; *New Orleans Picayune*, January 22–27, 1901; Sixteenth Judicial District Court Minute Books, no. 6, docket no. 304, Tangipahoa Parish Clerk of Court Archives.

37. *New Orleans Picayune*, February 28, 1909; May 16, June 20, 1899; October 30, 1901; *St. Tammany Farmer*, May 16, 1908; "Message of the Governor to the General Assembly of the State of Louisiana," *Louisiana Documents* I (Baton Rouge, 1908), 58–60.

38. *New Orleans Picayune*, June 15, July 12, 1897; October 26, 1896; April 4–8, 10, 12–14, 1899; *Kentwood Commercial*, March 27, 1897; *Franklinton New Era*, April 8, 1899; newspaper article, n.d., from *Greensburg St. Helena Echo*, in Robert Reid Papers (LLMVC). For discussion of the pattern of violence prevailing in the piney woods of the Florida parishes, see Hyde, *Pistols and Politics*, 203–07, 317–24.

39. *New Orleans Picayune*, January 24–26, 29, 1901; *Baton Rouge States*, February 21, 1901; *St. Tammany Farmer*, February 2, 1901.

40. Twenty-First Judicial District Court, Parish of Tangipahoa, Minute Book 21, State of Louisiana v. Joseph Reni et al., docket nos. 4925, 4926, pp. 54–55; *Ponchatoula Enterprise*, May 13, 27; July 1, 1921; John V. Baiamonte Jr., *Spirit of Vengeance: Nativism and Louisiana Justice, 1921–1924* (Baton Rouge: Louisiana State University Press, 1986).

41. *Amite City Florida Parishes*, May 13, 20, 27, 1922; March 3, 1923; *Amite City Florida Parish Times*, July 9, November 19, 1921; January 7, June 10, 17, 1922; April 14, 1923; May 10, 1924; *Ponchatoula Enterprise*, June 16, 30, 1922.

42. *Amite City Florida Parishes*, November 22, 1913; W. W. Draughon to Robert Reid, June 15, 1900, in Reid Papers (LLMVC); *New Orleans Picayune*, October

9–13, 1899; *Baton Rouge States*, February 21, 1901; *Journal of the Proceedings of the Constitutional Convention of 1898*, 378–79.

43. Constitution of the State of Louisiana, 1898, articles 116 and 117, pp. 42–43.

44. *New Orleans Picayune*, September 4, 7, 10, 16, December 11–21, 29, 1897; January 3–4, 6–7, 1898; *Greensburg St. Helena Echo*, December 17, 1897; *Kentwood Commercial*, December 18, 1897; *New Orleans Times Democrat*, December 23, 25, 1897; Reminiscences of Dr. J. W. Lambert, typescript, n.d., in John Lambert Papers (LLMVC).

45. FBI homicide statistics reprinted in Fox Butterfield, "Why the South's Homicide Rate Is So High," *New York Times*, July 26, 1998; Federal Bureau of Investigation, Uniform Crime Report, 2012 and 2015, and 2006–2007 Louisiana Commission on Law Enforcement, "Louisiana Index Crimes Reported to the FBI Through the Louisiana Uniform Crime Report," Center for Disease Control, "Louisiana Homicide Death Rate, 1999–2014," Louisiana Life Expectancy Report, 2015; Supreme Court of Louisiana of the Judicial Council of the Supreme Court, "Annual Report, 2013," pp. 44–47; *New Orleans Times-Picayune*, September 27, 2016.

46. Jeff Asher, Ben Horwitz, and Toni Monkovic, "Why Does Louisiana Consistently Lead the Nation in Murders?," *New York Times*, February 23, 2021.

47. California case Wharton v. Woodfork (case no. CV 92-3469-GLT), Louisiana case Wearry v. Cain (no. 01-FELN-015992); *Baton Rouge Advocate* and *New Orleans Times Picayune*, August 21, 2022; Franklinton *Era Leader*, August 23, 2022.

Chapter Six

EQUALITY FOR WOMEN IN LOUISIANA

AN UNFINISHED REVOLUTION

JANET ALLURED

The post–World War II women's liberation movement in Louisiana, as elsewhere in the country, used peaceful methods of protest as they fought violence, harassment, and prejudice against women. In addition to working against de jure and de facto gender-based discrimination, the participants were intent on destroying long-held damaging social and cultural stereotypes about men as well as women.[1] It is also key to note, especially for those that know little about second-wave feminism—the term typically applied to the groundswell of grassroots activism that characterized the 1950s through the 1970s—that while the face and voice of the movement were typically white, well-educated, respectable, and middle-class, the movement was in fact quite diverse. It included people of color, labor unions and tradeswomen, students and middle-aged women, lesbians and married cisgender women, as well as those who identified as nonbinary. What was required was a commitment to political activism that sought to overturn patriarchal oppression against all women, regardless of how they identified themselves or where they lived in the state.

Political scientist Erica Chenoweth's research into the success rates of violent versus nonviolent protests shows that peaceful movements such as feminism tend to succeed more often than violent rebellions because they are more inclusive of a larger proportion of the population. Peaceful types of protest do not require physical strength, so they can be gender inclusive, multigenerational, and multiracial, and they cut across lines of class, age, ability, educational, rural, and urban divides. This gives them claims to legitimacy that bring them more attention and ultimately help them to shift power within their opponents' pillars of support, that is, among economic, political, and religious authorities.[2] This was certainly true of the feminist movement in Louisiana, although the movement did not quite reach the critical mass necessary to move those pillars of the establishment as far as they had desired to.

The heterogeneous nature of second-wave feminism in Louisiana meant that it was also fractious, partly because so much was at stake for women's lives, opportunities, and careers. Ultimately organizing thousands of Louisiana women along with some male allies, participants did not see eye to eye about goals or strategies. A plethora of organizations fought for women's equality, including some older, single-sex, prowoman, feminist organizations that had been around for generations, with active branches across the state, like the Business and Professional Women's Clubs and the League of Women Voters. Others were new to the era, liberal nonprofits such as the National Organization for Women (NOW), which had chapters in major cities in Louisiana (and included sympathetic male allies as members). To the left of NOW were more radical groups that formed out of the hippie zeitgeist of the 1960s. The more extreme they were, however, the less appeal they had beyond their immediate cadre of members. Radicals (including socialist feminists) were located primarily in New Orleans, which had a more polyglot and bohemian population than the more staid urban centers like Baton Rouge and Shreveport.

Liberal feminists working through the existing political system achieved some legislative successes, although not all they wanted and not without a great deal of pushback and compromise. To their great dismay, some of their opponents included other women, such as Representative Louise Johnson from Bernice in north Louisiana, an insurance agent who successfully opposed the ratification of the Equal Rights Amendment (ERA).[3] She, of course, was not the only woman who opposed the ERA and other feminist goals. Perhaps predictably, the vigorous feminist movement produced its exact opposite among conservative women, particularly among evangelical Christians, Catholic laywomen, and housewives living in rural areas.

Most feminist organizing occurred in Louisiana towns that also included universities, and female faculty were often heavily involved in the bureaucratic liberal feminist organizations. But it is worth restating that not all feminists in Louisiana were privileged, white, or well educated. Many were "workplace feminists," also known as "labor feminists." These included Mexican American Fran Bussie and African American Sybil Taylor of the Louisiana AFL-CIO. Some were young, poor college students like Clay Latimer, Phyllis Parun, Sandra Karp, and poet Andrea R. Canaan. These last four also identify as lesbian, as did quite a few of the grassroots organizers, especially in New Orleans.[4]

Lesbians and with some cisgender Louisiana feminists, as part of their revolution against male-defined standards of beauty, rejected the trappings of femininity such as skirts and dresses, shaved legs, and makeup. Others, however, loved being women and dressing the part. For some feminists, refusing to get their hair done at the salon and refusing to apply makeup every day saved time and money to accomplish things that were more meaningful, including getting an education and embarking on a career. The rejection of feminine fashion opened opportunities for self-expression for women and helped to open even more job prospects as well. By rejecting confining clothing such as high heels, panty hose, and girdles and normalizing the wearing of traditionally male clothing such as pants and even overalls, women felt comfortable applying for jobs as mechanics and construction workers, or even white-collar occupations that required attire associated with men, such as chemists and bankers, rather than only secretaries and bank clerks.

In 1964, following the example of President Kennedy's establishment of the Commission on Women, Louisiana governor John McKeithen established the Commission on the Status of Women (now known as the Women's Policy and Research Commission) to gather statistics and to advise the governor about policies that would improve women's prospects in the state. Under director Pat Evans in the 1970s, the office pushed legislators to embrace many feminist measures, although its campaign to have the legislature ratify the ERA failed.[5]

Many gains that feminists scored occurred above the level of the state, such as Title VII of the Civil Rights Act of 1964, a federal law that outlawed employment discrimination based on sex (or gender, as defined today) as well as race, religion, and national origin; it also prohibited labor organizations from discriminating against these same "protected classes." However, the Equal Employment Opportunity Commission (EEOC) set up by this act barely enforced the provision prohibiting discrimination based on gender until attorneys working with NOW forced the issue. Sylvia Roberts, a Baton Rouge attorney for NOW, won the first great victory for Title VII in *Weeks v. Southern Bell*, in which the Supreme Court of the United States (SCOTUS) struck down arbitrary labor laws and practices based on sex, ending many artificial stumbling blocks to occupational advancement for women. Feminists such as Roberts used Title VII to win greater access for women to traditionally male occupations, from news anchors to mechanics to professionals and businesspeople. Running their own companies was unlikely, however, before Congress passed the Equal Credit Opportunity Act (1974), which prevented discrimination in lending on the basis of sex. In 1978, Congress passed the Pregnancy Discrimination Act, an amendment to Title VII, which made pregnancy discrimination against the law whether in the hiring process, pay, job assignments, promotions, employee benefits, and any other term or condition of employment. The EEOC enforces this law.[6] As a result, women in Louisiana today may be found in a variety of fields that previously were off limits to them.

Louisiana feminists joined the nationwide effort for the passage of federal laws that would improve outcomes for women. These succeeded in getting Title IX of the Education Amendments of 1972, that mandated that women be granted greater access to higher education and equality in sports. Colleges and then high schools began varsity sports programs for girls and women that had not previously existed and improved facilities for those sports. Far more women were admitted to and received scholarships to universities and professional schools because of Title IX. Consequently, a rich feminist scholarship burgeoned in many academic disciplines.[7]

Because language encodes so much of our thinking about gender, feminists worked within the academy and without to end sexist language tropes (such as the use of "man" to stand in for all people, substituting "humans" or "people") and to rewrite texts to use gender-inclusive language. This meant the sacred texts, too: the Bible and other ecclesiastical documents such as hymnals, the Book of Common Prayer, creeds, the Book of Discipline in the United Methodist Church, and so on. Figuratively storming the walls of churches and synagogues, feminists achieved greater access to the pulpit and additional roles in religious observances that had previously been denied them. While evangelical religious groups leaned conservative, mainline denominations backed feminist goals and assisted the women's movement in multiple ways. This included the National Council of Jewish Women (NCJW), the Woman's Society of Christian Service, a part of the Methodist Church (later the United Methodist Women) that supported ERA, abortion rights, and many other tenets of second-wave feminism. Pulpits that had previously been off limits to women now began to admit them into that inner sanctum. Today, female Methodist pastors in the Louisiana Annual Conference are appointed to serve churches in approximately equal numbers as males, and there are many more female rabbis and ministers in other religions, too. Touro Synagogue in New Orleans has had female rabbis for years, as have other temples throughout Louisiana.[8]

Revising standard English did not stop with the sacred texts but came to include scrutiny of textbooks and news outlets. Louisiana NOW chapters insisted that news organizations drop the trivializing practice of referring to women of all ages as "girls," and instead, if they were of age, call them "women." They demanded that newspapers not shunt all stories involving women to the "women's page" and instead put them front and center, that women not be identified as "blondes" or "brunettes" or have their figures described underneath their names (so as to satisfy the male gaze) but that instead, like men, their important identifying information be their educational achievements or other legitimate credentials. Local female journalists Patsy Sims, Kathleen Thames, and Joan Kent, among others, authored hard-hitting stories about violence against women, including sexual assault and the widespread problem of illegal abortion.[9] Slowly but surely, things began to change.

A deeply personal issue for second-wave feminists involved challenging the societal taboo against discussing subjects involving the female body, specifically sex, sexuality, sexual assault, unwanted pregnancy, birth control, and abortion. For women to remain silent about these ever-present and ongoing problems protected abusers and rapists and harmed women in myriad ways. When, for example, it was taboo to say the word "breast" in public, or for it to appear in or be heard in a respectable news outlet, it complicated the ability of the medical community to move forward in the detection and treatment of breast cancer and decreased women's willingness to seek medical care when they observed changes in their breasts. Few issues were as personal as sex, yet it was never discussed in public. Feminists dedicated themselves to liberating women's sexuality and acknowledging gender and sexual fluidity. As a result, LGBTQ+ issues became more widely accepted, particularly among young people, and so far, anyway, Louisiana has not followed the lead of other conservative-dominated state governments in banning gender-affirming medical care for people under the age of eighteen. However, it did enact an antitrans sports ban restricting transgender women and girls from playing on school sports teams that match their gender identity.[10]

Overturning the stereotype that ladies were to be timid and soft spoken in public, feminists spoke up and spoke out in ways that required tremendous courage. They raised awareness about issues that had always been considered private. They exposed the horrific level of violence and sexual abuse at the hands of cruel husbands and other men in the domestic circle (such as fathers and uncles and even priests) against women and children. They established the first domestic-violence shelters and made it a criminal offense to hurt women and children in the home. Domestic violence had not been considered a crime before, and children who "told" about their abuse typically were not believed as the problem had not yet been documented. Assault had always been illegal if it involved strangers, but not if it occurred within an intimate relationship. The new criminal codes included punishment of offenders.

To end the silence and shame around sexual assault, feminists held speak outs against rape, a crime that routinely happened to women—especially the most vulnerable women, meaning low-income women, sex workers, or women of color—but which no one ever talked about. They helped change the laws to make rape convictions easier, encouraged police departments to hire women (often called "matrons") for the first time to assist women through the process of bringing charges against their attackers, and established rape crisis centers throughout the state. However, none of these changes came without a tremendous outlay of energy and developing a very thick skin. When Senator Diana Bajoie cosponsored a bill making spousal rape a crime, the male legislators laughed, made jokes, and mocked it. But the bill passed after Bajoie called them out on it.[11]

Following the Supreme Court decision in *Meritor Savings Bank v. Mechelle Vinson et al.*, in 1986, feminists sounded the alarm bell about the problem of sexual harassment on the job and worked assiduously toward ending this exceedingly widespread practice that was so terribly detrimental to women's ability to advance in the workplace of their choice. Since 2018, all Louisiana state employees are required to receive annual training to identify and prevent sexual harassment, although this was at best a partial victory because it is the bare minimum the state can get away with and it only covers state employees, not those employed in the private sector.[12]

Women also won the right to serve on juries in Louisiana—finally, in 1975—yet this victory occurred not because of legislative action but because of a Supreme Court ruling involving a man who was convicted of a crime by a jury from which women had been barred. SCOTUS ruled in *Taylor v. Louisiana* (1975) that women could no longer be excluded as a class from jury service or be given automatic exemptions.[13]

Second-wave feminists encouraged women to seek political appointments and elective office, too, since that is where real power lies. Louisiana saw more and more women in positions of authority. While tokenism prevailed for many years, the stereotype that women were unfit for public office was broken. Cities elected their first female mayors, such as Willie Landry Mount in Lake Charles in 1993; voters elected their first female Congressional representatives in 1973 (Lindy Boggs became the first woman elected to Congress from Louisiana); and citizens sent to the governor's mansion the first female governor, Kathleen Babineaux Blanco of Lafayette, in 2004.[14] While those examples are white women, women of color also won elective offices, perhaps most famously Representative Dorothy Mae Taylor from New Orleans, the mother of seven who entered the Louisiana House in 1971. Taylor pioneered legislative activism not only on behalf of women but also on behalf of people of color.[15]

This first generation of women in elected office overwhelmingly championed and pushed forward democratic principles like equality and fairness. Studies have shown that when women hold public office, they are more actively involved in a variety of gender-salient issue areas, including healthcare, the economy, education, and the environment. They are more responsive to constituents, value cooperation over hierarchical power, and find ways to engineer solutions in situations where men have trouble finding common ground. Furthermore, having women's voices at the table can potentially influence policy choices in favor of benefitting all women.[16]

To counteract the conservatism of the Louisiana electorate, feminists established organizations to incentivize, recruit, and train women to run for political office such as Louisiana Women's Network; the committee of twenty-one in New Orleans and in Jefferson Parish; the Louisiana Center for Women in Government and Business at Nicholls State University in Thibodaux, Louisiana; and, after 2000, Emerge Louisiana.[17] Other groups have as their purpose mobilizing the female vote. This would include older single-sex organizations like the League of Women Voters; the Woman's Society of Christian Service, the missionary organization of the Methodist Church, which in 1950 established the "National Citizen's Roll Call of Methodist Women"; and the NCJW, which was particularly active in New Orleans. In 1991, Kim Gandy, the national president of NOW and a Louisiana native, established Women Elect 2000 to register and mobilize female voters in Louisiana.[18] In 2018, the NCJW joined with the League of Women Voters New Orleans to form the nonpartisan coalition, Engaging New Voices and Voters (ENVY) to register new voters, inform voters, and help get out the vote. It currently has more than three hundred volunteers and twenty diverse organizations working in the coalition.[19] However, these efforts did not produce a flood tide. In 2022, Louisiana ranked in the bottom ten for the percentage of women in state legislatures. While women make up 51 percent of Louisiana's population and 54 percent of registered voters in the state, they currently make up only 18 percent of the Louisiana legislature.[20] Furthermore, not all women elected to the legislature in recent years have been reliably prowoman in their politics.

While political power is important to any class of people, particularly those who have historically been subject to discrimination, of equal concern to feminists is the immensely personal issue of bodily autonomy. This includes the right to say "no" to sex without suffering harm or repercussions, and, on the flip side (the "prosex" side, as pundits would have it), the right to have enjoyable, consensual sex without fear of unwanted pregnancy. Along with male allies, liberals in the federal government helped make birth control services widely available (Title X), thanks to President Lyndon Johnson's Great Society and War on Poverty initiatives. Additionally, after public support for the decriminalization of abortion increased in the 1960s, SCOTUS ruled in *Roe v. Wade* (a Texas case) in 1973, that states could not restrict access to abortion in the first trimester, although they could restrict it within reason in the second and third trimesters if they allowed exceptions for the life and health of the mother. In other words, a grown woman's life was to take precedence over any potential life of a fetus or a fetus's claims to personhood. This was consistent with the Fourteenth Amendment's definition of citizenship, which said that a person must be *born* or naturalized in the United States to have citizenship rights or status. Since a fetus is, by definition, not born, it does not have protected status. Abortion was a given after *Roe v. Wade*, but in the 1980s, conservative Republicans decided to weaponize it to attract evangelicals and conservative Catholics to their party, a move that worked. But before discussing that, an examination of the history of abortion practices in Louisiana before *Roe* is required.

When abortion was proscribed in Louisiana, contrary to popular mythology, most providers were doctors, nurses, midwives, and paraprofessionals who routinely performed the clandestine operation. Given the secretive nature of the practice, there is no way to know how many were performed before 1973. Illicit abortions were often disguised in the records as dilation and curettages (D&Cs) necessary for legitimate medical reasons (e.g., blighted ovum, polyps). Hospital abortions were allowed for therapeutic purposes, although hospital boards made them difficult to get.

Abortion providers were usually only prosecuted if a woman died, and then they were often acquitted. If convicted, they served a short prison term and went right back into practice. Some providers were arrested multiple times, but most, especially if they were physicians, operated practically above ground, doing hundreds per year with no fear of prosecution. These physicians were "moral pioneers" who openly defied the law, believing that women had a right to this vital health-care service. Louisiana women of means sometimes traveled to Puerto Rico or Mexico rather than to a local provider. Regardless of where they went, women seeking pregnancy termination had the assistance of friends and family, who provided the funds and often transported them. Poor women availed themselves of the charity hospital system, where Louisiana State University (LSU) medical students did their residencies. Residents provided abortions (usually at night) and hysterectomies to women who had all the children they wanted. It is clear from the documentary record that abortion was widespread in the 1950s, among all classes, married and unmarried.

Nationwide, the movement for reform and repeal gathered steam in the 1960s due to several factors. One was the rubella (or German measles) epidemic. This disease, if contracted by a pregnant woman, caused severe and life-threatening damage to the fetus. Another was the thalidomide scare, a drug prescribed to pregnant women for nausea that caused terrible birth defects as well. When Sherri Finkbine, star of *Romper Room*, went to Sweden for an abortion when she could not get one in the United States even though she had been given thalidomide, 52 percent of Americans approved of what she had done, and 64 percent polled after that high-profile story became well-known favored liberalization of abortion laws. Professional associations like the American Law Institute, the ACLU, the American Medical Association, and Social Workers spoke out. Doctors began to challenge Louisiana's antiabortion statutes in court, and feminists (NOW, NARAL) argued for acceptance of the ethic of "voluntary motherhood" or "every child a wanted child." Doctors, clergy, the NCJW, and the YWCA, as well as independent feminist groups, established abortion referral networks that formalized and advertised in newspapers that young people were likely to read (e.g., campus papers or alternative publications). Those who provided this service were volunteers who never took any money for their services. They established a kind of Underground Railroad of abortion providers. They personally investigated providers for safety and respectful treatment of the patient. All these people (including the women who got abortions) were engaging in acts of civil disobedience, a technique learned from the civil rights movement.

The Clergy Consultation Service on Abortion (or Problem Pregnancy) (CCS), which had chapters all over the country, started by the pastor at Judson Memorial Methodist Church in New York City, included clergy of many different religions, Protestant and Jewish. CCS counselors referred women to abortion providers out of state as a matter of policy. One of their most trusted providers was Horace Hale Harvey III, a student at LSU medical school in New Orleans. He set up the first "clinic" in the Claiborne Towers, apartments for LSU medical students, in 1969. Because there was a direct flight between New York and New Orleans, the CCS leadership in NYC sent most of their clients to him. They knew him to be trustworthy and compassionate, motivated by concern for the women and not by profit (he charged on a sliding scale). When New York's new law went into effect on July 1, the nation's first and busiest legal abortion clinic opened its doors in NYC, and its director was none other than Horace Hale Harvey III.

Support for relaxing abortion restrictions came from many surprising quarters. Contrary to its current position, the Republican Party endorsed reproductive justice until the rise of the New Right in the late 1970s and early 1980s, when it flipped. Before that, Governor Ronald Reagan signed the law liberalizing California's statutes; Barry Goldwater, the 1964 Republican presidential nominee, who held libertarian views, endorsed its legalization, and First Ladies Betty Ford and Barbara Bush, married to Republican presidents, remained committed to a prochoice position their entire lives. Liberal

Protestant and Jewish groups, even Baptists, espoused reproductive freedom. Baptists saw it as a matter of individual conscience that the state should not be involved in. Representative Louise Johnson, the Louisiana version of Phyllis Schlafly, supported legal abortion. Even many Catholics thought similarly, such as Justice William J. Brennan, one of the Supreme Court justices who joined Justice Harry Blackmun in the majority decision in *Roe v. Wade*.

History demonstrates that banning abortions will not stop women from getting them, yet antichoice activists have acted as though it will. They have forced the issue in many states, including Louisiana, which had a trigger ban—a mélange of laws that went into effect upon the Supreme Court's ruling in *Dobbs v. Jackson Women's Health Organization* (June 24, 2022). Abortion bans, however, are unworkable in practice and do significant damage. This is the way it has always been and will continue to be, regardless of lawmakers' ill-informed decisions to change the situation.

As with all such socio-political revolutions, feminist victories were incomplete. Ruth Rosen said in *The World Split Open: How the Modern Women's Movement Changed America* that "each generation of women activists leaves an unfinished agenda for the next generation."[21] Historian and women's liberation movement participant, Sara Evans, summed it up by saying, accurately, that "Change was always partial."[22] There is always more to do, as the latest edition of the "Status of Women in Louisiana" (2020) report makes clear. Despite progress, the report reads, "so many gaps exist between women and men, women of color and white women, and between southern women and women in other parts of the country."[23] Women are undervalued in the home (the idea of wages for housework never got any traction) and underrepresented in elective and appointive office. Job and pay discrimination are technically illegal, although there are so many other stumbling blocks to women's advancements, it does not mean a lot. The masculinist structure of the labor force devalues labor associated with women and allows employers to escape responsibility for supporting families. Low-wage, full-, and part-time jobs that many poor women have as their only option provide no health care, paid sick leave, paid vacation, paid family or maternity leave, or retirement benefits, while at the other end of the scale, the work environment that professional women move in makes little or no allowance for the responsibilities of family life and children.[24]

The challenges that lie ahead include many of the same issues that feminists brought to the public's attention between forty and seventy years ago, where gains were either inadequate to begin with or have been rolled back as the state has become reliably red (Republican dominated). What follows is a list of those areas in serious need of reform, along with suggestions for a path forward toward equity for women.

SEXUAL HARASSMENT

While Louisiana state employees must receive annual training in the detection, prevention, and reporting of sexual harassment, it is the bare minimum (one hour online) and does not uphold best practices for sexual harassment training. Unfortunately, it is still all too common and is not addressed in the private sector, which employs over 80 percent of Louisiana workers. There is no law to prohibit the nefarious practice of forced arbitration in cases of harassment on the job in the private sector. Businesses are not mandated to establish prevention practices nor to stop requiring employees to sign nondisclosure agreements, which hide the true extent of sexual harassment and shield harassers from accountability.[25]

VIOLENCE

The rate of violence against women is still very high in Louisiana. The state has the fifth highest homicide rate for women in the nation.[26] No general-fund dollars go to domestic violence prevention and response in Louisiana, despite feminists' and domestic-violence victims' advocates' requests for several million dollars to be allocated in recurring state general funds to address the large unmet need for hundreds of shelter beds and program funding. Among the things this money would fund is training for judges. Victims' advocates also point to the need for higher prosecution rates for cases involving strangulation, pregnant victims, and domestic assaults where children are present and witnessing. The state should implement policies to ensure domestic-violence survivors do not end up in prison for crimes connected to their abuse (meaning that they defended themselves).[27] Laws in place now require the transfer of firearms from domestic abusers to sheriffs during the pendency of a protective order and following any conviction for domestic abuse/battery. However, there's no uniform system by which the enforcement of this law can be recorded. In the 2022 session, a bill was passed requiring that the Louisiana Commission on Law Enforcement implement a reporting system for firearm transfer. This will entail coming up with uniform standards to help the public ascertain which sheriffs are implementing the law by matching the number of restraining orders against firearm collection in each parish.[28] The battle continues, though progress is slow.

Women who are not economically independent are much more likely to be victims of domestic violence and cannot see a way out of their situation. The stress of poverty contributes to violent behaviors. If the state had stronger laws to achieve economic security and family stability, the rate of violence would fall. Indigent women are also much more likely to become unintentionally pregnant. The problem of pay inequity compounds in myriad ways.

It is clear from the evidence that Louisiana women face a significant gender pay gap, pregnancy discrimination, gender-based violence, lack of reproductive justice, lack of paid support for parents and children, and much more. The Fourteenth Amendment does not apply to women, conservative justices such as Antonin Scalia have said.[29] Therefore, only a constitutional amendment can prevent legislators, the executive branch, or the courts from changing, diluting, or ignoring laws that are supposed to protect women from sex discrimination.

EQUAL RIGHTS AMENDMENT

The ERA passed Congress in 1972 and was sent to the states for ratification. Its ratification seemed all but assured until Phyllis Schlafly and other enemies of women's equality geared up significant opposition to it in the mid-1970s. An artificial deadline for ratification had been placed at the front of the amendment—something that was not done with any other constitutional amendment—saying that proratification forces had until 1982 to get it ratified. They failed to meet the deadline, but, since then, the last three of the needed thirty-eight states ratified in 2017 (Nevada), 2018 (Illinois), and January 2020, (Virginia). Two years later, a resolution with 133 cosponsors was introduced in the House recognizing that the ERA has now met all legal requirements to be recognized as the 28th Amendment. Among the leading lights who say that it met the requirements are Lawrence Tribe and Russ Feingold (both attorneys). The US House has twice passed bills to eliminate the time limit and to credit the three recent ratifications toward the required three-fourths, but it has stalled in the Senate, where the southern-initiated practice of the filibuster that requires sixty votes instead of a bare majority stops most legislation from passing, including this one. President Donald Trump pressured the national archivist not to certify the ERA after ratification by the thirty-eighth state. Meanwhile, the attorneys general of Nevada and Illinois filed a lawsuit, arguing that under Article V, a time limit in a congressional resolution cannot stand in the way of an amendment that has now been ratified by three-quarters of the states. Their suit languishes in an appeals court. President Joseph Biden has expressed strong support for the ERA and has declared that the only action needed now must come from Congress.[30]

If ERA were in place, it would set a norm for equal pay, provide a basis for litigation, and would keep women from being segregated in lower paying job categories. It would ensure that victims of violent crime occurring within an intimate partnership would have protection. It would guarantee consistency from state to state.[31] It would require "strict scrutiny" of sex-discrimination cases rather than "intermediate scrutiny," which is what we have now. Women who sued Wal-Mart for sex discrimination lost because we do not have the ERA and the advantage of "strict scrutiny." Title IX and the Violence Against Women Act (VAWA) (passed in 1990) can be overturned at any time. (It was not renewed under President Trump but has been renewed under the Democratic Biden-Harris administration.)[32] Of increasing importance in today's medically advanced world, ERA would also cover LGBTQ+ persons, trans rights, and reproductive rights.

FOR LOW-INCOME WORKERS

PAY GAP

Louisiana has consistently ranked at the bottom in the United States for what women earn on average compared to men—$0.69 to the dollar. "This gap exists in all fields, regardless of profession or educational background, and jobs predominantly filled by women are paid less than jobs mostly filled by men."[33] A "mommy gap" exists on the job, meaning that mothers are automatically offered less, while fathers are automatically offered more (mothers are seen as less reliable). This obviously contributes to the wage gap.[34] Pay secrecy fuels this. Using salary history to screen applicants and to set compensation forces women to carry lower earnings and pay discrimination with them from job to job.[35]

It is worse for minorities. Black women make on average $0.47 to each dollar a white man earns, and Latina women $0.53. Due to systemic racism and policies, Black women in Louisiana face significant inequities, including higher rates of poverty, infant and maternal mortality, increased contact with the criminal justice system, and overall lower quality of life. In 2016, the median wealth for Black families in Louisiana was $17,600, compared to $171,000 for white families. Inheritance and other intergenerational transfers "account for more of the racial wealth gap than any other demographic and socioeconomic indicators." Most poverty-stricken Black families are hardworking taxpayers who hold lower wage jobs such as cashiers, store clerks, and food-service workers. They live paycheck to paycheck and do not make enough money to meet basic needs including housing, childcare, food, and transportation. Raising the minimum wage would drastically reduce the number of Louisianans who live at or below the poverty line.[36]

Solutions to the gender-based pay gap include ending pay secrecy and allowing freedom of speech in the workplace, meaning requiring pay transparency and ending the practice of forcing employees to sign nondisclosure agreements. What is lacking in the law is a specific prohibition against retaliation for talking about wages in the workplace to ensure workers are being paid equitably. The Fair Labor Standards Act (FLSA) has provisions to protect speech for the purposes of organizing unions. It is poorly enforced, punishment is a slap on the wrist, and it is not uniformly interpreted as a way to get equal pay. Some states require the posting of salary ranges during the hiring process, either when advertising the job or during the interview process or both. Arguments in favor of pay transparency are persuasive: it allows businesses to budget and prevents them from being culpable for salary discrimination suits.[37] That is what the Equal Pay Act would do, but it has been a nonstarter in Louisiana for years. Senator Regina Barrow (D, Baton Rouge) has authored and sponsored it recently, but the result is always the same—the legislature hands it to the partisan House Committee on Labor and Industrial Relations, which is stacked with procorporation representatives endorsed by the Louisiana Association of Business and Industry (LABI). Legislators send it to this committee because they know it will be killed there and will not make it to the House floor for a vote.[38]

Same with the minimum wage—legislators send it to the House Labor Committee to die. Louisiana is one of five states (all in the abortion-ban area) that have not raised their minimum wages above the federal level of $7.25 per hour even though a higher minimum wage helps all low-income workers. Approximately two-thirds of minimum-wage workers are women. Half are over twenty-five, many married, most working full time. Since 1997, in Louisiana, local governments have been banned from raising the minimum wage even though surveys confirm that Louisianans want higher wages and a fair chance at equal pay. A 2017 LSU survey reported that 91 percent of Louisiana residents support the state requiring equal pay, and a 2019 LSU survey indicated 81 percent of Louisianans believe the minimum wage should be raised.[39] Since 2009, fifty-two bills have been filed in Louisiana seeking to establish a higher statewide minimum wage. All have been shot down despite polls indicating strong public backing for laws requiring employers to pay their workers a decent wage, according to the Louisiana Budget Project.[40]

SUPPORT FOR LABOR UNIONS

Labor unions were helpful in advancing working-class women (labor feminism), but right-to-work laws decimated unions in general and the AFL-CIO in particular in Louisiana. Most female wage workers in Louisiana are not able to provide for themselves and their children on what they make, thanks in part to lack of unionization. This could be alleviated by fully funding day care and by offering employees paid sick and family leave. The federal government mandates a certain amount of leave time, but it is not paid, and most people cannot afford to take it. In not having paid leave, the United States is unlike any other industrialized country in the world. In 2021, the Louisiana legislature established a task force to study the issue (HR118) but loaded it with antis. It was a big fight just to allow the presentations explaining all the rational reasons why paid leave is desperately needed in Louisiana. Agenda for Children, a Louisiana-based female-led advocacy group, has long pressed for this reform. Its report showed that 82 percent of registered voters in Louisiana support paid leave, including 77 percent of Republicans.[41]

While this is not something that Louisiana can do on its own, the country as a whole needs a system of universal health care that will guarantee access to reproductive health care, including birth control, and abortion services. A system of universal health care akin to what exists in most other industrialized nations would make it far less expensive for individual parents to raise children, our next topic.

FOR CHILDREN

CHILD CARE

Louisiana (and the nation) needs fully funded day care and after-school care so workers can be trained and paid decently. This would greatly assist low-income workers and could be subsidized to help higher-income families, too. Women report missing work, quitting a job, turning down promotions, and going from full-time to part-time because of childcare issues at far higher rates than men. This costs employers in employee absences and turnover and costs the Louisiana economy $1.1 billion per year in consumer spending. Quality childcare can also save funds on remedial education later in life because children who start school behind generally stay behind. The only state-administered program for children under the age of four has been cut in the last ten years from serving almost forty thousand children to fifteen thousand in 2020. Additional federal funds and increased state funding for the Child Care Assistance Program (CCAP) increased that number to about twenty thousand in June of 2022.[42]

FOSTER CARE

Louisiana needs a better-funded child-welfare system to assist parents who are unable to care for their children. It is already overwhelmed, and it is about to get worse. Andrea Gallo wrote a series called "Suffering So Young" for the *Baton Rouge Advocate* documenting the worsening crisis. The funding for foster care has declined by half since 2007. The number of full-time employees in the Department of Children and Family Services has fallen from over five thousand in 2007 to about thirty-five hundred today. Meanwhile, children in Louisiana have died at a rate 50 percent higher than the national average over the past decade (since 2010). Louisiana youths were killed at the highest rate of any state in 2020. Yet the state has no plan for how to reform the system, which is about to be even more overwhelmed now that abortion is no longer available.[43]

For all families, but particularly for people of color, Louisiana needs to end mass incarceration. Racism explains Louisiana's extraordinarily high incarceration rate—about double the national average. White people have criminalized Black life, taking advantage of the loophole in the Thirteenth Amendment, and then used that criminal record to deprive them of the right to vote. Eighty percent of women in jail are mothers, and most are also the primary caretakers of their children. Incarcerated women have high rates of mental illness and substance abuse, and most have a history of sexual, physical, and emotional trauma, sometimes as high as 90 percent.[44] Louisiana would benefit from decreasing the number of individuals incarcerated pretrial. Louisiana incarcerates more people before trial than any other state, three times more than the national average. Over 60 percent of women in jails under local control are awaiting trial (not convicted), and more than 77 percent of those are charged with a nonviolent offense. Why spend money there instead of increasing funding for mental-health services and substance-abuse treatment? Louisiana needs to become a more compassionate, less carceral state.

Louisiana women would benefit, too, if the state provided more funding for programs that assisted successful transition and reentry from jails. Studies confirm that programs for higher education for women in prison greatly reduces recidivism rates (down to 5 percent). Unfortunately, due to entrenched racism, there is little political will to do this. Despite clear evidence of what works, the state's long history of racism has kept it from advancing policies in the best interest of the majority of the state's inhabitants. It sometimes lives up to its unofficial slogan of "Third World and Proud of It."[45]

Why does Louisiana repeatedly follow such backward policies? The answer is simple: conservative Republicans dominate the state's legislature. Republican opposition has prevented Louisiana and the national Congress from passing measures like family leave and an extended child tax credit that would expand the social safety net, leaving those things up to each state. (The tax credit was extended temporarily during the Covid pandemic, resulting in a dramatic drop in child poverty.)[46]

Gerrymandering has made the passage of greater social-welfare measures increasingly unlikely at both the federal and the state levels. The Louisiana state senate is particularly gerrymandered, and, as of 2022, Republican seats are safe. Facing no competition, Republicans in Louisiana continue to shore up corporations at the expense of workers and consumers. Elected officials can pass laws that disadvantage women—and primarily poor women of color, to boot—and suffer no political consequences. They do not seem nearly as interested in enacting legislation that has costs for people like them—white men of means.[47] The problem is much greater than voters can manage. In addition to gerrymandering, another reason that conservatives dominate the state legislature is because legislators are paid so little, they must be independently wealthy to serve. It is a demanding and time-consuming job that is impossible for nonwealthy people to do. This means that a lot of legislators—including women—are put up for office by corporations and their lobbying groups like the American Legislative Exchange Council (ALEC), a probusiness, procorporation lobby that funds conservative candidates who vote against, for example, raising the minimum wage and other proworker measures. While Democratic women (and men) are more likely to aid women's issues, that is not a given. For example, the sponsor of Louisiana's abortion ban, Katrina Jackson, is a Democrat and a Black female. Other examples of this same phenomenon are Lenar Whitney (D, Houma) and Dorothy Sue Hill from Allen Parish (a very rural parish in south central Louisiana). Some (like Jackson) are religious conservatives and have not only voted against women's best interests but also voted against LGBTQ+ protections. These include Sharon Hewitt (R, Slidell), a Shell engineer and a leading Senate conservative sponsored by ALEC. Hewitt has voted to end women's rights to bodily autonomy and reproductive choice and opposed pay equity measures. These women are in lock step with the power brokers, nearly all of whom are white males.

REPRODUCTIVE JUSTICE

No issue is more important to women's empowerment and equity than their right to bodily autonomy. In Louisiana, about 60 percent of pregnancies are unintended, yet the state refuses to mandate sexual education in public schools or to provide young women who want it with free access to long-acting reversible methods of contraception (LARC) such as IUDs. Implementing age-appropriate, trauma-informed, medically accurate comprehensive sexual education in public schools across the state, to include grades K–12, would lower the high rate of unintended pregnancies and sexually transmitted diseases that limit the success of Louisiana's youth and tax the state's resources. Instead, the state makes sexual education optional, does not allow any instruction about sexual orientation, and requires that all materials used must be submitted to and approved by the local or parish school board and by a parental review committee. It also requires that "the major emphasis" shall be to encourage abstinence.[48] This practice, which has been in place (with some changes) since 1979, clearly has not worked to prevent teens from engaging in unsafe, unhealthy, and unprotected sex, meaning they have unintended pregnancies at a time when they are not able to care for a child. Furthermore, disallowing discussions surrounding issues of sexuality places LGBTQ youth at higher risk of suicide due to mistreatment and stigmatization.[49]

Lack of real political opposition in Louisiana is perhaps the main reason why the "prolife" side emerged triumphant in the recent abortion wars. First, however, it is important to clarify that "prolife" is a misnomer (hence the quote marks). The more accurate term for those who support criminalizing abortion is "probirth." To claim the mantle of "prolife," they would also have to embrace pro-natalist policies such as Western European countries have, including "baby bonuses" that all new parents receive when they give birth to or adopt a child. These cash gifts and other items routinely given to families with new babies are not tied to income—a significant point because it means they do not carry any stigma and are considered part of the social contract. Yet the antiabortion forces and their allies holding political offices continue to stall progress on policies that would materially assist families.

That is no coincidence. States with restrictive abortion bans are reluctant to raise taxes or spend money on social programs (a legacy of institutional racism—Mississippi, the site of the *Dobbs* case that overturned *Roe*, just cut taxes) but banning abortion *seems* free of costs as well as consequences (it is not). Funding programs to assist working mothers has costs; voting for an abortion ban does not require state money. The beauty of defending a fetus is that the fetus demands nothing in return—no housing, no health care, and so on. It is easy, cheap, and a way to distract voters from more critical issues that affect those walking the earth now. Yet the *Dobbs* ruling and state abortion bans will have enormous costs. A lot more preemie and nonviable babies will be born, meaning astronomical expenses to the system. The child-welfare system will be overwhelmed, yet the same officials who voted in favor of banning abortion have publicly admitted they have no plan in place to expand the foster-care system.

The most vulnerable people in the state are the ones most burned by abortion bans. Abortion bans disproportionately affect low-income individuals and families who are marginalized by their race, poverty, or immigration status. Research reveals a strong link between state policy choices and outcomes for mothers and children. States that have the strictest abortion restrictions, including Louisiana, have some of the highest child-poverty rates in the nation (Mississippi being the worst, number 51), the highest rates of low birth weight babies, the highest infant and maternal mortality rates, the highest stillbirth rates, and the highest teen pregnancy rates, the worst (or no) policies on paid family- and medical-leave programs, less access to maternal (pregnancy) care—and women who do not get prenatal care are five times more likely to die of pregnancy-related causes. Because most of those states did not expand Medicaid—medical insurance for the poor—although this is not true of Louisiana—they have declining numbers of maternity hospitals.[50] Though Louisiana's Democratic governor John Bel Edwards accepted federal money to expand Medicaid (which pays for contraception), Mississippi rejected Medicaid expansion, leaving an estimated forty-three thousand women of reproductive age without health insurance.[51] Governor Edwards's expansion of Medicaid protected many rural hospitals that would otherwise have gone under. In that sense, at least, Louisiana is somewhat better off than the nearby states in the South where Republican governors refused it. Yet Louisiana has little to brag about, as it has some of the highest Black maternal death rates in the country: four Black mothers die for every white mother, and two Black babies die for every one white baby. Even with Medicaid expansion, more than one-third of Louisiana's parishes do not have a single OB/GYN, and in many parts of the state, it takes an hour or more of travel to reach the nearest provider.[52] Recently, in a perfect example of medical racism, Republican senator Bill Cassidy, a retired gastroenterologist, said in May 2022, "If you correct our population for race, we're not as much of an outlier as it'd otherwise appear."[53] But the United States is still way out of line with other industrialized nations, and Louisiana ranks last of the fifty states when it comes to overall health.[54] Restrictive abortion states make it harder for families to take time away from work, earn a living wage, and access affordable childcare, among other factors. None of these states offers new parents paid family leave to care for their newborns.[55] Conservative legislators are simultaneously sanctimonious and miserly, mean, stingy, and tightfisted. We can do better. We must.

States with restrictive abortion bans also make it harder for families to access TANF funds (Temporary Assistance to Needy Families, or "welfare"). The lowest-ranking states are Texas, Mississippi, Louisiana, and Arkansas, where only four out of every one hundred families in poverty have access to TANF because those states have diverted that money to "other areas." Louisiana spent less than 10 percent of its TANF funds on basic assistance in 2020 but increased its funding for crisis pregnancy centers, fake abortion clinics that dupe women seeking abortions. Mississippi spent 5 percent of TANF funds, and Mississippi has the least generous cash welfare assistance ($260 per month for a poor mother raising two children) and has misspent millions of welfare dollars.[56] Clearly, these states value embryos and fetuses more than needy children who are already born.

A more generous social safety net could easily be funded if Louisiana taxed the rich and corporations appropriately and stopped giving tax breaks to corporations that can most afford to pay. Louisiana does not have a spending problem—it has a revenue problem, that is, a problem with insufficient income from appropriate sources. Despite what corporations like to claim, Louisiana is not a high-tax state. The state's problem is that it makes the poorest households pay taxes at a higher rate than those at or near the top in income. This is bad policy for many reasons, one being that it perpetuates poverty among female heads of households. To solve the problem, the state should raise its property taxes (since these are progressive) and lower sales taxes (which are regressive). Nationally, the United States should enact a minimum tax on corporations, so they do not shop around and pit one state against another as they seek bigger tax breaks. Too many business tax exemptions, deductions, and credits mean that companies are not paying their fair share. To make the critically needed investments in women and children in Louisiana, the state (and localities) must have sufficient revenue. Other countries have figured out how to do this and create better outcomes for all. There is no reason—other than lack of political will—that Louisiana cannot do likewise.

Louisiana's antiabortion bill, written and proposed by Representative Katrina Jackson (D, Monroe)—one of very few antiabortion Democrats—was turned into three separate trigger bans in 2022 (by which time Jackson had moved to the Senate). It is currently being challenged because the bills are vague, contain different criminal penalties, and officials have made contradictory statements about what conduct is prohibited in Louisiana.

This makes it impossible for health-care providers to know what care they may or may not perform. Because the bills are so murky, on more than one occasion, health-care providers have called Senator Jackson to ask for clarification before performing a procedure. All three bans prohibit abortion after fifteen weeks. The only exceptions are to save the life of the pregnant person (although this is extremely limited—the mother has to be on death's door) and medically futile pregnancies. The Louisiana Department of Health has produced a list of what those conditions are, but it requires two physicians to certify the diagnosis, which is burdensome in a rural community. The bills do not contain a penalty for the woman, only the provider. Michelle Erenberg, cofounder and executive director of Lift Louisiana, a nonprofit dedicated to fighting for women's reproductive health, rights, and justice, told the author that "there was no way we were going to stop the trigger bans. We couldn't even get an amendment for exceptions for rape and incest."[57] Lift Louisiana issued a dire statement regarding the *Dobbs* decision that well summarizes the challenges facing the state in the wake of this harmful set of laws:

> The Supreme Court of the United States (SCOTUS) today turned its back on nearly 50 years of legal precedence, and in doing so has harmed millions of people who no longer will have access to abortion services. By overturning *Roe v. Wade*, the court has denied a pregnant person's right to bodily autonomy and to make critical health care decisions that impact their life and their future. . . . Let's be clear that this decision will not affect privileged people, mostly white, from accessing abortion services. Instead it empowers the state to continue to oppress Black, Indigenous, and other People of Color, people with low incomes, young people, people living in rural areas and other marginalized communities from accessing abortion care. This oppression is rooted in anti-Black racism, white supremacy, patriarchy, and misogyny. This decision unravels long-standing principles of privacy and freedom upon which many other rights are protected. We understand those rights are now at risk as well.[58]

Lift Louisiana was able to clarify that these bills did not include emergency contraception, and HB 1061 by Rep. Jason Hughes (D, New Orleans) ensures that Louisiana survivors of sexual assault have timely access to information and emergency contraception ("Plan B") to prevent pregnancy resulting from rape. There was unanimous approval for this because the woman who reports a rape is given a pregnancy test first.[59]

While that is a bit of good news, the unwelcome news is that the Louisiana Family Forum is currently trying to prevent the Louisiana Department of Health from working with anyone who provides abortion, such as Planned Parenthood, despite the fact that many clinics that closed after *Dobbs* provided comprehensive health care to women who otherwise could not afford it, not just abortion service.[60] Once again, government is making medical decisions about women's bodies—a discriminatory practice that does not impact men and that would not have happened if ERA was part of the US Constitution.

Access to abortion is classed and raced. Another example of how poor women are the ones most hurt by abortion bans is the Hyde Amendment, a 1980 congressional measure barring the use of federal funds to pay for abortion, meaning Medicaid will not cover abortions even in medically futile pregnancies. Hospitals will not perform an abortion when they know they will not be reimbursed for it. Repealing or modifying the Hyde Amendment would greatly assist poor women, but with the Republicans in control of the House (as of the 2022 midterms), this is highly unlikely to happen.

Even before *Dobbs*, more and more women had begun self-managing abortions (SMA) by purchasing pills online (Mifepristone and Misoprostol). Abortion with pills is safe and effective and does not need to take place in the presence of a doctor. While that is one advantage, another is that it allows the woman to avoid the stigma of having to walk into a facility and dodge the protestors. However, a bill sponsored by Representative Sharon Hewitt criminalizes tele-health appointments for abortion pills (Act 548) and limits medication abortion administration to physicians.[61] Act 548 will have a chilling effect on out-of-state providers, and of course it reduces options for poor women who cannot afford to travel out of state. Access to birth control and abortion has always been hardest for the poor. Well-placed women (typically white) have the money to pay for travel, although the wait times in states where it is legal are astronomical. States (all outside the South) that are protecting abortion rights passed physician shield laws to ensure that if a woman travels out of state for an abortion, her home state cannot prosecute the physician who provided the abortion.[62]

When the clinics closed in the summer of 2022 in Louisiana, they lost standing to sue, but the Medical Students for Choice chapters took up the cause and now serve as the complainants because Louisiana medical residency programs stand to lose accreditation as the Accreditation Council for Graduate Medical Education (ACGME) requires this training for every OB/GYN program. This means medical students will not go to or stay in Louisiana for training, and since physicians tend to practice where they do their residency, in the long term, this will reduce the number of OB/GYNs in Louisiana overall.[63] It is going to be hard to attract OB/GYNs to the state because the laws put them in a dilemma if they try to, for example, treat a pregnant woman with medication for diabetes, arthritis, or cancer. Those medications may damage the fetus and could put the treating physician at legal risk. Louisiana's law defines pregnancy (personhood) as beginning at fertilization, which is not a medically accurate definition (the zygote must be implanted). This means that drugs that might potentially harm an embryo can be denied women who need it for other reasons. Fetal personhood laws criminalize the person who seeks an abortion as well as abortion providers. One woman whose fetus had no skull was denied an abortion by the hospital's attorneys (Woman's Hospital in Baton Rouge).[64] Medical providers are confused about whether they can intervene to save a patient's life. How close to death does a mother have to be? This delays care, which will mean many more complications for her—and a lot more expensive care. Physicians need to be able to offer their patients all options to provide safe care. The law also throws many fertility practices such as invitro fertilization into question, impacting a far larger number of couples.[65]

Plus, antiabortion statutes will have a detrimental effect on the economy. Businesses are less likely to locate here, college students less likely to come to school here. Louisiana's other poor-quality-of-life measures have already driven away many of Louisiana's young people; adding a no-exceptions abortion ban will drive away even more.[66] At least one convention (American College of Obstetricians and Gynecologists or ACOG) has cancelled due to the abortion ban, and more are likely to follow.[67]

Though there is no recent polling data in Louisiana, nationwide polls establish that most Americans (60 percent) support abortion rights with restrictions. In a 2022 referendum in Kansas, a conservative (red) state, people of both parties overwhelmingly voted to keep it legal. The rhetoric in Kansas revolved around bodily autonomy: the government should not be making these decisions for women and interfering with medical care that she might need. Most people believe that whether the decision to terminate a pregnancy is moral varies according to the circumstances (i.e., most Americans agree that "it depends").[68] This practical position recognizes that one in four women in the United States will have accessed abortion care before they reach the end of their childbearing years. Kansas voters let it be known that abortion is a policy issue, not a "moral" issue, since what constitutes a moral decision differs from one person to another and depends on a variety of circumstances. Indeed, the decision to terminate a pregnancy may be just as moral as the decision to have a child. People's personal morality should not dictate policy. Banning abortion disrespects the pregnant person's values for why they seek it in the first place.

The most oft-cited reason that women cite for not continuing a pregnancy is the expense of it. A normal pregnancy costs around forty thousand dollars for the uninsured (or for the state if the person is on Medicaid). The woman may also add to that expense the lack of paid leave, medical insurance, and affordable day care (or finding day care, period, as there typically are not enough spots). The majority of those who seek abortions already have children and report that they are barely able to afford the ones they have, much less more. Having a child pushes many people into poverty in part because the United States has no "child allowance" that other nations have. Or perhaps the woman is not ready for pregnancy, especially if it will interrupt her schooling (and maybe a lot of people are helping them get that education, so they would be disappointing those people). In other words, the state of Louisiana's deficiencies in assisting women and families is exactly why some women choose abortion. A large body of research proves that being denied an abortion limits peoples' education, time in the workforce, and wages, with the economic consequences extending well into the lives of their children. Findings indicate that pregnant people who are unable to get a safe, legal abortion and carry the pregnancy to term will experience long-term physical and economic harm.[69] Politicians who genuinely want to defend life would seek to remedy this, rather than imposing greater burdens on poor families and/or the already overwhelmed foster-care system.

Male philosophers and theologians have argued about the morality of pregnancy termination for eons and have arrived at no consensus about it, but progressive people (and most women) today believe that it is immoral, unjust, and antifamily to fail to provide respectable financial assistance to families and to force pregnancy and birth on women. Feminists and their allies argue that it is immoral for the state to criminalize medical care around reproduction and that bankrupting families is immoral. Providing little support for mothers forced to carry out dangerous pregnancies is also immoral. Contrary to abortion opponents' propaganda, it is not true that women who choose abortion suffer lifelong guilt. Quite the opposite: the overwhelming reaction, even decades later, is relief. A longitudinal study conducted by the University of California, San Francisco, shows "that receiving an abortion does not harm the health and wellbeing of women, but in fact, being denied an abortion results in worse financial, health and family outcomes." Women who are denied a wanted abortion suffer elevated levels of poverty and stress, debt and eviction, and their existing children had worse development outcomes compared to the children of people who were allowed to have an abortion. Women who choose abortion have a multiplicity of reasons for doing so, but it is not done on a whim, and it does not indicate that they are antichild or antifamily. They are making the best decision for themselves and their families at that time.[70]

If we want a solution to the "problem" of abortion (as the antiabortion forces see it—the prochoice forces disagree that it is a problem), why do we not look to the example of other countries such as the Netherlands, which has low abortion rates and unplanned pregnancy rates because they have universal health care, age-appropriate sex education, easy access to contraception, and so forth? If an accidental pregnancy does occur, the mother knows that the state will help provide for her and her child, including through medical care, and that she will have paid leave time to care for her infant. We need to become a more generous country that supports low-income mothers. We are rich. We can do this.

The takeaway is that, despite decades of progressive activism, most prowoman legislation has either been stalled, rolled back, or erratically administered due to conservative opposition. Thus, Louisiana still languishes at the bottom of the fifty-one areas of the United States surveyed by nearly every measure of quality of life. The only real remedy to this is to ensure that women have power because from that all else follows. One way to do that is to increase salaries for legislators, a democratic reform that helps keep them out of the pocket of corporations and others with large campaign chests. A reform like that would help people who are not independently wealthy run and hold office, most importantly women of color who (despite the voting record of Katrina Jackson) have the most prowoman voting records. Senator Regina Barrow (D, Baton Rouge), for example, has been good on domestic-violence issues, advocates in favor of sensible gun control laws, and supports bills to provide employees with paid sick leave and minimum-wage laws. Finally, the governor and legislature could and should give the Women's Policy and Research Commission greater power to write and amend legislation, rather than making it purely advisory. But that will never happen, and women will never be able to achieve comparable status with men until people on both sides of the aisle begin to see them as full human beings with equal citizenship rights.

NOTES

1. This section on history of feminism in Louisiana is taken from Janet Allured, *Remapping Second-Wave Feminism: The Long Women's Rights Movement in Louisiana, 1950–1997* (Athens: University of Georgia Press, 2016), unless otherwise noted.

2. Erica Chenoweth, PhD, is the Frank Stanton Professor of the First Amendment at Harvard Kennedy School and has written a number of highly acclaimed books on the subject of nonviolent civil disobedience. https://www.hks.harvard.edu/faculty/erica-chenoweth Accessed 12/4/2022.

3. The proposed ERA read, "Equality of rights under the law shall not be denied or abridged by the United States or by any state on account of sex."

4. Andrea Canaan, *A Writer's Life*, https://andreacanaan.blog/about-andrea-canaan/.

5. RS 46:2525; Louisiana Women's Policy and Research Commission, https://gov.louisiana.gov/page/womens-policy.

6. https://www.eeoc.gov/pregnancy-discrimination.

7. https://www.justice.gov/crt/title-ix-education-amendments-1972.

8. Clergy Appointments as of July 1, 2022 (PDF), sent by Rev. Katie McKay Simpson, pastor of University Methodist Church in Baton Rouge, LA, personal correspondence, November 21, 2022. Janet Allured, "Louisiana, the American South, and the Birth of Second-Wave Feminism," *Louisiana History* 54 (Fall 2013): 389–423.

9. See chapters 4 and 5 in Janet Allured, *Remapping Second-Wave Feminism* for a full retelling of these issues.

10. Act No, 283, 2022 Regular Session, LA. Senate Bill 44, Fairness in Women's Sports Act, enacted 8/1/2022

11. Allured, *Remapping*, 126.

12. Prevention of Sexual Harassment Law, LA. Revised Statute 42:341-44, (Act 270 of 2018).

13. Taylor v. Louisiana, 419 U.S. 522 (1975).

14. Lillian W. Walker of Baton Rouge was the first woman elected to the Louisiana House of Representatives in 1964. Virginia Shehee of Caddo and De Soto Parishes became the first woman elected to the Louisiana State Senate in 1975, and Mary Landrieu, who went on to serve as the first female United States senator from Louisiana, began her political career in 1980 in the Louisiana House as a representative from New Orleans. Mount was later elected to Louisiana State Senate from 2000–2012.

15. Allured, *Remapping*, 243–45.

16. Emerge Louisiana, https://la.emergeamerica.org/about/about-us/.

17. Cheron Brylski, https://en.wikipedia.org/wiki/Cheron_Brylski; Louisiana Center for Women and Government, Nicholls State, https://www.nicholls.edu/lcwg/; Louisiana Center for Women in Government & Business, http://louisianawomen.org/; Emerge Louisiana: https://la.emergeamerica.org/.

18. Kim Gandy, https://www.discoverthenetworks.org/individuals/kim-gandy.

19. Email correspondence with Ina Weber Davis (New Orleans), December 1, 2022; Engaging New Voices and Voters PDF and Envvnola.weebly.com (accessed December 1, 2022).

20. Emerge Louisiana; Center for American Women and Politics, https://cawp.rutgers.edu/facts/current-numbers/women-elective-office-2022.

21. Ruth Rosen, *The World Split Open: How the Modern Women's Movement Changed America* (New York: Viking Penguin, 2000), 344.

22. Angie Maxwell and Todd Shields, *The Legacy of Second-Wave Feminism in American Politics* (London: Palgrave Macmillan, 2018), 15; Sara M. Evans, "Generations Later, Retelling the Story," in Maxwell and Shields, *The Legacy of Second-Wave Feminism*, 34.

23. Louisiana Status of Women report (2020), https://gov.louisiana.gov/assets/Programs/StatusOfWomenInLouisiana_Edition1_OnlineVersion.pdf.

24. Evans, "Generations Later," 34.

25. https://gov.louisiana.gov/assets/Programs/StatusOfWomenInLouisiana_Edition1_OnlineVersion.pdf.

26. https://lcadv.org/louisianas-female-homicide-rate-remains-fifth-highest-in-nation/.

27. Susan Willis, Donna Dees, Documentary Short, *Five Awake*, 35 minutes 36 seconds (May 25, 2016), United States, https://wdrv.it/845c5f689.

28. "Challenges in Louisiana's Efforts to Address Domestic Violence," Louisiana Legislative Auditor Performance Audit Services (December 16, 2021): chrome-extension://efaidnbmnnnibpcajpcglclefindmkaj/https://app.lla.state.la.us/publicreports.nsf/0/8ee1181936c16c6e862587ad0058c879/$file/0002556e.pdf?openelement&.7773098. United against Domestic Violence 2022: chrome-extension://efaidnbmnnnibpcajpcglclefindmkaj/https://www.unitedwaysela.org/sites/unitedwaysela.org/files/2022-03/DomesticViolence2022CaseBook.pdf.

29. Robin Bleiweis, "The Equal Rights Amendment: What You Need to Know" (January 29, 2020), American Progress, https://www.americanprogress.org/article/equal-rights-amendment-need-know/.

30. "ERA" project at Columbia Law School's Center for Gender and Sexuality Law, https://gender-sexuality.law.columbia.edu/content/research-policy.

31. https://www.lwv.org/ERAToolkit.

32. Fact Sheet: Reauthorization of the Violence against Women Act (March 16, 2022), https://www.whitehouse.gov/briefing-room/statements-releases/2022/03/16/fact-sheet-reauthorization-of-the-violence-against-women-act-vawa/#:~:text=The%202022%20reauthorization%20of%20VAWA,many%20cases%2C%20increasing%20authorization%20levels.

33. Status of Women in Louisiana report.

34. American Progress, https://www.americanprogress.org/article/breadwinning-mothers-critical-familys-economic-security/.

35. American Association of University Women, "Policy Guide to Equal Pay in the States," https://ww3.aauw.org/resource/state-equal-pay-laws/.

36. 4. See ALICE reports for Louisiana, https://www.unitedforalice.org/state-overview/louisiana. ALICE is an acronym for Asset Limited, Income Constrained, Employed. See also https://gov.louisiana.gov/assets/Programs/StatusOfWomenInLouisiana_Edition1_OnlineVersion.pdf.

37. Institute for Women's Policy Research/Rockefeller Survey of Economic Security, "Private Sector Workers Lack Pay Transparency: Pay Secrecy May Reduce Women's Bargaining Power and Contribute to Gender Wage Gap," December 20, 2017, https://iwpr.org/publications/private-sector-pay-secrecy/.

38. LABI grades legislators based on their business-friendly policies, and legislators pay attention to their grades. See the LABI scorecards, https://labi.org/research/score-card/ LABI: https://labi.org/; Labor and Industrial Relations committee: https://house.louisiana.gov/H_Cmtes/Labor (accessed November 18, 2022).

39. LSU Manship School of Mass Communication, "The Louisiana Survey 2017," http://pprllsu.com/wp—content/uploads/2017/06/LA-Survey-2017-Full-Report-v1.pdf.

LSU Manship School of Mass Communication, "Louisiana Survey Shows Bipartisan Support for Public School Teacher Pay Raises & Increased Minimum Wage," April 9, 2019, https://www.lsu.edu/manship/news/2019/april/2019lasurvey3.php.

40. Louisiana Budget Project, "The Gap Widens," June 27, 2022, https://www.labudget.org/2022/06/the-gap-widens/.

41. Gba strategies, "Paid Leave Research in Louisiana—PL+US: Paid Leave for the United States," September 2018, https://drive.google.com/file/d/1fyioVoGpyAT-lcGREk-WOl_nscvd88c2z/view, https://agendaforchildren.org/cms/wp-content/uploads/2021/08/Webinar-Slides-Paid-Leave-is-the-Foundation-of-a-Stronger-LA.pdf.

42. Louisiana Policy Institute for Children, https://policyinstitutela.org/; see "Local Taxation in Louisiana: Alternatives for Local Public Support of Child Care" (November 2022) on this website for more detailed information.

43. Andrea Gallo, "Suffering So Young" series, https://www.nola.com/news/collection_37ff73fc-1ff9-11ed-b105-374f67d3050f.html, https://www.nola.com/news/article_1d14054e-1f40-11ed-900c-cb4f9af23c6b.html, https://www.theadvocate.com/baton_rouge/news/article_0e3f5172-2a30-11ed-949c-9fd4763bf907.html.

44. 2. One example of how Louisiana fails its children is documented in the film *8 Days at Ware*, by Meg Shutzer and Rachel Lauren Mueller. A companion piece was published in the *New York Times*, https://www.8daysatware.com/ (accessed November 26, 2022).

45. Reentry Initiatives & Transitional Work Programs, Louisiana DPS&C, https://doc.louisiana.gov/imprisoned-person-programs-resources/transition-reentry/ (accessed November 26, 2022).

46. How the Expanded Child Tax Credit Could Cut Childhood Poverty in Half, https://www.npr.org/2021/07/19/1017891479/how-the-expanded-child-tax-credit-could-cut-childhood-poverty-in-half, July 19, 2021.

47. Democratic governor John Bel Edwards vetoed H.B. 1 and S.B. 5, the new congressional redistricting map, because it is so gerrymandered. It passed over his veto. The complaint filed against Secretary of State Kyle Ardoin noted that this "continues the State of Louisiana's long history of maximizing political power for white citizens by disenfranchising and discriminating against Black Louisianans." Robinson v. Ardoin, April 29, 2022.

48. Revised Statute 17:281.

49. Thetrevorproject.org—a suicide prevention program and website for LGBTQ+ youth—seeks to counter the damaging stereotypes that antitrans and anti-LGBTQ+ policies that are forced upon young people who identify as such. (accessed November 26, 2022).

50. Emily Badger, Margot Sanger-Katz, and Claire Cain Miller, "States with Abortion Bans Are among Least Supportive for Mothers and Children," *New York Times*, July 28, 2022, https://www.nytimes.com/2022/07/28/upshot/abortion-bans-states-social-services.html?searchResultPosition=1.

51. Mississippi ranked last in the Commonwealth Fund's 2020 score for health-system performances on measures including "overall preventable mortality" and "children without appropriate preventive care." *New York Times*, July 28, 2022; "States with the toughest abortion laws have the weakest maternal supports, data shows." *New York Times*, August 18, 2022, https://www.npr.org/2022/08/18/1111344810/abortion-ban-states-social-safety-net-health-outcomes.

52. Elizabeth Dawes Gay, "The Challenges and Solutions to Accessing Maternity Care in Louisiana," *Every Mother Counts*, November 30, 2017, https://blog.everymothercounts.org/why-louisiana-494cf0b487fc.

53. Cassidy made the comments in an interview with *Politico*. He insists his comments were taken out of context. NBC news, https://www.nbcnews.com/news/nbcblk/cassidy-defends-statements-louisianas-black-maternal-health-statistics-rcna30166.

54. Annual Report, 2021, America's Health Rankings, https://assets.americashealthrankings.org/app/uploads/americashealthrankings-2021annualreport.pdf.

55. The fact that women's status is lower in antiabortion states is nothing new. In addition to the July, 2022, *New York Times* piece cited next, see also Jean Reith Schroedel, *Is the Fetus a Person? A Comparison of Policies Across the Fifty States* (Ithaca, NY: Cornell University Press, 2000).

56. That scandal includes speeches that were never delivered by Brett Favre and a volleyball stadium for his daughter's college (University of Southern Mississippi). A motley assortment of political appointees, former football stars, professional wrestlers, business figures, and various friends of the state's former Republican governor (Bryant) were accused of pocketing or misusing money earmarked for needy families (most have pleaded guilty). Millions of dollars were transferred to friends and relatives of Bryant's appointees. Neil MacFarquhar, *New York Times*, September 22, 2022. Anna Wulf of *Mississippi Today*, a nonprofit news outlet, first broke the story. Wulf was interviewed on *PBS News Hour* September 26, 2022, https://www.pbs.org/newshour/show/brett-favre-under-scrutiny-for-allegedly-seeking-welfare-funds-to-build-a-sports-facility.

57. Michelle Erenberg, telephone interview, September 14, 2022.

58. https://liftlouisiana.org/updates/lift-louisiana-statement-supreme-court-overturning-roe-v-wade.

59. Lift Louisiana's mission is to educate, advocate, and litigate for policy changes needed to improve the health and wellbeing of Louisiana's women, their families, and their communities. Erenberg interview.

60. For Louisiana Family Forum's antichoice activism, see their website. https://www.lafamilyforum.org/action/. Lift Louisiana actively opposed LFF's policies.

61. Lift Louisiana, https://liftlouisiana.org/content/faqs-about-abortion.

62. Guttmacher Institute, State Legislation Tracker, https://www.guttmacher.org/state-policy (accessed November 26, 2022).

63. https://liftlouisiana.org/updates/lift-louisiana-takes-louisiana-lawmakers-court-over-abortion-restrictions-violate-state.

64. "Medical Students for Choice vs. Jeff Landry, Attorney General of Louisiana," Memorandum in Support of Motion for TRO and Application for Preliminary Injunction, filed June 27, 2022, in Civil District Court, in author's possession (supplied by Lift Louisiana).

65. Neelam Patel, "Abortion 'Trigger' Ban Statutes: Impacts on Plan B, Birth Control, and IVF Treatments," *Georgetown Journal of Gender and the Law* 23, no. 3 (2022), https://www.law.georgetown.edu/gender-journal/wp-content/uploads/sites/20/2022/04/Abortion-Trigger-Ban-Statutes-Impacts-on-Plan-B-Birth-Control-and-IVF-Treatments_N.-Patel.pdf.

66. Jacqueline Thanh, "Abortion Ban Will Drive Young People from State," October 5, 2022, https://www.theadvocate.com/baton_rouge/opinion/article_db874607-2c10-58d6-8e3a-3d20044467ea.html.

67. Anthony McAuley, "National OB-GYN Group Cancels New Orleans Conference, Citing La. Abortion Stance," NOLA.com, May 16, 2022, https://www.nola.com/news/business/national-ob-gyn-group-cancels-new-orleans-conference-citing-la-abortion-stance/article_15472c60-d526-11ec-9032-bb38bb6e1cc7.html.

68. Pew Research Center, "About Six-In-Ten Americans Say Abortion Should Be Legal in All or Most Cases," June 13, 2022, https://www.pewresearch.org/fact-tank/2022/06/13/about-six-in-ten-americans-say-abortion-should-be-legal-in-all-or-most-cases-2/.

69. University of California San Francisco, "The Turnaway Study" *News*, June 30, 2022, https://www.ucsf.edu/news/2022/06/423161/ucsf-turnaway-study-shows-impact-abortion-access https://www.ansirh.org/research/ongoing/turnaway-study.

70. https://www.ansirh.org/research/ongoing/turnaway-study.

SECTION THREE

Water and Weather

Chapter Seven

LOUISIANA'S COASTAL CRISIS, MANAGEMENT, AND PROGNOSIS CONSIDERING TIPPING POINTS OF CHANGE

JOHN A. LOPEZ

This study provides a perspective of coastal Louisiana by organizing under three headings: the coastal crisis, the coastal management response, and the long-term prognosis. Aside from describing these three topics, the chapter identifies "tipping points," which are periods when the nature of the problem or the approach to the problem has rapidly changed to a different reality. A tipping point may be a paradigm shift but may also be an acceleration of activity with the existing paradigm.

Hurricane Katrina was a tipping point toward a new integrated coastal planning paradigm manifested in the state's coastal master planning (CMP) process. After seventeen years under the new planning process, its performance can be critiqued in light of tipping points and for system effectiveness.

One possible advantage of understanding tipping points is that they may help anticipate key events in the future, so in the final section, I speculate on future tipping points. Historically, the tipping points are often precipitated by a disaster. Because the catastrophe triggered an accelerated change to improve, it may seem the disaster was worthwhile or at least necessary to force change. Ideally, a tipping point toward better coastal management is possible without the tragedy and expense that often result from disastrous events.

COASTAL CRISIS

A tipping point for Louisiana's coast was the period of the industrialization of the coastal wetlands from 1930 to 1980. Still, it is worthwhile to consider the prior period's impacts before the precipitous loss of wetlands post-1930. The most significant pre-1930 coastal impact was clear-cut logging of all coastal forests in the near complete absence of sustainable silviculture management. This commercial logging included all coastal forests dominated by a climax composition of cypress/tupelo species. Most places have not recovered to "old-growth" forest quality, and logging ditches still affect the wetland hydrology. Another preceding unfortunate activity was the harvest and mining of extensive barrier oyster reefs, which depleted the live reefs and removed the hard bottom foundation for new reefs to regrow. The loss of the coastal forests and the destruction of the oyster barrier reefs meant that two of the critical habitats of the coastal estuary were already severely compromised when the period of industrialization began in earnest in the 1930s.

This natural resource loss, and others, was driven by loosely regulated exploitation with a mindset of the most expedient means to economic gain. However, another profound early impact was caused by a desire to reduce flooding. Rudimentary and piecemeal artificial levees along the Mississippi River began just a few years after New Orleans was established in 1718. By 1890, continuous river levees had been constructed below Baton Rouge and south of New Orleans.[1] Therefore, before the industrial period, the loss of the process of deltaic wetland creation by the natural overflow of the river had eliminated the potential to offset wetland losses.

The industrialization of Louisiana's coast was the tipping point to a period of net loss of wetlands due to the conversion of emergent wetlands to upland or drained areas, mudflats, or open water.[2] In this case, the cause of the tipping point was the confluence of technological change and the rise of certain industries. In particular, the proliferation of bucket dredges with diesel engines made creating canals in coastal Louisiana a cost-effective way to access natural resources. The rise of the oil and gas industry took aggressive advantage of the technology and began creating canals to access well sites and pipelines (with canals) to transport oil or natural gas. However, many other canals were dug for general navigation, such as the Gulf Intracoastal Waterway, which spans the entire length of coastal Louisiana was completed around 1950.

The scientific discovery that a net loss of wetland was occurring in coastal Louisiana was made by Louisiana State University (LSU) researchers

Table 7.1. Compilation of Causes of Wetland Loss in Coastal Louisiana (* is anthropogenic)

Erosion

- Natural wave
- Navigation wave*
- Artificially enhanced channel flow (bank erosion)*
- Natural channel flow (bank erosion)
- Erosion sulphur operations*
- Hurricane breaching of Barrier Islands
- Hurricane marsh shears

Submergence (i.e., Chronic Flooding)

- Natural subsidence
- Induced subsidence*
- Insufficient sediment accretion due to artificial river levees*
- Insufficient sediment accretion due to natural delta abandonment
- Reduced sediment load of the Mississippi River*
- Insufficient sediment accretion due to sediment export (channel flow)*
- Altered hydrology—oil and gas canals and spoil banks*
- Altered hydrology—road beds*
- Saltwater intrusion—weakened or loss vegetation*
- Faulting natural
- Faulting induced*
- Natural waterlogging
- Failed land reclamation / flooded impoundments*
- Herbivory, e.g. nutria*
- Submergence sulfur-mine extraction activities*
- Submergence due to salt-mine collapse*
- Submergence oil and gas fluid extraction*
- Submergence loss due to industrial discharge, (i.e., produced water*)
- Loss of vegetation due to prolonged flooding*
- Loss of vegetation due to weakened root structure*

Direct Removal of Strata
Oil- and gas-canal access channel*
Pipeline-floatation canals*
Navigation channel*
Drainage channel*
Sewage pond*
Borrow pit*
Burned area*
Agriculture pond*
Logging canal or ditches*
Direct sulfur operations*
Direct Fill of Strata
Fill for development building, highways, etc.*
Spoil banks oil and gas and nav canals*
Draining of Wetlands
Successful levee impoundments without hydrologic exchange*

This list represents numerous sources, including Donald Boesch et al., Scientific Assessment of Coastal Wetland Loss, Restoration, and Management, 103; Robert Morton, J. C. Bernier, J. A. Barras, and N. F. Ferina, Rapid Subsidence and Historical Wetland Loss in the Mississippi Delta Plain: Likely Causes and Future Implications, USGS; Penland et al., Process Classification of Coastal Land Loss Between 193 and 1990 in the Mississippi River Delta Plain, Southeastern Louisiana, USGS; John Lopez, Chronology and Analysis of Environmental Impacts within the Pontchartrain Basin of the Mississippi River Delta Plain:1718 to 2002, 235.

led by Dr. Woody Gagliano.[3] Louisiana's coast had a net gain of wetlands for the past seven thousand years.[4] Until 1970, despite the prior scientific understanding that river levees had stopped the land-building process, it was still widely assumed that the natural process of the Louisiana coast was somehow functional. Contributing to this false assumption was that the extent of Louisiana's coastal wetlands was so vast that the human impacts were assumed to be insignificant. The 1970 study and subsequent publications[5] showed that wetland loss was significant, and the cumulative effect was already great. In 1972, the Clean Water Act (CWA) was passed, which recognized the value of wetlands and began installing regulatory protections for wetlands. In 1980, Louisiana established its Coastal Zone Management program within the Office of Coastal Management. The CWA and recognition of the Louisiana land loss problem were tipping points that shifted state and federal policy away from wetland exploitation and destruction and toward legal protections. The public's perception of wetlands also began to change. In Louisiana, Dr. Woody Gagliano (LSU), Dr. Len Bahr and Paul Kemp (office executive assistant to the governor for coastal activities), Dr. Bill Good (director, DNR Coastal Program-precursor to CPRA), and others started to champion the need to protect and restore wetlands, emphasizing the importance of using river diversions.

Subsequently, two other investigations systematically mapped the coastal land change in Louisiana. The US Army Corps of Engineers (USACE) mapped land loss in coastal Louisiana but stopped this program around 2001, and their records of mapped loss extend from 1932 to 2001.[6] The US Geological Survey (USGS) has an ongoing program and has mapped land change (gain and loss) from 1932 to 2016.[7] USGS and USACE had different methodologies, each with particular strengths and weaknesses. The USACE data reported a peak of wetland loss from 1958 to 1974, and the USGS data peaked a decade later.

In 1989, the recently created Coalition to Restore Coastal Louisiana published *Here Today, Gone Tomorrow*, dramatizing the coastal crisis as an existential threat to coastal communities. The report *Scientific Assessment of Coastal Wetland Loss, Restoration, and Management* in 1994 was foundational to the scientific community to define the many natural or anthropogenic causes of the coastal crisis in Louisiana. Now, more than thirty processes are known to contribute to wetland loss.

COASTAL MANAGEMENT RESPONSE

The disaster of Hurricane Katrina in 2005 was a tipping point toward accelerated coastal planning but also with a new planning paradigm. Pre-Katrina, planning was more traditional, that is, a less formal or quantitative process that was subject to populist influence. For example, the Coast 2050 plan was widely described as a "consensus plan" because it was a collection of locally popular restoration projects. However, it was a milestone because it had first-time 100 percent sign-on by all nineteen coastal parishes.[8] The plan also was the first to have an estimate of a total cost for coastwide restoration ($14 billion). Many of these projects were worthwhile concepts but lacked details or realistic cost estimates. Most importantly, there was no synthesis of the net benefits or objective modeling of project performance. There was no detailed budget. There was no realistic implementation plan. The plan was just an environmental plan, so it did not include levee construction or other structural or nonstructural approaches to risk reduction from hurricane surge. It was not intended as a plan to affect storm surges to reduce potential damages specifically. Levee planning, or construction, was institutionally separate from restoration due to an archaic patchwork of local levee boards and the Louisiana Department of Transportation and Economic Development. In the twelve months after Hurricane Katrina, all of this changed.

It is important to note that acute awareness of the coastal crisis existed pre-Katrina. Governor Mike Foster called for a "coastal jihad." Governor Kathleen Blanco strongly supported planning efforts such as Coast 2050. However, it was Hurricane Katrina that shocked the world and the country and even changed the Louisiana state political system. Change accelerated.

Just a few months before Hurricane Katrina, the multiple-lines-of-defense strategy again, this is the title of John Lopez's project and publication. MLODS was proposed as a holistic and system-engineering approach to coastal planning in Louisiana.[9] The concept was initially developed and advocated externally to any state or federal program. Local NGOs such as Pontchartrain Conservancy and the Coalition to Restore Coastal Louisiana vigorously proposed the new framework for planning and new projects conforming to MLODS.[10] Reports, in response to Hurricane Katrina, by the ASCE[11] and NASEM,[12] also advocated for unified coastwide planning by the state, such as MLODS.

MLODS is holistic because it includes traditional structural measures along with nonstructural and coastal restoration. It is integrated so that projects are synergistic and not mutually destructive. System engineering results from having "system compensators" for evacuation and insurance. That is, to the degree that the lines of defense cannot protect people; they must be evacuated. Similarly, insurance is required to the degree that physical assets cannot be protected. In theory, the system is made "whole" by the system compensators.

The idea that coastal wetlands buffer surge has been well documented, but the natural buffering effect has limitations. Surge reduction results from the physical resistance vegetation and topography exert on the surge as it moves into the coast. The resistance slows the surge movement but does not stop it. Therefore slower-moving storms have more ability to overcome the resistance, and the surge may continue to elevate.[13] Also, wetlands are subject to storm damage, but so are all other remedies except relocation.

Just four months after Hurricane Katrina, in a special session, the state legislature authorized Coastal Protection and Restoration Authority

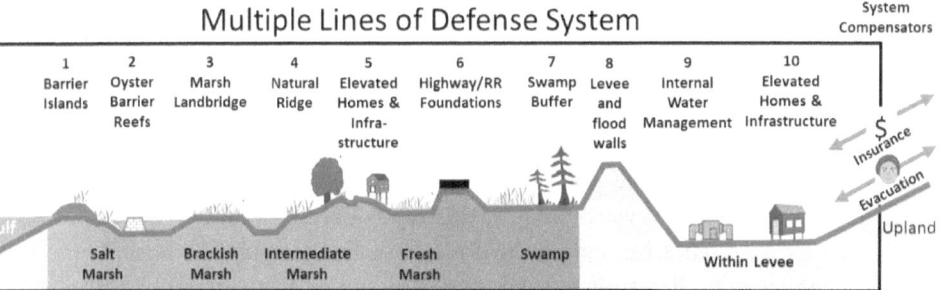

Figure 7.1. First proposed by Dr. John Lopez in 2005, pre-Katrina, the multiple-lines-of-defense concept evolved to include not just defensive elements of structural protection, non-structural and coastal landscape, but also system compensators, which hypothetically can make the system "whole" by addressing inadequacies of the protection of physical assets or human life.
(John Lopez, *The Multiple Lines of Defense Strategy to Sustain Coastal Louisiana*, 186–97)

(CPRA). By unanimous vote in 2007, the state legislature approved the first Coastal Master Plan (CMP), which included the restoration of flood protection with an MLODS approach.

However, the adoption of MLODS was not a fait accompli due to an influx of experts from around the world, particularly the Netherlands. The Dutch model of aggressive use of barriers with minimal accommodation of coastal habitats led to an extraordinary proposal of a continuous barrier levee being built far south on the Louisiana coast and placing much of the remaining coastal wetlands within a levee. The "barrier plan" would, like the barriers in the Netherlands, harm much of the coastal ecosystems. In contrast, the MOLDS approach attempts to work with nature by enhancing the ability of our coast to buffer storm surges but using complementary levees and home elevation to achieve the desired level of risk reduction. Although late, the USACE in 2009 embraced MLODS.[14]

So, within a few months following Hurricane Katrina, Louisiana had a new MLODS planning paradigm with an accelerated planning program under a new organization structure (CPRA). A few years later, mega funding began through the Deepwater Horizon (DWH) settlement. Since Hurricane Katrina, three master plans have been developed and approved by the state legislature. The fourth CMP will be before the legislature in the spring of 2023. Since 2006, the CPRA coastal budget has increased from less than $500 million per year to over $1.3 billion per year. Since 2007, billions have been spent under the post-Katrina planning model.

INTEGRATED PLANNING CHALLENGES

Although disasters such as Hurricane Katrina have legacies of both the value loss of damaged assets and the loss of life/human suffering, planning of the CMP does not include risk to human life. This is a commonplace practice for most state and federal planning of civil works projects. Appropriate sensitivity is warranted for this type of analysis, but this does not justify its absence from planning discussion. For example, the benefit of a levee project is determined solely by the reduction in economic damages. It does not assess possible loss of life with a levee failure, nor the lives possibly protected by a levee not failing. There is a significant tradition of loss of life analysis for dam safety,[15] but only more recently for levees or civil works projects in general.[16] Levees, like dams, increase water elevation on the flood side and, therefore, like a dam, may increase levels of inundation on the protected side if there is a failure, as happened in the Lower Ninth Ward of New Orleans during Hurricane Katrina.[17]

The CMP process has developed the Integrated Compartment Model (ICM), which is a spatially based analysis tool to simulate the vast array of physical and biological processes relevant to assessing various types of CMP projects. The ICM represents a state-of-the-art science to objectively quantify the performance of individual projects or a selected array of projects. However, the ICM must also be recognized realistically as a vast oversimplification of the real-world complexity of biological and physical processes interacting. An ICM tool is necessary and must cautiously advance, but improvements add more complexity. The challenge is that each new increase in complexity may improve the ICM but make it more difficult to understand or gauge its actual value. The CMP analyzes ICM results, but its overall reliability is still not wholly understood and becomes increasingly difficult to assess by scientists. The ICM, indeed, represents a significant challenge to the nonscientist.

INTEGRATED PLANNING POSITIVES

The CMP uses an MLODS approach, but more importantly, it should be viewed as a "kitchen-sink" process that is open to almost any type of project. Projects may fall under the broad banner of "structural," "nonstructural," or "restoration." Still, the open process of solicitation of projects allows consideration of new concepts or variations of old ideas. This is a living document's engine for robust improvement and reinvention. The CMP does limit new proposals to specific project types, but these have malleability. Most important is the attitude that there may always be a better mousetrap. The projects are analyzed individually and as project-arrays to assess compatibility or enhanced performance. The overall benefit of integrated planning is to avoid isolated unilateral activity that is not synergistic or may detract or conflict with the performance of other projects.

The CMP is mandated to be a living document and is required to be re-formulated every six years when it is subject to approval by the state legislature, but only *en masse* by an up or down vote of a House, Senate, or by joint resolution for the CMP during the session. This requirement is highly beneficial because it reduces the potential for alteration in the legislative process—the chance to have "pet projects" inserted or justifiable projects with minority dissent to be eliminated. The draft CMP is released to the public for review before submission to the legislature, allowing the public and political agents to express their views. Adjustments are often made before sending the CMP to the legislature for approval.

IMPLEMENTATION CHALLENGES

Implementation is the construction phase and, therefore, the most expensive component of the CMP budget. The CMP does analyze how to phase or prioritize projects broadly, but the completion of the project with construction is often at the mercy of specific funding availability. The difficulty is that most large tranches of funds have limitations on what types of projects can be funded, and these limitations are almost invariably narrower than the full breadth of project types in the CMP. The DWH settlements and the RESTORE Act were tipping points because they accelerated and increased funding for the CMP, but these funds are almost entirely for some form of ecosystem restoration or mitigation. DWH funds for levee projects are minimal, so levee projects are often funded through the unpredictable appropriation process Congress. Funding restrictions limit the ideal rollout of CMP projects.

The CMP process requires six years to complete, and within the first two years, the baseline conditions are established. The subsequent four years of analysis and drafting of the final CMP are based on the baseline conditions. Coastal change continues to occur, but the CMP does not allow adjustments while the analysis and drafting are completed. Hurricanes punctuate significant shifts in the coastal landscape and expose new coastal risks. A single hurricane may cause considerable land loss, such as impacts by Hurricane Ida in 2021, which will not be addressed by planning until 2029. Ida also revealed a new level of concern for the resiliency of the electric grid. The CMP is not well structured to make midprocess adjustments, so a plan to address the recent landscape change may be delayed several years.

OPERATION AND MAINTENANCE

By any standard, the CMP's aspiration of realizing an integrated functionality of the projects included in the plan requires the performance of a highly complex system. After Hurricane Katrina, the Interagency Performance Evaluation Task Force (IPET)[18] report described New Orleans's flood protection as a "system in name only." However, it was never referred to as a system, just a collection of isolated state and federal projects. An integrated system was not envisioned before Hurricane Katrina. However, the aspiration now in the CMP does not guarantee that successful system engineering is achieved. The International Council on System Engineering (INCOSE) suggests system engineering requires *"System Thinking—Thinking and Acting to Apply System Approaches to Address Complex Challenges and Thus Realize the Successful Sustainable Solution."*

INCOSE emphasizes the use of model simulations, and the CMP uses the ICM to select projects, but the operation and maintenance fall to many variable local authorities that are not modeling the whole system. An example of New Orleans system complexity was highlighted in a system engineering analysis of the post-Katrina Hurricane Storm Damage Risk Reduction System (HSDRRS).[19] This study highlighted the complexity of the operation of the New Orleans Surge Barrier and related structures, in which there is likely to be a simultaneous inward evacuation of marine vessels and outward evacuation of residential traffic across drawbridges and railroads that, if open, impede cars and if down impeded boats. Dual evacuation is coordinated through the levee boards, city police, state police, Coast Guard, railroad management, vessel captains, bridge operators, Corps of Engineers, and so on. This intense coordination occurs while the window of time for successful evacuation closes before the storm is close enough to preclude safe travel. This is a microcosm of a more extensive array of cross-parish coordination of evacuations, levee boards, and municipalities taking emergency actions as a storm's cone of uncertainty shifts its aim at the coast.

LOWER MISSISSIPPI RIVER MANAGEMENT

Geologists and engineers widely understand that the Lower Mississippi River is changing due to a number of influences, such as sea-level rise. The Corps,[20] NASEM,[21] and CPRA[22] have specific initiatives to begin analyzing the lower river's current and future characteristics. The "Changing Course" program attempted to develop consensus on paths forward, which suggested the lower river needs a new channel with a shorter route to the Gulf of Mexico.[23] The CMP process does not evaluate river-management alternatives and lags in applying the latest data or analyses of the Mississippi River. Altering the river management is an enormous undertaking and probably needs to work in parallel with the CMP, but the CMP needs to improve with formal intersection points of the CMP process and the ongoing studies of the Lower Mississippi River.

COASTAL PROGNOSIS

American geographer Peirce Lewis called New Orleans "the impossible but inevitable city."[24] The location of a major city and port on a delta landscape where land elevation rarely exceeds the average person's height can easily subside to more than a person's height below sea level, and if subject to storm surges can be several times a person's height seems impossible, but less so after three hundred years of settlement. There is much more in jeopardy on the coast other than New Orleans, but a south Louisiana coast without the Greater New Orleans Region would be diminished in almost every way, culturally and economically. So, is New Orleans and all it symbolizes and supports still inevitable?

After Katrina, many others and I have been asked this question many times, and of course, no one can answer this with certainty. Simple flooding scenarios assuming even modest rates of sea-level rise suggest New Orleans would be a narrow, perilous peninsula jutting into the Gulf of Mexico by 2100 and that the Mississippi River does not have sufficient sediment to keep pace with the flooding, even if all of the river's sediment was somehow captured to rebuild wetlands.[25] After the third generation of the CMP, the plan admitted for the first time that even with fully implemented and constructed projects at the cost of $25 billion, the coast long term would still have a net loss rate of wetlands.[26] Before Hurricane Katrina, *Scientific American* presciently published "The Drowning of New Orleans," which emphasized its sinking nature, below-sea-level landscape, and need for body bags.[27]

Considering the coastal crisis solutions from the aspect of first principles, coastal restoration in Louisiana is scientifically simple. Estuarine biology is defined by the physical conditions of the land and water.[28] The mud platform must simply be high enough for the plant biology to respond and grow wetland vegetation within a zone mixed with river and gulf water. Moving mud can be easily engineered, but for an extraordinary cost. The sediment supply of the river may be limited, but sediment supply is not limited when mining the existing widespread mud platforms of the coast and shelf. However, the river is helping. A 2022 comprehensive USACE study of the Mississippi River documents that the river above Baton Rouge has been accumulating sediment, causing the river to slow and force flood levels to rise.[29] A river building excess sediment and energy is a river primed to build land. Indeed, in the last decade, two major outlets have developed on the east bank (Mardi Gras Pass[30] and Neptune Pass[31]) and have begun the delta land-building process without the aid of engineering. If these outlets had been built by the state, the cost would have been over $1 billion.

In this sense of mud management, restoring the coast and protecting New Orleans and the coastal infrastructure is only limited by funding. Restoring the coast does not require a "Moonshot" of new technology, although this always helps and must be encouraged. Restoring the Louisiana coast can be done with sufficient funding; so, *is it worth the expense*?

A historical perspective on the value of wetlands begins with the Swamp Reclamation Act of 1849, which epitomizes the misguided view of wetlands of low value, primarily due to the difficulty of successful agriculture in wetlands and due to the association of swamps and wetlands to disease and pestilence. The timeline in figure 7.2 is from 1860 to 2100 and includes the USACE and inferred USGS net wetland loss rates. The figure suggests various significant causation events that were tipping point periods to some noteworthy effects.

After the Civil War, the Federal government began aggressively rebuilding and regionalizing river levees, and by 1890, levees were in place and stopped the deltaic land-building process downriver of Baton Rouge. The collapse of the preexisting wetlands began after the introduction of motorized bucket dredges in the early 1900s, which allowed canals to be dug in the coast cheaply and for any purpose but primarily to support oil and gas activity. The peak impact of the wetland loss from the industrialization period was between 1958 and 1985 and may have been as high as 42 to 68 square miles per year. In the 1970s, the public began to realize the value of wetlands because of their enhancement to water quality but also in coastal areas as a nursery for fisheries inshore and offshore. At this time, the severe loss of wetlands in Louisiana was also documented. Starting in 1980, federal and state Coastal Zone permitting requirements

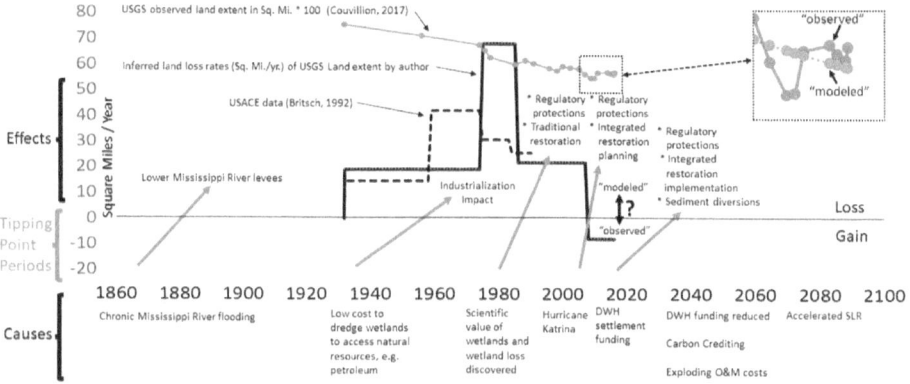

Figure 7.2. Graph of net land loss rates with possible influences and tipping points of change. Suggested causation of tipping points toward change is shown. Expected future events that may drive positive or negative change are indicated. (Net wetland loss rates by USACE–Britsch and Dunbar, 1992, and as inferred by the author for select periods of the USGS land extent data [also shown] from 1932 to 2016, by Brady Couvillon, *Land Change in Coastal Louisiana (1932–2016)*, 2017)

afforded new wetland protection. In the 1990s, modest coastwide restoration programs began, such as the Coastal Wetland Planning, Protection, and Restoration Act (CWPPRA).[32] Land loss rates fell to around 20 square miles per year by 2006, even including the severe impact of Hurricane Katrina, (that is, ~50 percent reduction from the peak loss rate). In the latest period of available data, 2006 to 2016, the USACE data suggest annual slight net gains or losses, but the subsequent hurricanes after 2016 have likely erased a possible net gain from 2006 to 2022. The USGS "modeled" loss for this period is 11.6 square miles per year. Considering that the 2006 to 2016 land-change data does not reflect the conditions when sediment diversions are operative or a $1.3 billion CPRA budget, it is reasonable to suggest no-net-loss is within reach in the short term.

In sum, from 1930 to 1980 industries were unleashed with dredges onto the coast in the absence of any consequential regulatory restrictions, a dysfunctional river, and without restoration efforts. From 1980 to 2006, with wetland protection in place and modest programmatic restoration, the loss rate was reduced. In the last period of data from 2006 to 2016, no net loss seemed possible in the near term, especially with significant projects or opportunities to restore the function of the Mississippi River.

In 2005, Hurricane Katrina precipitated the new integrated planning paradigm, but it was the DWH settlement that drove a significant new level of project implementation under the new paradigm. In 2022, the CPRA budget, for the first time, exceeded $1 billion and should sustain this level until at least 2032. In December 2022, the Mid-Barataria Sediment Diversion was permitted, and construction started in the fall of 2023.[33] These developments suggest that from 2016 to 2036, we will further reduction in the loss rate and possibly occasional net gain. The prognosis of completing sediment diversions is enhanced by the expanded involvement of NGO organizations after Hurricane Katrina. Key figures such as King Milling (formerly Whitney Bank),[34] Oliver Houck and Mark Davis (Tulane), and Jim Tripp (EDF) facilitated this NGO movement that culminated in a well-funded coalition between local and national environmental organizations (Mississippi River Delta Campaign Coalition).[35] The science and historical significance of river diversions was strongly supported by vocal scientists such as Drs. John Day and Robert Twilley (LSU), Drs. Denise Reed and Shea Penland (UNO), and David Muth (NWF).

When viewed in its entirety from 1849 to the present, the transcending and pivotal influence in coastal Louisiana was the recognition that the wetlands are of exceptional value to people and the environment. Science initially recognized that the special qualities of coastal wetlands were for water quality, a marine nursery, and a storm-surge buffer to enhance the protection of people and physical assets. Now, we also realize the potential value of wetland restoration to sequester carbon. During this period, US populations also shifted closer to the coasts, which amplified the coastal wetland's value further. Economists have attempted to sum up the actual dollar value of these major attributes and many other secondary attributes of wetlands.

A global synthesis found that the average value of wetlands to reduce storm-surge damages was $11,000/hectare/year ($4,400/acre/year).[36] A similar study for the United States found a value of $18,000/hectare/year ($7,200/acre/year).[37] An analysis of Louisiana wetlands value for water quality and storm-surge protection was $4,410/acre/year.[38] The global study also found that in the United States, lives saved by coastal wetlands average 469 per year. A synthesis of the value of all other benefits, *but* excluding reduced storm surge and reduced mortality, found a value of $135,000/hectare/year ($54,000/acre/year).

The 2017 CMP estimates that if implemented, it would build or maintain 512,000 acres at the cost of $25 billion, so the average cost per acre is $49,000. It is clear that the multidecadal value of an acre of wetland to the cost to restore is at or exceeds parity. A study of the economic impact of the projected Louisiana wetland loss in just fifty years estimated a total direct and indirect impact at risk to the state and country was $5.8 billion to $7.4 billion annually.[39] If all these coastal wetland benefits are included, the cost to restore an acre could be accrued in just one year and multiply through the years of the project's performance, aside from the fact that coastal wetlands save lives.

Figure 7.3. Canals cut by petroleum and timber companies, combined with the construction of levees that deny fresh water replenishment in the wetlands of Louisiana, have combined to allow salt water intrusion, which has proven devastating to the fragile ecosystem. Years of neglect have produced mass coastal erosion in Louisiana that has far-reaching implications. (Courtesy of the National Oceanic and Atmospheric Administration)

SUMMARY

The critique of the CMP indicates that it can be enhanced, as it was intended, and therefore, its performance will improve. Total investment (public and private) may well exceed the $50 billion CMP budget due to justified needs and economic opportunity. More importantly, science continues to expand the understanding of the extraordinary value of wetlands. Future scientific discoveries may show greater value and new ways to reduce the cost of restoring wetlands. But the wetland cost-to-benefit ratio seems to have tipped toward restoring wetlands for local and global expediency. There are signs that we may be entering a tipping point period in which the free market capitalizes on wetland restoration in Louisiana. Based on economic analysis, it is likely that entrepreneurial efforts have not yet fully capitalized or innovated the industry of restoring wetlands. The US value of the ports from New Orleans to Baton Rouge strongly suggests that US policy must support an adequate landscape to maintain, at least, the trimodal shipping infrastructure backbone of the Mississippi River to the Gulf.

In the next twenty years, we should expect a net gain in wetlands in coastal Louisiana. But longer term, there are other countervailing potential tipping points, such as the cumulative cost of operation and maintenance of coastal projects and, of course, the anticipated increase in the rate of rise of the eustatic sea level due to climate change. Global carbon dioxide emissions must be reduced to avoid the worst-case scenarios.

Nevertheless, it is conceivable that under the umbrella of disciplined, integrated planning with stronger wetland protections, utilizing the new emerging power of the Mississippi River, improved long-term management of the Lower Mississippi River, scientific innovation, national funding directed toward resilient infrastructure, a vibrant NGO community, and new commercial funding to restore wetlands, the scale will be tipped long-term again to a net gain in wetlands in coastal Louisiana. New Orleans and much of the coast will inevitably remain inevitable due to the unacceptable loss of monetary value and the existential threat to the cultural heritage of the coastal zone but also, no less due to the indomitable spirit of a city, a coast, a state, and a country.

NOTES

1. Craig Colten, *The Unnatural Metropolis, Wrestling New Orleans from Nature* (Baton Rouge: Louisiana State University Press, 2005), 245.

2. Donald Boesch et al., *Scientific Assessment of Coastal Wetland Loss, Restoration and Management*, Journal of Coastal Research, 1994 103.

3. Sherwood Gagliano, H. Kwon, and J. L. Van Beek, *Deterioration and Restoration of Coastal Wetlands*, 1970.

4. Donald Boesch, *Scientific Assessment of Coastal Wetland Loss, Restoration and Management*, 103.

5. Sherwood Gagliano, K. J. Meyer Arendt, and K. Wicker, *Land Loss Is the Mississippi Delta Plain*, Transactions Gulf Coast Geological Societies 1981, vol. 31, 295–300.

6. D. Britsch and J. Dunbar, *Land Loss in Coastal Louisiana—Map*, 1996, USACE, New Orleans District.

7. B. Couvillion, *Land Area Change in Coastal Louisiana (1932–2016)*, Scientific Investigations Map 3381.

8. Coast 2050 laid the political foundation of uniting the desire for coastal restoration. It had many extremely dedicated "consensus builders," such as Sue Hawes, Karen Gautreaux, and Cynthia Duet.

9. John Lopez, *The Multiple Lines of Defense Strategy to Sustain Coastal Louisiana*, 186–97.

10. John Lopez, N. Snider, C. Dufrechou, M. Hester, P. Keddy, P. Kemp, B. Kohl, S. Kulkarni, A. McCorquodale, M. O'Connell, J. Suhayda, B. Rogers, *Comprehensive Recommendations Supporting the Use of the Multiple Lines of Defense Strategy to Sustain Coastal Louisiana—2008 Report*, Pontchartrain Conservancy & Coalition to Restore Coastal Louisiana.

11. American Society of Civil Engineers, *The New Orleans Hurricane Protection Systems: What Went Wrong and Why*, 2007.

12. National Academy of Sciences, Engineering and Medicine, *The New Orleans Hurricane Protection System, Assessing Pre-Katrina Vulnerabilities and Improving Mitigation and Preparedness*, 2009.

13. T. D. Resio and J. Westerlink, *Modeling the Physics of Storm Surge in Physics Today* (2008).

14. US Army Corps of Engineers, Louisiana Coastal Protection and Restoration-Final Technical Report, 2009.

15. *Department of Army Engineering and Design Safety of Dam-Policy and Procedures (2014)* Regulation 1110-2-1156.

16. *Department of Army Risk Assessment for Flood Risk Management Studies (2019)* Engineer Regulation No. 1105-2-101.

17. Ezra Boyd, "Fatalities Due to Hurricane Katrina's Impacts to Louisiana" (dissertation, Louisiana State University, 2011).

18. *US Army Corps of Engineers, Hurricane Katrina Interagency Performance Evaluation Task Force (2007)*.

19. E. Boyd, R. Storesund, and J. A. Lopez, *A System Engineering Based Assessment of the Greater New Orleans Hurricane Surge Defense System using the Multiple Lines of Defense Framework (2014)*, Pontchartrain Conservancy.

20. *Water Resources and Development Act 2021 Section 213—Lower Mississippi River Comprehensive Management Study*.

21. National Academy of Sciences, Engineering, and Medicine, *Gulf Research Program—Delta Transitions*.

22. Coastal Protection and Restoration Authority, Lower Mississippi River Management Program.

23. Changing Course circa 2017 overseen by the Environmental Defense Fund.

24. Craig Colten, *The Unnatural Metropolis: Wrestling New Orleans from Nature*, 245.

25. Michael D. Blum and H. H Roberts, *Drowning of the Mississippi Delta Due to Insufficient Supply of Sediment and Sea-Level Rise*, 4.

26. Coastal Protection and Restoration Authority, 2017 Coastal Master Plan.

27. Mark Fischetti, "Drowning New Orleans," *Scientific American*.

28. William Mitsch, and James Gosselink, *Wetlands*, 920.

29. US Army Corps of Engineers, *Technical Assessment of the Old, Mississippi, Atchafalaya, and Red River: Main Report MRG&P Report 41 (2022)*.

30. D. Ryan Cordell Jr., "The Mardi Gras Pass: Coastal Restoration and Public Rights in a Mississippi River Distributary Channel," *Tulane Environmental Law Journal* (2017).

31. "Corps Eyes Solution for Neptune Pass, A Mississippi River Channel That Is Blocking Navigation," *New Orleans Times-Picayune*, October 3, 2022.

32. CWPPRA was enacted in 1990 and is managed by the State of Louisiana and five federal agencies.

33. In February 2024 a suit filed by Plaquemines Parish, Louisiana, to halt the project was upheld by the court effectively stopping continued work. What the future holds for the diversion project remains in doubt. Baton Rouge *Advocate*, February 29, 2024.

34. The Coalition to Restore Coastal Louisiana gave a lifetime achievement award to King Milling in May 2002.

35. The Mississippi River Delta Campaign Coalition included Pontchartrain Conservancy, Coalition to Restore Coastal Louisiana, National Audubon Society, National Wildlife Federation, and the Environmental Defense Fund.

36. Robert Costanza, et al., "The Global Value of Coastal Wetlands for Storm Protection," *Global Environmental Change* 70 (2021): 102328.

37. F. Sun and R. T. Carson, "Coastal Wetlands Reduce Property Damage during Tropical Cyclones," *Proc. National Academy Sciences* 117, no. 11 (2020): 5719–25.

38. R. H. Caffey, H. Wang, and D. R. Petrolia, "Trajectory Economics: Assessing the Flow of Ecosystem Services from Coastal Restoration," *Ecologic Economics* 100 (2014): 74–84.

39. LSU–Rand Corp, *Economic Evaluation of Coastal Land Loss in Louisiana (2015) for the Coastal Protection and Restoration Authority*, 118.

Chapter Eight

SMALL WATERSHEDS, BIG CONFLICTS

Managing Floods in the Florida Parishes

CRAIG E. COLTEN

A pair of intense rainstorms in March and August 2016 overwhelmed several watersheds in Louisiana's Florida parishes. Total precipitation varied, but some locations endured what the National Oceanic and Atmospheric Administration referred to as a one-thousand-year event—or a downpour with a 0.1 percent chance of occurring any year. The largest local total reached thirty inches, which overflowed the banks of rivers, drowned the adjacent landscape, and caused extensive property damage. Although the raging waters caught many inhabitants by surprise, the 2016 floods were not the first to impact these river systems. The Amite, Tangipahoa, and Pearl have lengthy records of irregular, damaging floods.[1]

These disasters resulted from a combination of factors and processes. The watersheds themselves, or the territory that feeds runoff into a waterway, are physical factors. The size of the water-collecting area, the slope of the land, the vegetation cover, and the density of tributaries all contribute. Precipitation, whether caused by spring frontal systems, summer thunderstorms, or tropical cyclones, provides the moisture that flows through the tiny tributaries, feeding the main channels that drain into the Lake Pontchartrain system or the Gulf of Mexico. The impact of large discharges can be accentuated when winds push lake waters into the river mouths, causing backwater flooding in the low-lying wetlands that fringe the lakes and coast. The other principal element contributing to property damage, and what makes these events disasters, is the human uses of the land. Construction of homes, commercial structures, and public buildings and infrastructure adjacent to the waterways and down onto the floodplain—the area subject to overflow—and also agriculture or other economic pursuits carried out in flood-prone areas are exposed to risk. Disasters are not natural phenomena; they are the result of human decisions about where to live and pursue livelihoods. Human settlement in and management of watersheds is shaped by history, politics, risk culture, economics, and the underlying set of private property rights. Flood losses are not merely "acts of god."[2]

In response to the 2016 floods and a spate of other inundations across the state, Louisiana authorities launched "a new watershed-based approach to reducing flood risk in Louisiana." This Watershed Initiative seeks to deploy scientific data and tools to enable transparent and objective decision making to maximize the natural functions of floodplains in establishing regional, watershed-based management of flood risks.[3] This approach seeks to foreground the watershed as the appropriate geographic unit to manage floods and uses science as shield against criticism that there might be political or other influences that might bias objective decision making. Sound science must be relied on in making management decisions, but it is important to keep in mind that by selecting science as the guiding principle, a political decision has been made. And science is not immune to local political, economic, or cultural turbulence. Science is not a flawless insulator that can completely separate decisions from social, cultural, and political biases. Science demands comparable efforts in other arenas of human interaction to solve problems. Watershed management operates within geopolitical units that do not conform to the physical territories being managed. Much of the initial work of the Watershed Initiative has been directed towards modeling flood risk in watersheds. This is essential, but there has been no comparable effort toward contending with the historical political, cultural, private property, and economic tensions found in the various watersheds. Additionally, the simple geographic issue of upstream versus downstream (often expressed as interparish concerns) has generated conflicts that are as common in these watersheds as floodwaters.

This chapter will address the long-term historical geography of managing water and floods within three watersheds that traverse the Florida parishes. Louisiana has turned to the watershed repeatedly for managing water, generally following national attempts to promote this approach. Yet, as elsewhere, political territories, which frame the reach of jurisdiction, ultimately shape local flood risk. The Amite, the Tangipahoa, and the Pearl all have extensive records of flooding but with very different impacts because of the physical configuration of the basins and the particular patterns of human settlement, the geopolitical landscapes they flow through, and the resulting local approaches to mitigating flood impacts and guiding development. This discussion will focus on these human aspects of flood management. I will introduce the concept of watershed management in the United States, describe the three watersheds, and then discuss the settlement and flood history of each of the three basins, and conclude with observations on the implications of the Watershed Initiative on flood management in the Florida parishes.

"Watershed" is a term applied to the topographically determined territory that collects water and funnels it into a stream. Depending on the scale of analysis one can consider the watershed of a mighty river such as the Mississippi or lesser tributaries such as the Missouri and Ohio, or even small tributaries such as Thompson's Creek in West Feliciana Parish. Precipitation, rainfall or snow, that accumulates in any part of a watershed ultimately flows toward its outlet via surface streams or in aquifers beneath the land surface. Managing water within a basin relies on relatively simple accounting—measuring the amount of water arriving and departing. These fundamental measurements allow for assessments of how much water is available for use within the basin. Simple accounting for basins has prompted public officials to promote watersheds, at all scales, as the appropriate unit for managing water.[4] Of course, watersheds contain more than water, and land use within a watershed contributes to the rate of runoff and water quality. Heavily vegetated watersheds release water slower than desert or cleared farmland. Diversion of water for urban and agricultural use renders the lower Colorado River to a mere trickle as it enters Mexico, and riverside industries' use of the Mississippi River for waste removal polluted downstream water supplies. The relationships between land and water, thus, make watershed management more than simply a massive plumbing project and complicate the hydrological accounting.

National concern with water resources in the nineteenth century prompted the dispatch of scientific surveys to the American West to assess the quantity and utility of western rivers. These scientific teams and subsequent public officials saw a sound logic to managing water at the watershed scale.[5] From their upper sources to the mouths of rivers, the arrival of water and its movement occurs within the geographic boundaries of the basin. Drought or excessive rainfall in the upper basin impacts the lower basin. Hence, wise use, a guiding principle of the conservation movement in the early twentieth century, demanded watershed-scale management.[6] There were several programs that drew on conservation principles to link land and water management within watersheds, such as the ambitious Tennessee Valley Authority. The Natural Resources Committee attempted to address an integrated land and water approach by developing plans for major basins in the late 1930s. Their task was to consider flooding, water quality, navigation, irrigation, and public water supplies.[7]

A follow-up effort in the 1960s and 1970s revitalized interest in watersheds and called for the creation of several river basin commissions. These commissions sought to implement flood control and water quality and quantity management. While well-intentioned, they had limited authority over land use and consequently tended to rely on structures for flood control and waste treatment for quality concerns—actions largely detached from land use. Consequently, watershed management at the national level prioritized water within particular basins over a more comprehensive approach that fully linked water and land resources.[8] Indeed, industrial and urban development pressures since the nineteenth century drove water policy towards tolerating consumption and disassociated land-use management.[9] And most importantly, unsustainable land uses contributed to watershed degradation. Water, as a common resource, is managed differently than private property. US land law fundamentally promotes settlement and development of land regardless of its impact on water, which has led to water quality degradation and an increase in flood risks.[10] In the 1990s, there was still another reawakening to the watershed as the ideal geographic unit for protecting water supplies. Yet, imposing land-use controls on local governments and private landowners remains a stumbling block to fully integrated watershed management.

Louisiana, at least conceptually, followed the national ambition to manage water at the watershed scale. The State Board of Engineers in 1908 recognized the utility of relying on the geographic and topographic unity of basins as the most comprehensive and satisfactory approach to manage drainage.[11] Implementation of this approach did not match the aims of the state engineers, and drainage remained complicated by the lack of congruence between watersheds and political territories—namely, parishes. In the 1940s, the national river basin initiative spawned a rebirth in state-level watershed-oriented management. Louisiana launched a Water Basin Study as part of the National Resources Committee's study of basin problems and programs. A prime motive was drainage of excess water from agricultural land and, secondarily, flood control. Under the auspices of the Department of Public Works, state officials observed that drainage of one basin seldom took into account the impacts on downstream basins.[12] The lack of overarching integration rendered the use of small-scale watersheds ineffective for basin-wide solutions. Additionally, the patchwork of local districts, each created to address a specific problem, undermined the goal of a unified drainage system based on natural watersheds.[13] One basin's solution could produce a problem elsewhere. The state offered engineering assistance to parishes that shared a watershed to coordinate drainage for the entire watershed "rather than some arbitrary political boundary."[14] The state assigned fiscal management to parish governments. Voters in each parish had to approve bond issues to secure funding. So even if the design was coordinated at the watershed scale, political differences within the basin could stymie implementation of drainage projects. The Department of Public Works reported it had completed projects for the Amite, Tangipahoa, and Pearl Rivers by 1955, but the maps suggest they did not encompass all of Tangipahoa and St. Tammany Parishes. The state program continued into the 1960s, when reporting ceased.[15]

A series of floods across the state in the 1980s prompted another state-level response. In 1985, the state mapped floodplains and flood problem areas and launched a program to provide funds for locally directed flood mitigation.[16] Although envisioned as a state-wide program, it depended on local units of government requesting funds and implementing specific projects.[17] Additionally, the governor convened a task force in 1990 to consider a range of techniques to minimize flood damages. The most prominent suggestion linking water and land was the recommendation that communities adopt floodplain regulations that aligned with the National Flood Insurance Program.[18] While the task force considered flooding in particular watersheds, it did not recommend mitigation or regulation at the basin scale. Rather, it assumed management would remain a parish or municipal matter.[19] While various projects received funding, the 1990 program perpetuated the piecemeal approach that used parishes as the administrative units for mitigation and allowed local governments to respond to the pressing needs in the wake of floods irrespective of larger watershed issues.

The glaring shortcoming of watershed management, particularly for the small basins in the Florida parishes, is the fact that each watershed straddles multiple political jurisdictions. While the state attempted to provide coordination among multiple parishes, it had no influence beyond the state's borders. The federal Water Resources Committee's efforts at watershed management were relatively short lived and did not coordinate land use within basins. To cope with interstate pollution for example, Congress created a process for resolving disputes between upstream and downstream states in the 1950s and eventually enacted measures to provide national water-quality standards.[20] The US Army Corps of Engineers (USACE), which had increasing responsibilities for managing floods, worked at the basin scale for rivers such as the Mississippi and Ohio, but in the Pearl, it tended to deal with upstream and downstream flooding independently. The numerous river basin commissions formed in the late twentieth century had varied responsibilities including flood management. From the earliest to the most recent, flood mitigation relied on monitoring and warning systems along with structural controls. The river basin commissions did not employ land-use approaches, which would have required legislative action across several states and possibly infringed on private property concerns at the local level. Granted the National Flood Insurance Program does rely on various land-use policies, but local governments must enact them in order for their citizens to qualify for coverage, and there is room for uneven standards and enforcement. Consequently, flood management, while reliant on science and engineering to determine risks, remains fragmented in terms of dealing with the human uses of riparian landscapes and the political coordination of policy across jurisdictions.

The early twentieth-century conservation movement guided water resource management at the time. It relied on scientific expertise as did subsequent iterations of watershed management. From the fledgling conservation efforts, through the formation of river basins commission in the 1960s, and the reemergence of the watershed approach in the 1990s, science has remained the guiding methodology. It is not surprising that the Louisiana Watershed Initiative's early efforts follow this approach and follow the logic of managing floods at the watershed scale. A closer look at the three basins reveals their similarities and differences as watersheds.

This chapter considers three rivers that share several traits as they flow across the Florida parishes, yet each is also highly distinctive. Flood damages are the result of the complex relationship of hydrology and society within a watershed. Each of the rivers considered here rises in the adjacent state of Mississippi, flows southward, and traverses an elevated landform known as the Pleistocene Terrace. At the northern border of the Florida parishes, this terrace is about three hundred feet above sea level and the underlying geology tilts seaward. The rivers flow across the terrace and have carved valleys into a gently sloping landscape. They have noticeable currents in their upper reaches, but no rapids. The upper Amite and Tangipahoa Rivers pass through entrenched valleys with virtually no floodplains. Settlement consists mainly of farms and cultivated forest and several small towns all on the higher ground above the rivers. The Pearl, in contrast, has cut through the Pleistocene Terrace and consists of multiple channels that meander across a sizable floodplain that is several miles wide as it forms the southeastern boundary of Louisiana. The wetlands immediately adjacent to the river have few residences, and settlement, like in the other basins, concentrates on the elevated terrace, although set back from the braided channels of the lower Pearl River.

Both the Amite and Tangipahoa have formed wider valleys with more extensive floodplains in their middle courses—where they approach the lower edge of the terrace. Along the Amite, there has been considerable urbanization and encroachment on the floodplains since the 1970s. Proximity to Baton Rouge has enabled employees who work in business and government in the state capital to occupy suburbs in the Amite River valley. The Tangipahoa has less urbanization but has high value agriculture in the middle stretch of the river.

Along their lower reaches, each river leaves the terrace and passes along a broad low-lying floodplain before entering either Lakes Maurepas or Pontchartrain or the Gulf of Mexico. These areas have very little relief and are highly susceptible to inundation—both riparian and from storm surge. The Pearl branches into multiple channels as it meanders across the coastal plain toward the Gulf. Urbanization has been extensive in the lower Amite and in recent decades and has sprawled down to the fifteen-foot contour above the Pearl near Slidell. There is much less development in the lower Tangipahoa, and below Lee's Landing, the river traverses an extensive and unpopulated swampland, with numerous camps near Lake Pontchartrain.

According to the National Weather Service records, these rivers have flooded with some frequency since record keeping began. Yet there is an amazing consistency in the recency of the most significant crests. With three exceptions, the top ten record crests for all three rivers have occurred since 1973. The Amite and Tangipahoa share a top-ten flood in May 1953, accounting for two of the aberrations. Given their proximity and climatic similarity, it is not surprising that they also all share prominent crests in April 1983, January 1990, and 2016—in August for the Amite and Tangipahoa and March for the Pearl.

The Tangipahoa and Amite are relatively small basins, which means they are subject to flash flooding due to localized rainfall—as was the case in both 1983 and 2016. The Amite is the larger of the two with 2,200 square miles within the drainage basin. It is broader and fed by a sizable tributary, the Comite. The Tangipahoa has a narrow watershed that contains some 790 square miles—a sizable share is in Mississippi. The Pearl, in contrast, contains some 8,000 square miles and most of it is in Mississippi. This makes it less volatile in terms of flash flooding, and the wider floodplain along the lower stretch has been less appealing to urban encroachment. The most severe flooding has occurred in the upper basin near Jackson, Mississippi. Some of those floods also significantly impacted the Louisiana territory adjacent to the lower Pearl in 1979, 1980, and 1983.[21]

Prehistoric settlement in the Tangipahoa River valley followed the common practice of selecting sites overlooking streams, but perched on the terrace. This placement gave residents access to both forest and stream resources and minimized flood risks. European agricultural settlement accelerated after 1800 and followed a similar pattern. Rural communities tended to emerge along land routes where fords enabled river crossings. There were a few mills built on tributaries of the Tangipahoa, but the absence of steamboat traffic on the middle and upper course of the river restricted urbanization upstream from the terrace.[22] The swampy and marshy land south of the terrace inhibited agricultural activity there.

There was considerable evaluation of river basins in the South in the decades following the Civil War. The USACE conducted a survey of the Tangipahoa in 1879. Its report focused primarily on the navigability of the waterway and the potential for waterborne transport of agricultural and forest products. Engineers traversed fifty-three miles of the river and reported there were numerous obstructions including low branches, fallen trees, and sand bars—features familiar to today's tubers and boaters. It also noted there were rich timber resources in the watershed and opportunities for shipping cotton, vegetables, and poultry. It made no mention of flooding.[23] A follow-up investigation in 1912 reported that the removal of obstructions and snags had opened the river to navigation on its lower twenty-five miles. Nevertheless, the largest obstacle to navigation was a bar near the river's mouth. It resulted from the deposit of river-borne sediments where the stream entered the lake. A hurricane in 1909 obliterated the channel and disrupted navigation. The USACE noted that dredging a channel through the bar was not expected to last more than a year.[24]

In terms of flooding, the Tangipahoa's settlement history has minimized damages in the middle portion of the river—between the Mississippi state line and Robert, Louisiana. Hammond, the largest city, is not immediately adjacent to the river and has escaped most major flood impacts. Two exceptional events illustrate the relationships of natural processes and human decisions. Heavy rains in the watershed in April 1983 swelled the Tangipahoa River. There was extensive backwater flooding along a tributary stream in Hammond, despite its perched location, and the river knocked out the Louisiana Highway 16 bridge.[25] High water in Ponchatoula prompted approximately four hundred people to evacuate.[26] Inundation of strawberry fields also damaged much of the valuable crop near Ponchatoula.[27]

This 1983 downpour caused the failure of a dam in Percy Quin State Park upstream in Mississippi. Water from the impoundment rushed downstream, flooding the village of Amite, and causing Ponchatoula Creek to back up and flood portions of Hammond. Additionally, some thirteen hundred families near Robert, upstream from the Interstate 12 bridge over the Tangipahoa, suffered extensive damage and sued the state of Louisiana. They claimed that the highway bridge impeded the surging waters, which backed up into their homes and properties. After years of litigation, the plaintiffs won a $91.8 million judgement in 2006 but never received payment from the state. The suit focused on the highway obstruction, and not the dam failure,

Figure 8.1. A local resident casually bails water from his apartment following one of the region's regular floods. Immense rainfall amid insufficiently maintained drainage systems and a lack of coordination between political jurisdictions make flooding a perpetual problem in the Bayou State. (Courtesy of the Center for Southeast Louisiana Studies)

which contributed to the immense discharge.[28] Although rainfall was exceptional, the second highest crest of the Tangipahoa in 1983 stemmed from an upstream dam failure, construction in risky areas, and highway structures. Following the 1983 floods, Congressman Henson Moore requested funds for the USACE to expand its ongoing investigations of the Amite and Pearl to include the Tangipahoa and other Florida parish rivers. He hoped such studies might lead to solutions to the flood hazard.[29]

Despite recent floods, the Tangipahoa River came under intense scrutiny due to poor water quality. Tubing on the river was a thriving recreational activity in the 1970s and early 1980s. When members of a Girl Scout troop became ill after swimming in the river, public health officials became alarmed and intensified monitoring of water quality. Following tests, the river earned the undesirable designation as an Impaired Waterway. The pollution source was fecal coliform bacteria from dairy farms, municipal wastewater treatment plans, and small private treatment works. A concerted program led by the state improved treatment and lowered the fecal coliform levels to a safe level by 2008 when it was removed from the Impaired Waterway listing.[30]

Flood issues reemerged in 2012 as Hurricane Isaac drenched the basin as it moved slowly inland. The heavy precipitation caused slumping on the dam impounding Lake Tangipahoa in Percy Quin State Park in Mississippi.[31]

Emergency personnel attempted to lower the water level using pumps.[32] Mississippi officials considered an artificial breach to allow a controlled release and avoid a devastating "wall of water" rushing into Tangipahoa Parish.[33] With the dam's stability in question and fearing a repeat of 1983, Louisiana and parish officials ordered evacuation of Kentwood and other areas near the river. Some twelve hundred people took refuge in a parish shelter. Meanwhile, Mississippi park officials drained water from the lake to lessen pressure on the dam and averted its failure.[34] Nonetheless, some forty-five hundred homes suffered damage in the lower river basin.[35] An editorial claimed that Tangipahoa Parish residents, who had yet to receive damage payments from 1983, were still haunted from the previous flood and called for Mississippi to secure funds to improve the dam. The state boundary had impeded a coordinated watershed approach to flood mitigation since the 1983 event.

In March and August 2016, a pair of exceptional rainstorms produced flood crests that ranked among the river's top five. The Tangipahoa and its tributaries threatened the strawberry crop around Ponchatoula after some thirteen inches of rain fell in the basin in March.[36] Small communities suffered extensive flooding in both downpours. Tangipahoa had more than five thousand homes damaged in each event. Likewise, nearly every home in the Twin Lakes subdivision of Ponchatoula took on water in both March and August.[37] Residents upstream from the Interstate 12 bridge once again claimed damage due to the highway bridge. Yet, the circuit court denied these claims, citing the long interval between the highway's construction and the suit.[38] In a basin that had experienced major floods (twenty-one feet) three times since 1983, inattention to the highway structure merely accentuated frustrations with flood management. Although there were several federal studies of the Tangipahoa River for navigation by the early twentieth century, the floods in 1983 and thereafter did not motivate a watershed approach for flooding before 2016.

Louisiana delegates flood mitigation responsibilities to the parishes. For much of the Tangipahoa River watershed, a single parish provides uniform administrative opportunities. The parish addresses flood risks through a variety of means including restricting development in flood-prone areas and requiring that land uses in flood-prone areas include protections at the time of development. It also can regulate drainage and filling along with preventing the construction of barriers to floodwater movement.[39] Since the 2016 floods, the parish, in collaboration with university researchers, revamped portions of its ordinances. The parish changed the standards for new developments and required more water detention and expanded the requirements for green space and retention of wetlands as well.[40] This will reduce flood risk for new developments in the parish but makes no changes to existing land uses and has no reach into the basin within Mississippi.

The bulk of the Pearl River watershed is in Mississippi and experienced a prehistoric settlement pattern similar to the Tangipahoa. As Native Americans began permanent agricultural settlements, they selected sites on the higher ground adjacent to rivers. European settlers relied on trails and settlement sites previously used by indigenous people and created individual farmsteads and rural hamlets on lands near the river and fording sites but above frequent flood risk. Jackson, established as the state capital in 1821, grew during the 1830s and thereafter. Several other towns line the river in Mississippi. In Louisiana, both Bogalusa and Slidell were late arrivals and were the creation of commercial interests. Slidell came into existence as a railroad town in the late 1880s, while the Great Southern Lumber Company established Bogalusa as a company town in 1906. Founders set them both on land above normal flood levels near the West Pearl River.

As with the Tangipahoa, the federal government sponsored surveys to assess the feasibility of navigation on the Pearl in the late 1800s. An 1879 survey noted that European settlement transformed the river from a clear stream with few obstructions to a river with human-made cutoffs and forest clearance had created snags and bars obstructing navigation.[41] Between 1880 and 1916 the USACE cleared and dredged portions of the channel as far upstream at the town of Edinburg (443 miles from the mouth). Their efforts created a three-foot channel 211 miles upstream to Monticello which enabled regular navigation. Commerce on the waterway peaked in 1901 when some 258,700 tons of cargo, mainly logs and timber, floated down the river. With the depletion of forest resources, commerce declined, and officials terminated maintenance of the channel in 1916. The lumber industry by this time had shifted to rail transport.[42]

Flooding was a chronic concern along the Pearl, which had a "very unstable regimen."[43] The USACE reported that some five hundred square miles along the river were subject to inundation. Of that, only about forty square miles were cultivated and the rest was largely woodland, a reflection of decisions to avoid flood risks. There was frequent, if irregular, high-water damage near the state's leading city, Jackson. Between 1907 and 1926, the river reached flood stage on 935 days. Damage in Jackson resulted primarily from backwater flooding when Town Creek was unable to drain into the Pearl, which resulted in damage to urban infrastructure and inundation of principal roadways.[44]

In its 1930 report, the USACE recommended modifying the stream channel to create a nine-foot channel as far upstream as Jackson along with two reservoirs that, with locks, would increase navigational potential. These reservoirs, it estimated, would eliminate major flood damage between Jackson and Columbia but offer no real reduction in flood risk on the lower Pearl as it flowed by Louisiana. When comparing the costs of the navigation and flood protection system and the estimated benefits, the USACE concluded the project was not economically justified.[45] Congress did however authorize a seven-foot channel for the West Pearl to near Bogalusa, which required three locks. This improved channel opened to navigation in 1953.[46] There was no flood control as part of this project. The dismissal of flood control was due in part to the physical geography of the river as it passes Louisiana. The lower Pearl has multiple channels that meander through a broad wetland that tends to reduce the risk of flooding to towns situated on the adjacent terrace.

Continued investigations of the Pearl continued into the 1960s. The USACE held several public meetings in the 1940s to gauge local interest in flood mitigation in Mississippi. Jackson officials made the case for flood protection to enable growth out onto the floodplain. They also pressed for upstream storage, which would provide the dual benefits of water supply and flood control.[47] A 1960 report observed that bottomlands along the upper river were subject to "frequent floods" and that there had been floods at Jackson 183 times between 1902 and 1955.[48] Intense local precipitation produced the most noteworthy floods, which were more severe along the numerous tributaries of the main stream. The principal focus of the USACE's concern was with flooding in the upper basin—principally the Jackson urban area. Urban and industrial growth had expanded the territory at risk of flooding east of the river into the town of Flowood. Local interests built a ring levee that partially protected several manufacturing operations, commercial structures, and residences, but there was also considerable unprotected development. Urbanization also enlarged the property at risk on the west bank. The USACE projected that a flood equivalent to the 1902 event would cause over $6 million in damages in the Jackson area. Although there had been approval of a project to provide flood mitigation via channel improvements in 1936, it never materialized when Jackson declined to assume maintenance for the project.[49] The 1960 plan recommended by the USACE included levees protecting Jackson and East Jackson, plus channel modification to expedite drainage. Among the benefits touted by the USACE would be development in areas previously exposed to flooding.[50] The plan focused exclusively on the upper river flood risks.

After a flood in 1961, the USACE received authorization for a mitigation project and constructed some thirteen miles of levee in the Jackson area and channelized the river to accelerate discharge. Raging floodwaters that rose fifteen feet above flood stage in 1979 overwhelmed these defenses when some twenty inches of rain caused record flooding. Runoff coursed down the waterway, entered over two thousand homes and seven hundred businesses, covered streets, and threatened Jackson's drinking water and sewerage facilities along with critical electrical and communication infrastructure.[51] In 1983, heavy rainfall again caused the Pearl to flood in the Jackson vicinity. A pair of locally funded floodway clearing projects followed the 1983 flood, along with a hearing to consider additional flood protection plans. Local, state, and federal officials have debated several options in the ensuing years, with no significant infrastructure built.[52]

The precipitation causing upstream flooding contributed to a wave of serious floods in the lower basin as well. Bogalusa and Slidell, Louisiana, along with nearby Pearlington, Mississippi, endured damages in rapid succession in 1979, 1980, and 1983. Although both Slidell and Pearlington are susceptible to hurricane storm surge, this series of floods resulted from heavy rainfall in the upper basin, and all occurred outside hurricane season during April. In 1979, an average of 5 inches of rainfall fell across the Pearl River basin, with peaks exceeding 19 inches above Jackson. Runoff pushed the river to a crest of 19.3 feet at Pearl River, Louisiana. Even more rain descended into the watershed in 1980. The basin-wide average reached 8.6 inches, with 15 inches falling in the middle basin. The crest at Pearl River hit 19.8 feet. More copious rainfall produced even more flooding in 1983. As much as 18 inches fell in the middle basin, leading to a new record crest of 21.2 feet at Pearl River. The most extensive impacts were recently built subdivisions and trailer parks in eastern Slidell that had sprawled onto previously avoided low land. Some seven to eight hundred homes suffered water damage, many of which had been built in the one-hundred-year floodplain.[53]

The USACE evaluated mitigation options following the 1983 flood and considered fifteen miles of levee to protect Slidell. Public discussions of mitigation efforts revealed interstate differences. Slidell residents were most concerned about the ability of floodwaters to pass beneath the Interstate 10 bridge and favored levees to guard the city's eastern front. Residents of Pearlington, Mississippi, however, were skeptical of the levees. They feared these bulwarks would displace floodwaters into their state.[54] Thus, in the lower basin, communities on opposite sides of the river and in different states sought different solutions to flood threats.

Lower Pearl River flooding in 2016 resulted from a slow-moving March cold front. There was no devastating inundation in August as in other basins. The geography of rainfall simply did not impact the Pearl watershed as dramatically as the two watersheds to the west. Nonetheless, the spring downpours did cause damage to neighborhoods in eastern Slidell, nearest to the Pearl River. Some of the same neighborhoods impacted in 1983 took on water again, reinforcing concern with flood risk along the lower Pearl. In response, the St. Tammany Parish Council passed an ordinance to acquire some properties in flood-prone areas to mitigate the impacts of future floods.[55]

When allowed to participate in public meetings concerning an upstream mitigation project, lower river residents expressed diverse opinions about the local impacts. The USACE held a hearing in 2017 about a proposed reservoir on the upper Pearl to reduce flooding at Jackson. Critics voiced concern that reduced flow would result in siltation in the lower river and damage important wildlife habitats. Some also mentioned a belief that the reservoir completed in 1963 increased flood risk in the lower basin.[56] Oyster producers in Mississippi Sound, near the river's mouth, opposed the plan because they feared it would reduce the flow of fresh water and disrupt the balance of salinity needed for successful oyster cultivation.[57] In addition, the St. Tammany Police Jury passed a resolution in 2018 stating its opposition to the mitigation efforts in the Jackson area.[58] Congress approved a bill to support the project with the provision that final approval address lower river concerns.[59] Heavy rains in August 2022 once again caused flooding in Jackson. This event finally prompted approval of funding through a federal infrastructure bill that would enlarge the channel, build a dam, and raise levees. While gaining praise among Mississippi politicians, the projects did not assuage concerns in Louisiana. Lower basin residents feared the upstream projects would limit freshwater into lower-river wetlands and destroy habitats of endangered species.[60] Upstream-downstream tensions persist.

Despite the spate of recent floods, St. Tammany Parish has continued to grow in areas near the Pearl River. In a recent draft master plan, the parish outlined a goal to allow growth only outside the one-hundred-year floodplain and even encourage replacement of "intense" land uses in higher risk zones. For development within the one-hundred-year floodplain, the parish seeks "low-impact" development and elevation of any critical infrastructure. This approach acknowledges flood risk and takes a turn toward a land-use approach.[61] The real challenge will be implementing such a program and coordinating with interests throughout the basin.

The Amite River basin rises in southern Mississippi and flows in a southerly direction between East Baton Rouge and Livingston Parishes. As it moves off the Pleistocene Terrace and across the coastal plain, it veers southeastward through Ascension Parish toward Lake Maurepas, which is connected to the larger Lake Pontchartrain. The river has cut a fairly deep channel across the uppermost portion of the basin and farms and rural residences, along with several small communities, exist upon the terrace. As the river meanders across the middle section of the watershed, it has created a wider floodplain that fringe suburbs that have pushed eastward from Baton Rouge. This lower segment of the river has little gradient and has long been subject to the most intense flooding. However, this region was also the most thinly settled historically. Nonetheless, sprawl from Baton Rouge has given rise to rapid development in Ascension Parish since the 1980s.

The USACE examined the Amite beginning in 1880 and launched a project to remove obstructions as far upstream as Bayou Manchac to improve navigation potential.[62] Congress authorized a project to create a seven-foot channel from the river's mouth to Port Vincent in 1927. The lower river meandered across the coastal plain where there was little settlement. Along the stream's middle course, the river passed through a timber-covered valley with areas near its banks subject to overflow. Bluffs rose about twenty-five feet above the river. Further upstream, there was more cultivation and villages and farmsteads on the bluffs. The principal cargo of the river at the time was timber and lumber. A 1930 investigation reported about 160,000 acres of land were subject to inundation but observed that most of it "consists of forest and swamp." Damage from floods had been confined to the loss of livestock and to the flooding of some highways. Because the lower course overflowed its banks three to four time a year, this area "remained unpopulated and generally uncultivated."[63] The inquiry noted that although these lands could be protected by levees, such structures would be "economically unjustified." Likewise, the report concluded that wetland reclamation or upstream flood retention reservoirs were not economically feasible.[64]

A substantial flood in 1953 impacted Baton Rouge, the largest city in the watershed, and prompted a basin-wide response to flood risk. The state's public-works department developed a plan for improving drainage in the urbanizing middle basin along with modest levee protection in the lower basin.[65] While taking both the upper and lower basin into account, the program relied on accelerating the movement of water downstream. This tactic meant displacing risk to the lower basin, which still had far fewer people and established a framework for enduring tensions between the residents in the different segments of the basin. Additionally, the USACE responded to local appeals for flood protection. It held public hearings and found there was support for mitigation efforts throughout the basin. With efforts to accelerate drainage from the upper basin, the USACE suggested a canal that would accommodate the increased flow directed downstream and send it to the lake along a nearly straight course. Congress funded what became known as the Amite River Diversion Canal in 1955, and the USACE completed the undertaking in 1964.[66]

The combination of numerous floods between 1973 and 1983 and increasing suburban sprawl into the basin intensified public consideration of flood mitigation. While the USACE investigated several structural flood-control measures, it reported in 1981 that none was economically justifiable and instead recommended land-use approaches.[67] Although the parishes participated in the National Flood Insurance Program (NFIP), they took minimal action to regulate development in flood-prone areas. They relied on homeowners to bear the cost of meeting the NFIP standards.

A record-setting flood in 1983 caused extensive damage to more than five thousand homes in the middle and lower basin and traumatized residents in Baton Rouge and Denham Springs. The consequences of this event motivated a reexamination of the structures considered but rejected by the USACE a few years earlier. A host of local and state-level initiatives highlighted the public concern with flooding in a rapidly growing watershed. Options considered reservoirs in the upper basin to protect downstream residents, a diversion canal on the Comite, and local drainage to accelerate downstream flow. The state directed attention to a midstream diversion canal that would redirect water from the Amite's largest tributary, the Comite, westward to the Mississippi River.[68] This infrastructure would substantially reduce discharge near Denham Springs and Baton Rouge's eastern suburbs, along with Ascension Parish communities. Thus, it had appeal throughout the basin unlike a flood retention reservoir that was opposed by upstream landowners who argued it would take their land and offer them no benefits. Louisiana's legislature launched a statewide flood-control program that offered funds to allow localities to develop plans for flood protection works. While this program encouraged protecting existing development and discouraged sprawl into flood-prone areas, it reinforced the local authority over flood management and did not provide a means for a more unified flood-control system at the watershed scale.[69]

Among the critical observations coming out of the post-1983 flood were the interparish conflicts over mitigation strategies. Baton Rouge tended to blame upstream, rural areas for flood runoff. In the lower basin, Ascension Parish had built levees and drainage canals but complained that it could not keep pace with the additional and accelerated runoff from middle-basin communities.[70] Another target of criticism was the Amite River Basin Commission, formed in 1981. It provided a forum for discussing interparish flood management, but it had no authority to enact taxes for mitigation programs or to impose land-use regulations to reduce property risk.[71]

Additional floods in 1990 and 1993, amidst continued suburban sprawl in the basin, further accentuated the need for effective mitigation. On the back burner during these floods was the Comite River Diversion which had received congressional authorization in 1986 but no real progress in terms of its construction. It was the compromise mitigation project that would address flooding basin wide without displacing risks. Nearly two decades after the 1983 flood, voters in the three parishes destined to receive direct benefits approved a tax to cover the state's cost-sharing commitment in 2000.[72]

Yet, the project languished and a flood in 2016 obliterated the 1983 record crest. Several days of massive rainfall pushed waters through the river system and outward into neighboring communities. Some ninety-six thousand homes suffered serious damage, and total damage estimates surpassed $8 billion.[73] This event motivated public officials to press more aggressively for completion of the diversion canal. Since 2016, funding for the canal has been secured, and the project is underway. Initial projections called for completion in late 2022, but that has been pushed back, and construction will likely continue into 2025.[74] The underlying goal of the diversion canal is to improve protection for existing developments—which is far more extensive than when the project was authorized in 1986. This approach supports a common desire of parish officials to retain residents and the taxes they pay. It does not include any related land-use restrictions and basically perpetuates the existing policy that promotes development over safety. Although the Comite River Diversion receives some federal funding, it imposes no new land-use requirements on the parishes.

In the wake of the 2016 flood, parishes took immediate steps to encourage the rapid return of residents to their residences. They permitted property owners to bring in trailers as temporary shelter as they gutted and restored their houses. Parish councils waived fees and procedures for restoration construction. Some parishes even declared the 2016 flood was such an exceptional event, that they would continue to use the 1983 flood as the flood of record. Local codes called for rebuilding severely damaged properties one foot above the flood of record. By ignoring the 2016 crest, the parishes encouraged residents to return and rebuild homes that would be at risk from future floods.[75] Yet, the fact that Houston, Texas, has had two rain events in recent years with double the thirty inches that produced the 2016 Amite River flood highlights the fact that the 2016 event can be exceeded.

Despite the immediate policy adjustments to encourage return and to promote further development, there has been increased opposition to unchecked development, and citizens have voiced opposition to new developments in flood-prone areas. Skeptics of unchecked development are keenly aware of the potential displacement of runoff from new construction. Additionally, there have been programs instituted in Livingston and Ascension Parishes to buy out flood victims and encourage relocation away from high-risk flood zones.[76] Buyout programs seek to eliminate repeat flood insurance claims and to transform residential properties into open space. There have also been temporary moratoriums placed on new development. Still, there is great expectation that the diversion canal will be the magic bullet for flood control and enable economic growth and sprawl to continue.[77]

The chronic issue of multiple jurisdictions and uncoordinated flood management among the parishes remains. A recent report on Amite River basin flooding by the Louisiana Coastal Protection and Restoration Authority emphasized this very point. The authors argue for a watershed management approach and to expand the jurisdiction of the basin authority to the entire basin. They also advocate for delegating regulatory and permitting functions to the basin authority in order to achieve consistency.[78] An attempt to delegate greater authority to the basin commission failed in the legislature in spring 2022.

Returning to the general concept of watersheds, the authors of the report offer a sensible geographic framework for managing floods, at least until people, property, and political entities enter the equation. The Louisiana Watershed Initiative builds on the long tradition of turning to a physical territory, rather than political units, to address flooding across the state. Initial efforts focused on hydrologic modeling to determine risk in the numerous watersheds in order to prioritize projects for funding. Subsequent efforts have directed funds to assist with an array of flood mitigation efforts, with six projects funded in the Florida parishes.

Louisiana's Watershed Initiative is addressing issues exposed during the recent spate of severe floods. There are funds for voluntary buyouts of homeowners in Livingston, Washington (on a tributary to the Pearl), and St. Tammany Parishes. Drainage and infrastructure improvements to facilitate runoff removal have received funding in the Amite River basin. The most fundamental change between past watershed efforts and the current one is the inclusion of property buyouts. While limited in geographic scope, they do help reduce the number of homes that have been subjected to past floods and take those properties out of the residential real estate market. Buyouts

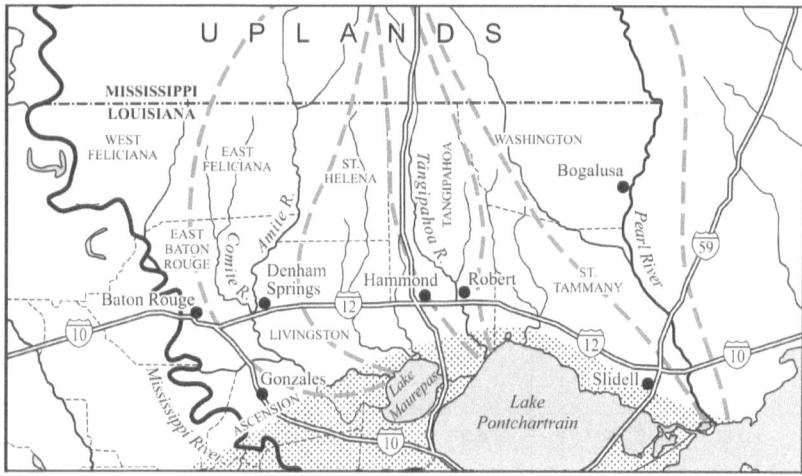

Figure 8.2. Lower Watersheds for the Amite, Tangipahoa, and Pearl Rivers. (Cartography by Mary Lee Eggart)

reject the traditional approach of encouraging development and then building infrastructure after floods. This strategy seeks to reverse development, at least to a modest degree. Parishes have also imposed temporary limits on new developments and are requiring builders to provide protection against more extreme storms than in the past.

The real challenge for watershed management of floods remains a truly unified approach for the entire physical territories within basins. The Watershed Initiative leaders attempted, unsuccessfully, to have the legislature create a Watershed Management Council that would enable collaborative management of watersheds by all governing bodies to overcome that challenge. Yet, each of the watersheds discussed here is interstate and continues to face discharges from Mississippi. And at the local level, differing views among those different sections of the basin create conflict on how to manage stream flow during floods. Public officials have turned to reservoirs, canals, pumps, and levees as flood mitigation tools in different segments of these streams. Each has local benefits but displaces risk to other communities. The persistence of political territories that do not conform to the hydrologic geographies makes equitable flood management extremely difficult. These political units stem in part from settlement histories and the tendency of governing bodies to seek new development to boost tax revenue within their territories. In Louisiana, the primacy of local political control will hinder the resolution of interparish conflicts, to say nothing of the interstate issues across these basins.

Table 8.1. Ten Highest River Crests for the Amite, Tangipahoa, and Pearl Rivers						
Amite River at Denham Spring		Tangipahoa River at Robert		Pearl River at Pearl River		
Crest	Date	Crest	Date	Crest	Date	
46.20	8/14/2016	27.33	8/13/2016	21.05	4/9/1983	
41.50	4/8/1983	27.10	3/14/1921	20.35	3/14/2016	
41.08	4/23/1977	25.87	04/07/1983	19.75	4/2/1980	
39.88	1/27/1990	25.52	3/12/2016	19.70	4/19/1900	
39.27	3/15/1921	23.95	9/1/2012	19.60	1/30/1990	
38.34	6/9/2001	23.13	5/3/1953	19.25	4/26/1979	
38.15	1/22/1993	22.43	1/22/1993	19.23	12/12/1971	
36.70	4/24/1979	21.76	5/23/1974	19.18	4/1/2009	
36.50	3/27/1973	21.55	4/19/1973	18.60	6/16/1921	
36.33	5/20/1953	21.46	1/27/1990	18.59	9/4/2012	

Source: NOAA, NWS, Amite River at Denham Spring, Historic Crests; Tangipahoa River at Robert, Historic Crests; Pearl River at Pearl River, Historic Crests.

NOTES

Ria Mukerji and Audrey Grismore provided substantial research assistance, which is greatly appreciated. Funding for Amite River basin research came from the National Academies of Sciences, Engineering, and Medicine and the Robert Wood Johnson Foundation.

1. Kara M. Watson, John B. Storm, Brian K. Breaker, and Claire E. Rose, "Characterization of Peak Streamflows and Flood Inundation of Selected Areas in Louisiana from the August 2016 Flood," *Scientific Investigations Report No. 2017-5005*, US Geological Survey, https://doi.org/10.3133/sir20175005, 2017.

2. Craig E. Colten, "Eroding Memories and Erecting Risk on the Amite River," *Open Rivers: Rethinking Water, Place & Community* 16 (Winter 2020), https://editions.lib.umn.edu/openrivers/article/amite-river/.

3. Louisiana Office of Community Development, Louisiana Watershed Initiative, https://www.watershed.la.gov/about, accessed February 2022.

4. James Westcoat Jr. and Gilbert White, *Water for Life: Water Management and Environmental Policy* (New York: Cambridge University Press, 2003); Isobel W. Heathcote, *Integrated Watershed Management: Principles and Practice* (New York: John Wiley & Sons, 2009).

5. Daniel J. Pisani, *To Reclaim a Divided West: Water, Law, and Public Policy, 1848–1902* (Albuquerque: University of New Mexico Press, 1992).

6. Samuel P. Hays, *Conservation and the Gospel of Efficiency: The Progressive Conservation Movement, 1890–1920* (New York: Atheneum, 1969).

7. Natural Resources Committee, Water Resources Committee, *Drainage Basin Problems and Programs* (Washington: US Government Printing Office, 1938).

8. Beatrice H. Holmes, *A History of Federal Water Resources Programs, 1800–1960* (Washington: US Department of Agriculture, Economic Research Service, 1972); A. Dan Tarlock, "Putting Rivers Back in the Landscape: The Revival of Watershed Management in the United States," *Hasting West Northwest Journal of Environmental Law and Policy* 14 (2008): 1068–69.

9. Chris Rosen, "Costs and Benefits of Pollution Control in Pennsylvania, New York, and New Jersey, 1840–1906," *Geographical Review* 88, no. 2 (1998): 219–40.

10. Tarlock, "Putting Rivers Back," 1085.

11. Louisiana Board of State Engineers, *Biennial Report, 1906–08* (Baton Rouge: 1908), 64–65.

12. Louisiana Department of Public Works, *Biennial Report, 1944–45* (Baton Rouge: 1945), 84.

13. Robert W. Harrison, "Louisiana's State-Sponsored Drainage Program," *Southern Economic Journal* 14, no. 4 (1948): 389.

14. Louisiana Department of Public Works, *Biennial Report, 1946–47* (Baton Rouge: 1947), 99.

15. Louisiana Department of Public Works, *Biennial Report, 1954–55* (Baton Rouge: 1955), map facing 76; Louisiana Department of Public Works, *Biennial Report, 1954–65* (Baton Rouge: 1965).

16. Rod Emmer, Rebecca B. Sonnefeld, Todd Davidson, Peggy Autin, and Richard McCulloh, *Louisiana Atlas of Flood Plains and Flooding Problems* (Baton Rouge: Louisiana Geological Survey, 1983).

17. Louisiana Joint Legislative Committee on Transportation, Highways, and Public Works, *Louisiana Statewide Flood Control Program* (Baton Rouge: Louisiana Legislature, 1985).

18. Scott Knowles, Scott Gabriel, and Howard C. Kunreuther, "Troubled Waters: The National Flood Insurance Program in Historical Perspective," *Journal of Policy History* 26, no. 3 (2014): 327–53.

19. Governor's Interagency Task Force on Flood Protection and Mitigation, *Final Report* (Baton Rouge: State of Louisiana, 1990).

20. Murray Stein, "Federal Water Pollution Control Enforcement Activities," *Proceedings of the Eighteenth Industrial Waste Conference* (Lafayette, IN: Purdue University Industrial Waste Conference: 1964), 264–72. The Clean Water Act of 1972 established a procedure to set discharge standards and issue permits.

21. Andrew Beall and Jack Kindinger, *Environmental Atlas of the Lake Pontchartrain Basin*, US Geological Survey, Open-file Report 0002–206, 2002; Kara M. Watson, John B. Storm, Brian K. Breaker, and Claire E. Rose, *Characterization of Peak Streamflows and Flood Inundation of Selected Areas in Louisiana from the August 2016 Flood*, US Geological Survey, Scientific Investigations Report 2017–5005, 2017, https://pubs.usgs.gov/sir/2017/5005/sir20175005.pdf.

22. Richard Beavers, Malcolm Webb, Teresia Lamb, and John Greene, *Archaeological Survey of the Upper Tangipahoa River* (New Orleans: University of New Orleans Archaeology Research Program, 1985).

23. US Army Corps of Engineers, "Survey of the Tangipahoa River," in *Report of the Secretary of War*, v. 2, pt. 1, appendix K–14, 1879, 946–49.

24. US Congress, House of Representatives, *Tangipahoa River: Letter from the Secretary of War*, House Doc. 1068, 62nd Cong., 3rd sess., 1912, 4–6.

25. "Highway 16 Bridge Collapses," *Hammond Daily Star*, April 7, 1983, 1, 3.

26. "Workers Rescue Ponchatoula Families," *Hammond Daily Star*, April 8, 1983, 1.

27. "Water Takes Toll on Berries," *Hammond Daily Star*, April 10, 1983, 1.

28. "Flooded Home Owners Want Federal Court to Force the State to Pay 16-Year-Old Judgment," *Baton Rouge Advoccate*, March 19, 2020, https://www.theadvocate.com/baton_rouge/news/politics/legislature/article_f4944238-6a32-11ea-b2a8-3bd6efaa54fe.html.

29. "Moore Request Area River Study," *Hammond Daily Star*, April 13, 1983, 1.

30. Lake Pontchartrain Basin Foundation, *Final Report: Targeted Water Shed Grant #WS-96618701-1, Tangipahoa/Natalbany Watersheds* (New Orleans: Lake Pontchartrain Basin Foundation, 2010), 6, 61.

31. "Dam Threatened by Breach at Percy Quin," *McComb Enterprise-Journal*, August 30, 2012, Newsbank database.

32. "Fire Fighters Work to Relieve Pressure on Percy," *McComb Enterprise-Journal*, August 30, 2012, Newsbank database.

33. "Officials Plan Breach to Relieve Pressure," *McComb Enterprise-Journal*, August 31, 2012, Newsbank database.

34. "Tangipahoa Parish Maintains Evacuation Order," *New Orleans Times-Picayune*, August 31, 2012, Newsbank database.

35. "Floods Swamp Thousands in Livingston and Tangipahoa Parishes," *Baton Rouge Advocate*, September 7, 2012, 1A.

36. "Tangipahoa Parish Strawberry Farmers, WWL TV New Orleans, March 16, 2016, Newsbank database.

37. "Second 500-year Flood," *New Orleans Times-Picayune*, August 17, 2016 A8.

38. "Tangipahoa Residents' Lawsuit Over I-12's Role in Flooding Dealt Blow by Louisiana's Top Court," *Baton Rouge Advocate*, November 8, 2017, Newsbank database. In 2022, Louisiana agreed to release funds to victims of the flood, Mark Ballard, "40 Years Later, Louisiana Agrees to Pay $100 Million in I-12 Flooding Lawsuit," March 24, 2022, https://www.theadvocate.com/baton_rouge/news/politics/legislature/40-years-later-louisiana-agrees-to-pay-100-million-in-i-12-flooding-lawsuit/article_63da95ae-aba2-11ec-b4b7-8fb0b47323e9.html.

39. Tangipahoa Parish Council Code of Ordinances, Chapter 17—Planning and Development, Article X—Flood Prevention and Protection, 76, https://library.municode.com/la/tangipahoa_parish_council/codes/code_of_ordinances?nodeId=PTIICOOR_CH17PLDE.

40. *Tangipahoa's Big Idea: LSU Helps Flood-Prone Louisiana Parish Rise to Challenges*, July 1, 2021, https://www.lsu.edu/research/news/2021/0701-tangipahoa.php.

41. US Congress, House of Representatives, Pearl River, Mississippi and Louisiana, House Doc. 445, 71st Cong., 2nd sess., 1930, 7.

42. US Congress, House Doc. 445, 3.

43. US Congress, House Doc. 445, 7.

44. US Congress, House Doc. 445, 4.

45. US Congress, House Doc. 445, 5.

46. US Congress, House of Representatives, Pearl River, Mississippi and Louisiana, House Doc. 482, 89th Cong, 2nd sess., 1956, 16.

47. US Congress, House of Representatives, Pearl River and Tributaries, Mississippi, House Doc. 441, 86th Cong., 2nd sess., 1960, 25.

48. US Congress, House Doc. 441, 18.

49. US Congress, House Doc. 441, 23.

50. US Congress, House Doc. 441, 28–32.

51. George Wynne (president, Pearl River Basin Development District) testimony to US Congress, House of Representatives, *Hearings before the Subcommittee on Water Resources, Committee on Public Works and Transportation*, 97th Cong., 2nd sess. 1982, 3–8.

52. Rankin-Hinds Pearl River Flood and Drainage Control District, Integrated Draft Feasibility and Environmental Impact Statement, Pearl River Basin (Jackson: US Army Corps of Engineers, Vicksburg District 2018), 21–27.

53. US Army Corps of Engineers, Vicksburg District, Pearl River Basin, *Slidell, Louisiana and Pearlington, Mississippi Interim Report on Flood Control*, Final, Main Report (Vicksburg: 1986), 14–19.

54. US Congress, House of Representatives, Slidell-Pearlington, Louisiana and Mississippi: Communication for the Assistant Secretary of the Army, House Doc., 101–250, 101st Cong., 2nd sess., 1990, 68, 112.

55. St. Tammany Parish Council, Ordinance 5694, Ordinance to Authorize St. Tammany Parish Government, through the Office of the Parish President, to Acquire Certain Parcel(s) of Immovable Property through the Flood Mitigation Assistance Grant Program, November 3, 2016.

56. "Opponents of Pearl River Project Voice Opposition," *St. Tammany Advocate*, August 17, 2018, Newsbank database.

57. "Mississippi Oyster Producers Question Pearl River Dam," *New Orleans Times-Picayune*, August 16, 2018, Newsbank database.

58. St. Tammany Parish Council, Resolution in Opposition of the Proposed Pearl River Basin Flood Control Project in Jackson Mississippi, Resolution C-5045, August 2, 2018.

59. "Bill with Pearl River Dam Provision," *New Orleans Times-Picayune*, October 16, 2018, Newsbank database.

60. Wicker Perlis, "Help Is Coming: Army Corps Says Jackson Area Could Get $221M Federal Funds to Prevent Flooding," *Jackson Clarion Ledger*, October 3, 2022, https://www.clarionledger.com/story/news/local/2022/10/04/jackson-ms-flooding-pearl-river-flood-control-project-funding/69536981007/; Sara Pagones, "Controversial Mississippi Flood Control Project Gets $221M More, but Louisiana Worries Remain," *New Orleans Advocate*, October 13, 2022, https://www.nola.com/news/northshore/article_473b1834-4999-11ed-9e4e-5363d74dabd6.html.

61. St. Tammany Parish, *New Directions 2040: St. Tammany Parish Comprehensive Plan—Draft* (Covington: St. Tammany Parish, 2022), 16–23.

62. US Congress, House of Representatives, Amite River, Louisiana, House Doc. 480, 71st Cong. 2nd. sess., 1930, 6.

63. US Congress, House, Amite River, 1930, 11.

64. US Congress, House, Amite River, 1930, 14–15.

65. US Congress, House of Representatives, Amite River and Tributaries, Louisiana, House Doc. 419, 84th Cong., 2nd sess., 1956, 6.

66. US Congress, House, Amite River, 1956, 6–8; and US Army Corps of Engineers, *Lower Mississippi River Valley Division, Water Resources Development in Louisiana 1981* (Vicksburg: US Army Corps of Engineers, Lower Mississippi River Valley Division 1981), 89.

67. US Army Corps of Engineers, *Water Resources Development*, 89.

68. Louisiana Department of Transportation and Development (LADOTD), Office of Public Works, *Amite River Basin Drainage and Water Conservation District* (Baton Rouge: LADOTD, 1984).

69. Flood Control Project Evaluation Committee, *Louisiana Statewide Flood Control Program: Guidelines and Procedures* (Baton Rouge: Louisiana State Legislature, 1985).

70. Chamber of Commerce of Greater Baton Rouge, *Flood Control in the Baton Rouge Area: Report of the Task Force on Drainage and Flood Control* (Baton Rouge: Chamber of Commerce of Greater Baton Rouge, 1986).

71. Amite River Basin Drainage and Conservation District, *Amite River Basin Floodplain Management Plan* (Baton Rouge: Amite River Basin Drainage and Conservation District, 2015).

72. Amite River Basin Drainage and Conservation District, *Project Fact Sheet: Comite River Diversion Canal, 2003*, www.amitebasin.org/fact.htm.

73. Federal Emergency Management Agency, *100 Days Later: Signs of Recovery Multiplying as Work Continues*, 2016, http://wwwfema.gov/news-release/2016.

74. Congressman Garrett Graves, "Comite River Diversion Canal Project Expected to Be Completed by December 2022," press release, March 30, 2022, https://garrettgraves.house.gov/media-center/2022

75. Craig E. Colten and Audrey M. Grismore, "Can Public Policy Perpetuate the Memory of Disasters?" *RCC Perspectives* 3 (2018): 43–52.

76. Louisiana Office of Community Development, Statewide Buyout Program: Denham Springs, https://www.watershed.la.gov/buyouts#denhamsprings, 2022; *Baton Rouge Advocate*, May 17, 2021; Gonzales *Weekly Citizen*, August 5, 2020.

77. Inland from the Coast, Baker, *Louisiana Scenario Building Workshop*, Baker, Louisiana, April 15, 2019.

78. Louisiana Coastal Protection and Restoration Authority, *Report of Study and Recommendations Regarding Management of the Amite River Basin in Response to HCR 46* (2021 Regular Session of the Louisiana Legislature) (Baton Rouge: Louisiana Coastal Protection and Restoration Authority, 2021).

SECTION FOUR

Determining Who We Are

Chapter Nine

THE POLITICS OF OPPORTUNITY

EDUCATION REFORM IN THE JINDAL ADMINISTRATION

PEARSON CROSS

> Policy entrepreneurs reveal themselves through their attempts to transform policy ideas into policy innovations, and hence, disrupt status quo policy arrangements.
> —EVANGELIA PETRIDOU, MICHAEL MINTROM, "A RESEARCH AGENDA FOR THE STUDY OF POLICY ENTREPRENEURS."

> You had this huge number of new members and . . . I think [they] wanted to give the governor what the governor had earned in the election. He had campaigned on education, and I think there [was] a general sense that "we're going to support him."
> —INTERVIEW, JOHN WHITE

> These bills went through in twenty-three days. And that's just unheard of in any process. And it's probably unlike anything I've seen since I've been here.
> —INTERVIEW, WILL SENTELL[1]

When Louisiana passed ground-breaking education reform legislation in 2012, it was national news.[2] The legislation, contained in four massive bills, reached nearly every aspect of public education in Louisiana. Voucher programs were expanded statewide, new categories of charter schools were created, the relationship between school administrators and boards was changed, teacher tenure was reshaped, and early childhood education was brought out of "childcare" and into the educational system proper. Perpetually mired in last or next to last place on every national survey of education quality and achievement, Louisiana was, for once, leading the country in something besides incarceration rates.[3] Credit for the wide-reaching reforms fixed on Louisiana's charismatic governor, Bobby Jindal. Speculation swirled: Was education reform a real interest of Jindal, perhaps part of his oft-stated desire to break Louisiana's long legacy of poverty, outmigration, and stagnation? Or did education reform reflect Jindal's presidential ambitions, a badly kept secret in the Pelican State? Two narratives competed to explain education reform in Louisiana: one, Governor Jindal, looking to make a name for himself in a policy area, trod a well-worn path frequented by other governors with similar ambitions, using education reform to demonstrate his seriousness, policy expertise, and accomplishment. A second narrative held that Louisiana's education reform was a wholly predictable product of Republican politics and the conservative policy mill, exemplified by the American Legislative Exchange Council's (ALEC) practice of drafting "model" legislation ready for adoption in states around the country.[4] In this view, having achieved the conquest of Louisiana government with his overwhelming reelection in 2012, Jindal was instituting the education reform agenda sought by conservatives and Republicans all the way back to Milton Friedman. His success in achieving these education-policy goals was thus an accompaniment to the lately realized Republican ambition of seizing entire control of Louisiana government and changing governance in the Pelican State.[5]

While these explanations seem reasonable, neither captures the dynamics of Louisiana's policy breakthrough, an accounting of which would include previous education initiatives, the opportunities created by Jindal's landslide reelection victory in 2011, and the complex web of educational institutions and groups shaping education policy in Louisiana. Also needing mention would be the networks linking reformers and entrepreneurs together in the policy process and the parents determined to achieve a better education for their children. Historical perspective aside, Louisiana's 2012 education reform opens a window into the world of public-policy theory. Researchers employ several theories to describe the public-policy process. These theories have been used to explain policy change and innovation in any number of areas, including health care, agriculture, economics and finance, foreign affairs, immigration, energy, environment, and transportation. In recent years, education policy has joined these other policy areas, shedding its sui generis status.[6]

In looking at Louisiana's education-policy explosion in 2012, the questions to be answered are how did such massive and far-reaching education legislation become law, surmounting the many obstacles that work to limit or curtail such initiatives? What explains Louisiana's policy achievements? Who were the actors, who were the groups, and what were the stakes? To answer these questions, I will be placing Louisiana's reform in the context of several public-policy models. I will briefly summarize the five or six policy models most frequently cited in the literature and show their fit for describing reform in Louisiana. The evidentiary part of my argument will rely on interviews conducted with the persons responsible for bringing the 2012 policy changes to fruition.[7] Seen as a case study, Louisiana's 2012 education reform reveals the dynamics of creating and passing reform legislation. Its study has implications for public-policy theory and education-policy reform in Louisiana and other states as well. I argue that the "multiple-streams" theory, focusing on policy, problems, and politics, policy entrepreneurs, and policy windows offers the best explanation of education reform in Louisiana when matched with the oral record of the participants in the process.

As Evangelia Petridou aptly put it, the object of policy research "is the understanding of the interactions among the machinery of the state, political actors, and the public," leading to an explanation of how policy develops and changes over time. However, this is not a simple task partly because policy research has produced what Petridou calls a "prolificacy of scholarship," requiring regular surveys of the literature to chart new developments, extensions, departures, and elaborations.[8] Given this prolificacy, the current review will be brief, focusing most attention where warranted.[9]

Public-policy theory is divided into five, six, or seven main branches, with extensions and related theories.[10] Petridou counts six main theories, which include advocacy coalition framework, institutional analysis and development, social construction and design, punctuated equilibrium, innovation and policy diffusion, and multiple streams. Working with a colleague seven years later, Petridou delineated a slightly different list of "classic policy process theories" including incrementalism, institutionalism, multiple streams, punctuated equilibrium, advocacy coalition framework, policy entrepreneurs, and narrative-policy framework. Nomenclature issues aside, what each of these theories and, indeed, what any public-policy theory does, is to show how policy develops and changes over time and the forces influencing its direction and pace.

An advocacy coalition framework (ACF) is made up of "people from a variety of positions (e.g., elected and agency officials, interest group leaders, researchers) who share a specific belief system—i.e., a set of basic values, causal assumptions and who show a nontrivial degree of coordinated activity over time." These "coalition participants seek to ensure the maintenance and evolution of policy in specific policy domains." The strength of the ACF theory is that it focuses on the large number of actors, agencies, and organizations that may influence policy development. Another strength of the ACF theory is that it considers what people in the coalition believe and thus, the influence of ideas on policy. It has been employed to analyze many different cases in different policy areas.[11]

A second theory is institutional analysis and development, which looks to "understand the influence of institutions on individuals." This form of policy analysis fell into disuse as behaviorism surged in the twentieth century but reemerged strongly in the late twentieth century with the work of James March, Johan Olsen, Theda Skocpol, and others. Institutionalists study the "importance of rules in incentivizing the actions of individuals; the fallible nature of people and learning through mistakes; and the centrality of choice in institution change and policymaking arrangements."[12] Another theory, "incrementalism," suggests that "most change within policymaking occurs through small steps pursued by risk-averse policymakers." In this view, policy makers are constrained by complexity and disagreement and operate within a web of rules and provisions created by "constitutions, legislative acts, administrative rulings, executive orders and judicial decisions." Policy changes then emerge from "structured interactions among proximate policymakers."[13]

An extension and refinement of the incrementalist theory is "punctuated equilibrium theory (PE)." This theory is based on the commonplace observation that "political processes comprise long periods of stability spiked by points of disequilibrium." PE theory focuses on the pace of policy change, explaining both long-term stability and rapid change, in the process responding to the limits of both the hyperrational and the incremental models of policy making. Research in this model focuses on the factors that prompt a "gap between the status quo and observed policy outcomes," such as when new information prompts major change.[14]

In contrast, "innovation and policy diffusion" research "focuses on the processes through which a government adopts innovative policies." As students of state government recognize, governments learn from each other continually, borrowing practices and policies that work. States also compete for competitive regional and national advantage. How other states are doing in this race for citizens and economic development is a matter of keen interest to state actors. Those working in the innovation and policy-diffusion paradigm focus their attention on how policies diffuse (spread from one locality or state to another) and what (which policies) gets spread. Diffusion theory assumes that the policy being diffused is an innovation or at least new to the governmental entity adopting it. As a model, innovation and policy diffusion makes some sense for the Louisiana education example, particularly as research has indicated that a "high concentration of administrative professionals increases the possibility of innovation." Another point in its favor is the spread of "choice" legislation and practices across the United States as states and districts have sought to raise their district scores, increase efficiency, and improve their pedagogy.[15] Yet, the diffusion-and-innovation model does not do a very good job of explaining why one district and not another, or one state and not another, would adopt a practice or policy. A model that may offer a better state-specific explanation is the "multiple-streams framework (MSF)" model.

MSF first emerged out of the "garbage-can logic" of Cohen, March, and Olsen but has since been most associated with the work of John Kingdon.[16] MSF is a "relatively intuitive policy process framework that has been used to explain agenda-setting in the US federal context." MSF "hypothesizes that a *policy problem* is more likely to gain decision-makers' attention when it is 'coupled' with a *policy solution* in the context of a supportive *political environment*."[17] MSF has "five structural components: three distinct streams: policy, problems, and politics," which combine with "policy entrepreneurs; and policy windows." Policy change occurs when "entrepreneurs couple the streams during short-lived, propitious moments in time—policy windows."[18] What does it mean to "couple the streams?" It means to link the policy problem, solution, and environment with a compelling narrative during a moment in political time when change is possible. The MSF model acknowledges that

> policy processes are permeated by ambiguity, randomness, and irrationality . . . in which policy participants hold unclear preferences and access incomplete information. Under these conditions, the policy process often does not proceed in a linear fashion in which a problem is identified, and then, solutions are investigated and assessed; instead, policy problems and solutions may be identified or developed independently of one another and coupled at a later time.[19]

Put more simply, a "problem," either arising or long-standing, comes to public attention through some highlighting process. Policy experts or entrepreneurs advance solutions to meet the now-salient problem. At some point, but not inevitably, the broader sociopolitical environment such as the "public mood, pressure group campaigns, election results, and partisan or ideological distributions" proves receptive to the framing of the problem and the proffered solutions.[20] Clearly, there is a great deal of contingency built into in the MSF model, prompting criticism that the model cannot be "falsified." Despite this and other criticisms, the strength of the MSF model is in its commonsense hypothesis that "an issue's chances of gaining agenda status dramatically increase when all three streams—problems, policies, and politics—are coupled in a single package." This, in turn, is "most likely to occur when a policy window opens in the problem or politics stream that emphasizes the need for policy action."[21]

One area that an MSF analysis addresses is the idea that a "problem" must come to the public's attention as something that needs to be solved. This is where the "policy entrepreneur" comes to the fore. Policy entrepreneurs "work at problem framing, team building, networking, leading by example, and exploring ways to scale up change processes." They "assembl[e] new evidence" and make "novel arguments," all with the "intention of changing political alignments and, hence, the status quo." They play the role of "meaning maker and interpreter of problems." Their description of the policy world is constructivist, meaning that the "policy problems . . . strongly depend on the meaning attached to them by the actors involved."[22] Policy entrepreneurs can be located within the state in departments and agencies, outside the state in activist organizations and think tanks, and sometimes, in elected positions, as was the case with Louisiana in 2012. Over the next few paragraphs, I will sketch out Louisiana's 2012 education reform initiative following the MSF model, first focusing on the "problem stream," then the "politics stream," and finally the "policy stream and entrepreneurs."

It is unclear whether Governor Jindal thought of himself as a "policy entrepreneur" when he stepped to the microphone at the 2012 Louisiana Education Summit in Baton Rouge, but he quickly made it clear that he was preparing to lead ground-breaking education reform. Titled "Leadership for Change," the summit, organized by House Education Chair Steve Carter, brought a number of distinguished figures in the education field to Louisiana to launch what was to become Jindal's signature policy achievement as governor.[23] In his speech, Jindal noted that his plan was "about taking the power out of the hands of bureaucrats and putting it in the hands of parents and teachers" by accomplishing three things: empowering teachers, empowering parents and empowering school leaders." Continuing to talk about changes for teachers, Jindal said, "The coalition for the status quo is going to say my plan hurts teachers and it hurts public education. . . . [T]his shouldn't be a Republican issue or a Democratic issue. This should be an American issue.

Every child deserves an equal opportunity in education. . . . Education has always been the backbone of the American Dream."

Jindal sketched out the mandate for education reform in Louisiana:

> The reality is that for students at failing schools, that dream doesn't always come true. . . . These failing schools are setting up our children for a life that we as parents would never want for them. . . . Whether you want to decrease general government spending, whether you want to improve our economy, whether you want to improve healthcare outcomes, whatever your goal, it comes back to education. . . . We're currently spending nearly a billion dollars at these failing schools in Louisiana. That's not good government. That's not good financial stewardship of taxpayer dollars. That's not good planning for the economic future of our state. And it's simply unfair. The reality is it doesn't have to be this way. It doesn't have to, and it won't be with this package of reforms. . . . Our kids deserve an opportunity to succeed, and it's a basic right that everyone should be afforded in America. The time to act is now.[24]

What Jindal had done in a few short minutes was focus attention on the inadequacies of a Louisiana K–12 education for many students and issue a clarion call to do something about it. What Jindal was pointing out should have been obvious to even the most casual observer: the problems facing Louisiana K–12 education were immense, as was the evidence documenting the depth, breadth, and seriousness of these problems.[25] The state's own figures showed that "fewer than 40% of Louisiana students met the benchmark . . . on the English section of the most recent LEAP test." While dismal, that "figure is lower for economically disadvantaged students (31%), minority students (28%) students with disabilities (13%), and English language learners (9%)."[26] Speaking frankly, former Senate Education Chair Conrad Appel said that "the scores are abysmal."[27] Nancy Landry, former chair of the House Education Committee, testified that poor Louisiana public schools made her son "lose interest in school and go from being engaged and eager to not wanting to go to school at all."[28] Chairperson Landry's experience was not unique; all across Louisiana, mothers and fathers were looking for relief from schools that were not meeting their children's needs.

Taking the long view, Louisiana education has improved significantly since the 1950s and '60s, yet it still falls short of national standards and has been an unyielding adversary for those intent on improving it as education reporter Will Sentell noted, "Classroom achievement . . . has largely eluded more than two decades of efforts by governors, state lawmakers, teachers and others."[29] House Speaker Chuck Kleckley agreed: "You know when you have a school system in Louisiana as a whole that is suffering and that has been near or at the bottom of our country for so many years, I think it is time to think outside the box, time to do something different, something separate from what we've done in the past and look for new ways and new ideas. So, I was open to any new suggestions, any ideas that [Governor Jindal] had; any ideas that his team brought forth. I was in."[30] There was near unanimity about the need for reform extending from good government groups like Council for a Better Louisiana (CABL), the Public Affairs Research Council (PAR), Blueprint Louisiana, and the Committee of 100 to powerful lobbying groups like the Louisiana Association of Business and Industry (LABI). Prominent figures in the reform movement and press editorials agreed that Louisiana K–12 education needed new ideas.[31] The "narrative of need" clearly established, Jindal's highlighting of the issue put education reform on the public agenda. His efforts in 2010 and 2011 to elect Republicans, stack the state education board, and compel the nomination of a reform-minded superintendent of education, dictate the membership of crucial legislative committees, and place his considerable influence behind the process created the political window of opportunity for education legislation to be passed.

Even prior to winning a (nearly) unprecedented 66 percent of the vote in his 2011 reelection campaign, Bobby Jindal began to plan a striking change in public education.[32] Control over K–12 education in Louisiana is shared between a mostly elected state board, called the Board of Elementary and Secondary Education (BESE),[33] the Department of Education (DOE), and the Superintendent of Education, who is appointed by BESE with a two-thirds vote. These are joined by education committees in both House and Senate and some seventy school districts, each led by a superintendent and with its own elected school board, principals, teachers, and staff. The entire education bureaucracy is responsible for the education of nearly seven hundred thousand public-school students and must be responsive to the wishes, hopes, and demands of their parents. Teachers' unions such as the Louisiana Federation of Teachers (LFT) and the Louisiana Association of Educators (LAE) and a number of activist organizations complete the picture. Additionally, the federal government provides regular monies as well as rules and regulations that states must abide by or risk loss of funding. As might be guessed by the many different governments, organizations, actors, and agencies involved, education is a forbidding and intractable area for policy change.

This point is confirmed by Jeffery Henig, who writes that "what constituted rough waves of change in other social policy arenas . . . were felt as only minor ripples in education governance, buffered and apart as it was."[34] Innovation is both hard to come by and hard to implement. Struggles over curriculum, attendance, tenure, funding, and the rest resemble trench warfare with dug-in constituencies vigilant for incursions on their territory. Finding an opportunity to make major reforms is rare and can only proceed from serendipitous circumstances or from lengthy planning. In the case of Louisiana, it was both: the opportunity for education reform was created by Jindal's victory in 2012 and the accompanying victories of a proreform team with him.

Campaigning in 2011 for a friendly BESE board, Jindal turned normally quiet BESE races into hot contests by vetting candidates and supporting them with resources and encouragement.[35] Jindal's efforts were rewarded as he helped elect a board that would later appoint his hand-picked state superintendent of education, John White. Working with the Committee for a Republican Majority, Jindal sought to achieve historic Republican majorities in both House and Senate, succeeding in 2010 and 2011, respectively. Using his unique powers as Louisiana governor, Jindal named proreform allies as Speaker of the Louisiana House (Chuck Kleckley) and president of the Louisiana Senate (John Alario). Through Kleckley and Alario, Jindal's team selected the legislators who would chair the influential House and Senate Education committees, Representative Steve Carter and Sen. Conrad Appel, respectively. Reaching nationally to tap like-minded reform proponents, Jindal brought in education-policy experts, appointing them to positions such as policy director and education-policy director. Focusing his attention on education, Jindal coordinated a broad team of allies and staff across several state agencies around a plan of action to remake K–12 education in Louisiana. As Erin Bendily, the assistant secretary of education, said, "I think after the results of that election, where the governor won by a strong margin, and also, you know a number of changes happened on the BESE board, where a very pro-reform board was elected, there was alignment. The signals were ready, we [had] the leadership in place. And everyone [was] ready to . . . take reform to a high level."[36] For his part, Jindal was ready to "go all in" on legislation. According to *Advocate* Reporter Will Sentell, Jindal's team was "convinced that this was going to be a singular achievement that people might be talking about in 20 years." Continuing, Sentell says, "I think Jindal decided he was going to spend every bit [of capital] that he had in year one, and put it all into place, put all his chips on the table on the whole public-school overhaul."[37]

With the parts in place, the time was right to push for education reform. Confirming this perception, Jindal's education-policy adviser, Stafford Palmieri, said, "I [had] a conversation with the Governor and with Wags [Steven Waguespack] and . . . with Timmy [Teepell], and the plan was that the session after reelection is sort of the new mandate. It's like . . . the president's first one hundred days, like you can get a lot done the first session after a reelection. And the plan was that the main thing we were going to do was education policy . . . [T]hat was why they had hired me. . . . [T]he whole end game was the 2012 session."[38] Jindal stayed involved as the plan began to unfold. House Speaker Chuck Kleckley notes that "it was pretty public what we were looking at, and to Governor Jindal's credit, I think he met with all the different groups. He met with just about every legislator and told them what he was doing and what his plan was."[39]

Jindal's plan for education reform was not just revealed during the 2012 Education Summit in Baton Rouge; he also spoke of it during his second inaugural, making it symbolically the centerpiece of his second term. While celebrating his administration's successes in other areas, Jindal stated,

> As long as there are children who are not receiving a quality education here in Louisiana—our mission is not accomplished. . . . Equal opportunity in education is a core underlying value we all share. But that is not the reality today in America. Every child does not receive an equal opportunity to a quality of education today. That is a matter of fact, not a matter of opinion. . . . There is not much that you and I can do about educational opportunities afforded to children in 49 other states, but we can do something about it right here at home.[40]

Acknowledging that remaking education was a tough job, Jindal called for checking "our party affiliations, our ideologies, and our political agendas at the door when it comes to improving our schools." Continuing, Jindal noted that children

> don't choose what family to be born into. They have no control whether they are born into a wealthy family, a middle-class family, or a poor family. . . . [In] America, you do not have everything your neighbor has . . . but I would suggest that we long ago decided that every kid does have a right to a quality education from an excellent teacher. . . . Real reform lies in providing more choices and more opportunities for parents, for families and for children. Kids only grow up once; waiting for the system to reform itself is not an option; it is time to act.[41]

In public-policy terms, what Jindal accomplished was to announce the problem and then open the "opportunity window," creating the space for the passage of education reform legislation. In this sense, Jindal acted as a policy entrepreneur. Returning to the multiple-streams model introduced above, "reform is 'most likely to occur when a policy window opens in the problem or politics stream that emphasizes the need for policy action.' Additionally, a problem must be coupled with a solution in a way that is attractive and coherent to receptive policymakers and, potentially, the public *while the window is open*."[42] With the 2012 legislative session following closely on the heels of Jindal's capture of the governorship, remaking of BESE, naming of the legislative leaders and the rest, the timing was perfect. Of course, it is hard to separate Jindal's actions in support of education reform from actions taken in his own self-interest, including reelection and potentially, future elective office. Would successful education reform aid Jindal's career? Of course. However, as Petridou notes, "the role of self-interest . . . is part of the policy entrepreneurs' calculus."[43] Still, with his very public announcements about the need for education reform and commitment to make education reform the signature accomplishment of his second term, the question is moot. The need for broad reform was clearly established and it was time to act. Jindal and his team were "all in."

One theory advanced to explain Louisiana's 2012 education reform has focused on the role of "outside" powers in originating, promoting, and shaping the legislation. The "powers" most often mentioned were Teach for America (TA), the American Legislative Exchange Council (ALEC), Michael Bloomberg, Joel Klein, education activist Betsy DeVos, funding titans David and Charles Koch, and homegrown institutions such as Louisiana Association of Business and Industry.[44] In this telling, outside powers and influences were intent on privatizing public education, looking for any opportunity to channel public money into private pockets while increasing religious-aimed education and undermining the "public" in public education. Brandishing their catchword "choice," education reformers were accused of grafting a "one-size-fits-all" reform package downloaded from ALEC onto the body of Louisiana education. Is this depiction of Louisiana's 2012 education reform true? Was the 2012 education reform homegrown, or was it grafted onto the Louisiana system by outsiders? To address this question, the author conducted interviews with the persons responsible for writing the reform legislation as well as those facilitating its passage through the Louisiana Legislature.

As the words and insights of those involved reveal below, there was very little that was "cookie-cutter" about Louisiana's 2012 education reform. Extensive conversations with insiders reveal a much more nuanced origin for the movement to reform Louisiana education. Those involved were motivated by their desire to improve Louisiana education and decrease its dysfunction. The story these reformers tell is one of legislative achievement, compromise, collaboration, and opportunity. The fact that they succeeded in this effort is a credit to their determination.[45] The remainder of this chapter will use insider voices to sketch the passage of education reform in Louisiana in 2012, allowing those who did it to show how it happened.

The team assembled by Jindal to change education in Louisiana was made up partly of outsiders, policy experts, and activists from across the United States, and partly of like-minded reformers already in Louisiana.[46] Their motivation was sometimes personal, sometimes policy oriented, and sometimes altruistic. For House Education Committee member Nancy Landry, it was personal: "My son ended up with a bunch of gaps . . . and it took him a while to catch up. . . . And you know, I couldn't afford to take him out and put him in private school. . . . [I]t was a real difficult year for me and my son to just watch him lose interest in school and go from being engaged and eager to not wanting to go to school at all. It was awful." As a result, Landry "wanted people on my committee who were passionate about the different areas. I wanted somebody who was going to take early childhood and run with it. I wanted someone who cared about charter schools. I wanted somebody [who] cared about high standards [and] accountability. . . . [W]e felt like . . . we were all soldiers together in this fight for the kids of Louisiana. . . . [W]e felt like 'we're doing the right thing for the right reasons.'"[47] Erin Bendily, formerly an education-policy director in the governor's office and later an assistant superintendent of education at DOE during the reforms, described her motivation this way, "I very much viewed my role, and I think a lot of my co-workers viewed their role [as] not being within a particular camp, you know reform or establishment, but we're individuals who care deeply about the work and care deeply about the opportunities that we're creating for kids." [48] Leaving her position at the Thomas B. Fordham Institute to join the Jindal administration as education-policy adviser, Stafford Palmieri said, "I went to Louisiana, and I interviewed, and I was 24, and I was just really excited about the kind of energy around education reform, about this passion for trying new things to produce better educational outcomes and a willingness to try things . . . the big picture reason that Governor Jindal cared about this was the same reason that I got involved in education, which is how education can change the life trajectory of someone. And the fact that a poorly educated person is not employable."[49] Senate Education Committee chairperson Conrad Appel said, "The real goal for me in my life, my reform thinking was, we have to solve the big picture. You can't fix seven thousand voucher kids and say you've done a great job. You've got to fix it for seven hundred thousand kids."[50]

Jindal's reforms were contained in three major bills, which became Acts 1, 2, and 3 of the 2012 legislative session and other legislation, including Act 25.[51] Through extensive and frequent conversations with his education reform team, Jindal worked through the issues with the proposed legislation. As Palmieri says, Jindal "likes to kick the tires. So, I had many conversations with him, presenting the ideas to him and him poking holes in them, my coming back with solutions to that, thinking through exactly how we were going to propose them." Representative Landry remembers, "Jindal was very hands-on with the legislature. He called us up to his office frequently to talk about the bills that were priorities for him, that were part of his agenda. . . . [H]e was a very hands-on governor."[52] Palmieri confirms that "all the way through the process he [Jindal] was asking what was happening, what amendments we were taking, what amendments we weren't taking."[53]

Taking the lead on crafting the legislation was Stafford Palmieri, although many other persons worked on it. Appel, leading the Senate Education Committee, said: "There were occasional meetings with Teepell and Jindal and Stafford and Waguespack, but those were more strategic meetings about how legislation would be passed. Stafford was the content person."[54] This was confirmed by the superintendent of education, John White, who said: "I wasn't . . . a designer or architect of the Jindal administration plans . . . I think there were people who [were] really involved there . . . Waguespack, [and] probably most of all, Stafford Palmieri."[55] Palmieri confirmed her role in the process, "So I wouldn't say that I can take authorship of the final product in its entirety, but it was my job to pitch the ideas, and so I was the one that came to the table with the bare bones of what we were going to do and then through conversations internally with . . . legislative staff, with John [White], with some of the BESE members, we refined the ideas and figured out how we would structure it."[56]

Given Palmieri's integral role in the creation of the legislation, it seems reasonable to ask if she was cribbing from ALEC or some other source? Addressing this specifically, Palmieri said, the ideas for the legislation "came more from a set of principles that I had and that I shared with the governor . . . and they got refined through a variety of conversations with people like John Walters, with the childcare people, with the principals in New Orleans, with principals in Bossier, with a variety of different people that I [met] traveling around the state . . . and that's kind of where the bills come from, putting all those different pieces together. So, it wasn't like there was some cookie-cutter reform model I had in the back of my head, and I was like, I'm going to apply that to Louisiana. It wasn't like that at all."[57]

Deeply involved in the effort were the committee staff, particularly Jeanne Johnson about whom Palmieri said, "She pushed back on me a little bit. I don't think she's ideologically aligned with what Governor Jindal wanted to do, but we had a lot of conversations and . . . she [was like], 'Ok, this is actually a good idea.' But she drafted that bill and helped figure out how to actually put the ideas into the law."[58] Addressing the question of ALEC-inspired legislation, Palmieri said, "There was no 'I picked up these bills from other states.' That didn't happen. It was a combination of principles and conversations. And then number two, from a writing standpoint, it was a very collaborative effort with the legislative staff, with Senator Appel, with Representative Carter. . . . [We had] multiple meetings, over multiple weeks in February and March 2012 to get the bills drafted."[59] Senator Appel confirmed: "The governor's office would put together their ideas . . . make a draft. And then it went to people like Jeannie Johnson in Senate Education, and they would look at it from the perspective of conflicts with other existing law and language changes that had to be made. So, there was a whole lot of that intermingling of ideas and discussions going on prior to the filing of the bills. . . . [W]hile general concepts and maybe some language came from the governor's office, the final product came out of the two committees."[60]

Contributing to the process was Erin Bendily in the Department of Education: "That was a lot of my role, taking in some cases what Stafford would initiate or the governor's office would initiate as an idea or a priority and then figure out how do we do that?" Continuing, Bendily said, "There were times that I would just spend hours in front of the computer drafting or working on a draft started by someone else . . . and so it was a lot of independent work and group work across a large number of people because there were so many issues we were trying to move ahead."[61] Those writing the bills looked ahead to the passage process. As Bendily says, "No one wanted to move ahead twenty-nine different bills. And we knew that we only have so much political capital. How could we then package these things into something that's manageable [that] also . . . tells a story?" "Ultimately, we coalesced around . . . an early childhood package. We also came together around a package that involves structural changes to the local educational system in terms of personnel and leadership and governance. And then the third package was around school choice. And so, ultimately, that's how we ended up with three different bills that ultimately were passed and became Acts 1, 2, and 3."[62]

Even with the legislation crafted and the team in place, education reform is always a struggle. As Senate Education Chair Conrad Appel said, "A lot of people get their feet stuck in concrete, and they don't see outside the small bubble we all live in."[63] Speed was of the essence. It's a standard rule in the Louisiana legislature that the longer legislation languishes in committee, the less likely it is to make it out in one piece. Palmieri confirms this, noting:

"Part of our strategy was to get [the bills] heard, week one, and out of the session as fast as possible. . . . That was part of our strategy so they wouldn't get bogged down in the horse trading and budget deals and all the other nonsense that was going to happen latter."[64] Other parts of the strategy included lengthy and detailed planning sessions in Senator Appel's office prior to the session and then Monday mornings during session. Other members in the House and Senate were recruited to help pass the bills. As Palmieri tells it,

> We actually recruited a number of other Reps to help us. There was like a small group of people. . . . [T]here was a lot of me walking them through what was in there [the bill]. Writing them talking points. Making sure they could answer all the questions in the well. Writing them Q and A. We could try to guess all the questions that somebody was going to ask them at the well because I can't be up there with them. They were on their own on the floor. And the same thing when those House bills went over to the Senate side, Senator Appel had to take all those questions at the well. And so . . . we prepped for that too.[65]

Directing and encouraging the process behind the scenes was Governor Jindal, who met with every legislator individually.[66] Some of the participants felt they might not be up to the task. House Education Committee Chairman Steven Carter said, "I had no idea how to be a chairman, I mean, I was a tennis coach. And so, when they came to me and said we want this to be the very first bill, I'm thinking, 'Man, what in the heck have I got myself into with this thing?'" To help speed the meeting along, Carter instituted a time limit on testimony saying, "We knew it was going to be a long and contentious meeting. I thought, if we don't put a time limit on the people coming in, we'll never get through. That's when we came up with the idea of a timer. It was a little controversial and had never happened before."[67] That the maximum-speed strategy worked was obvious to *Advocate* reporter Will Sentell, who was following the progress of the bills closely, "These bills went through in 23 days. And that's just unheard of in any process." Part of the reason for the bills' speedy passage was the Jindal team's reluctance to amend or change the legislation. Sentell confirms this: "I think the feeling from Jindal was that 'we've got our plan; we're not really interested in a lot of input even from our allies. And we're going to push it through before the opposition has time to organize and resist.'"[68] Despite their unwillingness to consider amendments, Speaker Chuck Kleckley insisted that legislators' concerns were addressed, "but the compromise and horse trading was done up front" rather than through the amendment process, where it might imperil passage of the legislation. Additionally, Chairman Carter was "very cautious about how the legislation would be heard in committee because he didn't want . . . [members to feel they] didn't have an opportunity to speak for or against it." Carter "wanted to make sure that his committee was very transparent . . . very open . . . that his committee would listen to the folks that were there that would come in to speak."[69] Even though, as Speaker Kleckley points out, they had the votes and did not really need to entertain changes or suggestions. Yet, "We dedicated a full day to education reform. . . . [T]here were no attempts to cut debate."[70]

After the passage of Jindal's education legislation, those involved looked back at their accomplishments. Erin Bendily said, "I'm very proud of the work that we did to initiate those changes and to see how they have played out over time and impacted thousands of children and families. . . . If you look at where we are with early childhood [education], we are leading the country."[71] Nancy Landry agrees, "I was very happy with what got passed. I think that it was a great bold start" and may have changed some perceptions of Louisiana education nationally: "When we go to conferences, national conferences . . . legislators come up to us and say, 'How did y'all get so much done in such a short time? We've been trying to do this one little thing like expand charter schools for years and years, and we've never been able to do it, and you guys pass so many reforms in one session.'"[72]

Louisiana's 2012 education reform demonstrates the episodic nature of policy reform, where innovation may happen quickly when the window of opportunity opens. I've argued above that this process in Louisiana is best described by the multiple-streams framework (MSF) model of public policy, although the testimony of those involved in the reform provides some support for the punctuated equilibrium theory and the innovation and diffusion model as well. One fact seems clear: education reform was made possible through the support and leadership of Governor Jindal, without whom the passage of the massive education package would have been unlikely. Jindal orchestrated the politics of reform masterfully, building a team, developing plans, gathering funds, advancing allies, and then choosing the most propitious moment for passage. This governor-led initiative was somewhat unusual as Will Sentell notes: "For the most part, the [education] initiatives come from the superintendent. What was unusual in 2012 was Jindal wanted to turn things upside down. He wanted to make changes in the state law, and BESE and DOE's input was more incidental."[73] It is hard to imagine education reform of this magnitude taking place without Jindal's complete commitment. The result was the passage of major legislation reshaping public K–12 education in Louisiana.

APPENDIX A: INTERVIEWEES

Senator Conrad Appel, chair, Senate Education Committee, interviewed April 17, 2020
Erin Bendily, associate superintendent of education, Louisiana Department of Education, interviewed July 26, 2021
Representative Steven Carter, chair, House Education Committee, interviewed March 19, 2020
Representative Chuck Kleckley, Speaker, Louisiana House of Representatives, interviewed November 16, 2017
Representative Nancy Landry, House Education Committee, interviewed August 3, 2019
Stafford Palmieri, education policy director, Jindal administration, interviewed July 22, 2 022
Will Sentell, education reporter, the *Advocate*, interviewed August 16, 2019, and October 24, 2022
John White, superintendent of education, Louisiana, interviewed February 22, 2017, and September 4, 2019

NOTES

1. Names and dates of interviewees may be found in appendix A.
2. Editorial, "Jindal's Education Moon Shot: Louisiana Governor Pushes Vouchers and Tenure Reform," *Wall Street Journal*, January 31, 2012; for a negative view of the same legislation, see Jonathan Tilove, "Bobby Jindal's Education Bills 'Obliterate Public Education,' Former Reformer Says," *New Orleans Times-Picayune*, May 10, 2012.
3. Staff, "How Louisiana Became the World's 'Prison Capital,'" *Fresh Air*, NPR, June 5, 2012.
4. Molly Jackman, "ALEC's Influence over Lawmaking in State Legislatures," *Brookings*, December 6, 2013, https://www.brookings.edu/articles/alecs-influence-over-lawmaking-in-state-legislatures/.
5. See Julia O'Donoghue, "Louisiana Political Trends That Took Off in 2014 and Are Likely to Stick Around in 2015," *New Orleans Times-Picayune*, December 29, 2014.
6. A point argued in Jeffrey R. Henig, *The End of Exceptionalism in American Education: The Changing Politics of School Reform* (Cambridge: Harvard Education Press, 2013).
7. A complete list of the interviewees can be found at the end of this chapter.
8. "Theories of the Policy Process: Contemporary Scholarship and Future Directions," *Policy Studies Journal* 42, no. S1 (2014).
9. This, of course, could lead easily to the charge that I've fitted the material to the theory or the theory to the material.
10. This depends on which scholar is doing the counting.
11. Several of the models end up on both lists. Paul A. Sabatier, "An Advocacy Coalition Framework of Policy Change and the Role of Policy-Oriented Learning Therin," *Policy Sciences* 21, nos. 2–3 (1988): 129–68, quoted in Evangelia Petridou and Michael Mintrom, "A Research Agenda for the Study of Policy Entrepreneurs," *The Policy Studies Journal* 49, no. 4 (2021): 943–67.

12. Petridou and Mintrom, "A Research Agenda," 943–67. See Mintrom, "A Research Agenda"; James G. March and Johan P. Olsen, *Rediscovering Institutions: The Organizational Basis of Politics* (New York: Free Press, 1989); Peter V. Evans, Dietrich Rueschemeyer, and Theda Skocpol, eds., *Bringing the State Back In* (New York: Cambridge University Press, 1985).

13. Petridou and Mintrom, "A Research Agenda," 943–67.

14. Petridou, "Theories of the Policy Process: Contemporary Scholarship and Future Directions" *Policy Studies Journal*, 42, Special Issue, 2014, 12–32.

15. Alan Greenblatt, "School Choice Advances in the States," *Education Next* 21, no. 4 (Winter 2021).

16. J. W. Kingdon, *Agendas, Alternatives, and Public Policies*, 2nd ed. (New York: Longman, 2003).

17. Elizabeth A. Koebele, "When Multiple Streams Make a River: Analyzing Collaborative Policymaking Institutions using the Multiple Streams Framework," *Policy Sciences* (2021), 609. Emphasis by Koebele, 2021.

18. Petridou, "Theories of the Policy Process," 12–32.

19. Koebele, "When Multiple Streams Make a River," 611.

20. Kingdon, *Agendas, Alternatives, and Public Policies*, quoted in Koebele, "When Multiple Streams Make a River," 611, possessive added by Cross.

21. N. Herweg, D. HuB, R. Zohlnhofer, "Straightening the Three Streams: Theorizing Extensions of the Multiple Streams Framework," *European Journal of Political Research* 54, no. 3: 435–49, quoted in Koebele, "When Multiple Streams Make a River," 609–28.

22. Petridou and Mintrom, "A Research Agenda" 943–67.

23. Other speakers at the February 1, 2012, conference included Joel Klein, Ben Austin, Senator Mary Landrieu, Jeb Bush, Senator Conrad Appel, John White, Tony Bennett, and organizer Steve Carter. https://www.youtube.com/watch?v=LAFtOltiKkY&list=PL669F00EF3F9475C2&index=2.

24. Bobby Jindal, speech, https://www.youtube.com/watch?v=-QXIynHSatY&list=PL669F00EF3F9475C2&index=6 (part 1 and 2), February 1, 2012.

25. *US News and World Report* placed Louisiana K-12 schools forty-sixth in the country. https://www.usnews.com/news/best-states/rankings/education. This ranking was better than WalletHub, which rated Louisiana forty-ninth out of fifty-one.

26. Leigh Guidry, "Analysis: Louisiana Public Schools Are Third-Worst in the US Who's No. 1?," *Lafayette Daily Advertiser*, July 28, 2022; The state's own figures may been accessed at https://www.louisianabelieves.com/resources/library/performance-scores.

27. Quoted in Will Sentell, "Louisiana Public Schools Still Struggle in National Rankings," *Advocate*, August 3, 2019.

28. Interview, August 4, 2019.

29. Will Sentell, "Louisiana Public Schools Still Struggle in National Rankings," *The Advocate*, August 3, 2019.

30. Chuck Kleckley, interview, November 16, 2017.

31. Editorial Board, "Louisiana's Education Reform Is a Dramatic Plan for Schools and Our Children: An Editorial," *New Orleans Times-Picayune*, April 8, 2012.

32. The only governor with a wider margin of victory than Jindal was the legendary John McKeithen who won the 1967 Democratic gubernatorial primary with 80.64 percent of the vote and then was unopposed by any candidates in the general election.

33. BESE has eight members elected in districts and three members appointed by the governor. https://bese.louisiana.gov/ Revised Statue 17:21 sets the parameters for the superintendent of education.

34. Henig, *The End of Exceptionalism in American Education: The Changing Politics of School Reform* (Cambridge: Harvard Education Press, 2013), 120.

35. Staff, "Jindal Largesse Benefits Legislative and BESE Candidates around La.," *Business Report Staff*, September 21, 2011.

36. Erin Bendily, interview, July 26, 2021. Bendily began on Jindal's staff before moving to the Louisiana DOE as assistant superintendent of education.

37. Will Sentell, interview, August 16, 2019.

38. Stafford Palmieri, interview, July 22, 2022.

39. Kleckley, interview.

40. Bobby Jindal, "Second Louisiana Gubernatorial Inaugural Address," January 9, 2012, *American Rhetoric.com*.

41. Jindal, "Second Louisiana Gubernatorial Inaugural Address."

42. Koebele, "When Multiple Streams Make a River, 612, emphasis mine.

43. "Theories of the Policy Process," S22.

44. Thomas Aswell, "ALEC Spreads the Wealth among Louisiana Legislators to Get Reform Agenda Passed While Trashing Employees, Teachers," March 14, 2012, *Louisianavoice.com*.

45. The success referenced here is passage of the legislation. The results-based evidence on the effectiveness of increasing choice in Louisiana education generally is inconclusive to date. See Anna J. Egalite, Jonathan N. Mills, "Competitive Impacts of Means-Tested Vouchers on Public School Performance: Evidence from Louisiana, Education," *Finance and Policy* 16, no. 1 (2021): 66–91; Jabbar et al., "The Competitive Effects of School Choice on Student Achievement: A Systematic Review," *Educational Policy* 36, no. 2 (2022): 247–81.

46. I've been lucky enough to interview most of the critical members of the Jindal education "team," although a few remain to be interviewed.

47. Nancy Landry, interview, August 3, 2019.

48. Bendily, interview.

49. Palmieri, interview.

50. Conrad Appel, interview, April 17, 2020.

51. These Acts are available online, Act 1: http://www.legis.la.gov/legis/ViewDocument.aspx?d=793654; Act 2: http://www.legis.la.gov/legis/ViewDocument.aspx?d=793655; Act 3: https://www.legis.la.gov/Legis/ViewDocument.aspx?d=800894.

52. Landry served on the education committee during Jindal's second term, and as chair of the House Education Committee during Governor John Bel Edwards's first term, 2015–19, interview, August 3, 2019.

53. Palmieri, interview.

54. Appel, interview.

55. John White, interview, September 4, 2019.

56. Palmieri, interview.

57. Palmieri, interview. John Walters was vice-president of government relations at Chevron.

58. Palmieri, interview.
59. Palmieri, interview.
60. Appel, interview.
61. Bendily, interview.
62. Bendily, interview.
63. Appel, interview.
64. Palmieri, interview.
65. Recruited were Kirk Talbot, Cameron Henry, Alan Seabaugh, and Chris Broadwater. Palmieri indicated there were others as well. Palmieri, interview. The "well" is the area in the front of the legislative chamber where the presenters of bills stand to answer questions.
66. Reported by Speaker Kleckley, interview.
67. Carter noted the timer worked well: "It worked, pretty well. After we did that, a number of other committees did the same thing." Carter, interview, March 19, 2020.
68. Sentell, interview.
69. Kleckley, interview.
70. Kleckley, interview.
71. Bendily, interview.
72. Landry, interview.
73. Sentell, interview.

Chapter Ten

SHOULD I STAY OR GO?

THE SOCIAL, POLITICAL, AND ENVIRONMENTAL CAUSES OF LOUISIANA'S "BRAIN DRAIN"

ROBERT MANN

Writing in the *New Orleans Times-Picayune* in 2014, this author argued that young people disillusioned with Louisiana should consider staying: "You're frustrated with the intolerance of this state? Will your leaving—taking your broadmindedness with you—make Louisiana any more tolerant? Stay here, find like-minded people, organize them, expand your influence, demand change, but don't give up on this amazing, beautiful place. Its good people—flawed as we might be—are worth your efforts."[1]

Three years later, the idealism in that column yielded to harsher reality. Louisiana, even under a more progressive governor committed to investing more in Louisiana's young people, would not soon change course. If the state ever began to address and resolve its myriad social and economic problems, enough to reverse the state's "brain drain," it would not likely happen soon enough to allay the fears and worries of the current generation of Louisianians between the ages of eighteen and thirty—or the generation of young adults after that.

For that reason, I wrote in 2017: "It's time to admit this is a place with no visible promise and little hope. To pretend otherwise is to engage in delusional thinking. We must face facts. I'm not saying everyone should give up and leave. I'm staying and fighting for our future. . . . But if we're staying, we must be honest about Louisiana's deplorable condition and bleak future. . . . It's time to admit that Louisiana is sick and dying."[2]

The concerns expressed in both columns were products of despair over Louisiana government's decades-long refusal to make the state a more progressive state that might attract more young people than it repelled. Even though we know the results we could expect from better state-funded schools, including strong universities, combined with serious and sustained investments in infrastructure and measures to increase social capital, Louisiana's lawmakers have consistently failed to invest in education and other programs aimed at the state's young residents.

Two decades ago, in 2002, Louisiana was among the worst states in almost every category on the annual Annie E. Casey Kid's Count survey. Then, the state was forty-ninth in overall child well-being. In 2022, its position was unchanged. According to the 2022 Kids Count survey, Louisiana remained forty-ninth in overall child well-being. In addition, in the 2022 survey, Louisiana ranked fiftieth in economic well-being, forty-eighth in education, forty-ninth in health, and forty-ninth in family and community. The public outrage in 2022 arising from the tragic, needless deaths of several young children in the Baton Rouge area directed the news media's attention to the chronic underfunding by the state's Department of Children and Family Services, a vital state agency that leaders of both parties have starved of resources for decades.[3]

Evidence that Louisiana is on the cusp of a sustained, broad-based commitment in the well-being of its people is nonexistent. Under Governor John Bel Edwards, the state moved in a more progressive direction, especially regarding health insurance for the working poor. Among his first acts as governor, Edwards moved to expand the Medicaid system to extend health insurance coverage to more than four hundred thousand individuals previously denied coverage. While he stopped the deep cuts to education that his predecessor, Bobby Jindal, instituted, Edwards was unable to persuade the Republican-controlled legislature to invest significantly more state resources in education or any other social or education program.

The administration of these programs may have changed, and the policies might be more progressive in some cases, but since Jindal left office, Louisiana has generally not made any significant new investments in its people beyond expanding Medicaid. And, with Edwards's departure from the state's political scene in January 2024, it is unlikely he will have been replaced by someone more progressive.

Even under Edwards, Louisiana's subservience to industry—particularly the oil and gas and chemical industries—has barely changed. To his credit, Edwards tried to reform the Industrial Tax Credit system that once provided a blank check to industry. (Those reforms may vanish under the next administration.) And he attempted to focus the state on the dangers of climate change and the need to attract industries that are carbon neutral. (Those reforms will also surely disappear under a more conservative successor.)

In other words, under Edwards, Louisiana made incremental progress toward creating a government and economy more hospitable to its highly trained and well-educated young people. That progress can be seen in the fact that, while Louisiana has been among those states with the highest percentage of "brain drain," it is not the worst state in that category. In 2019, a report by the Joint Economic Committee's Senate Republican staff concluded that Louisiana's net brain drain in 2017 put it firmly in the middle of the states with high percentages of brain drain. Still, the report cited Louisiana as a state with high gross and net brain drain but low out-migration, explaining that "the impact of brain drain in these states is lessened by the relatively small share of people born in the state who leave, but this may be cold comfort, as the leavers are better educated than the stayers and the entrants." The committee report further concluded that between 1970 and 2017, Louisiana was among states that saw the biggest increases in gross brain drain (calculated by subtracting the percentage of highly educated stayers from the percentage of highly educated leavers). Separate research by University of Louisiana business economist Gary Wagner (using US Census and American Community Survey data) concluded that from 2007 to 2017, among the nine southeastern states, Louisiana ranked near the bottom (eighth place) in net in-migration of college-educated residents per ten thousand.[4] Another study from 2022 put Louisiana near the middle of the pack of states in the percentage of brain drain, but the results also suggested that Louisiana loses almost a quarter of its college graduates each year to states like Texas and New York. In real numbers, that would be almost ten thousand newly minted college graduates who flee Louisiana each year. If such a trend continued for a decade, it would equal the loss of one hundred thousand college graduates—more than the total of college graduates statewide for two years.[5]

As the US Senate report made clear, to the extent that any state is losing more high-skilled workers than it attracts, that state's economic future is threatened. The committee concluded that "highly-educated [sic] adults flowing to dynamic states with major metropolitan areas are, to a significant extent, leaving behind more rural and post-industrial states. The geographic sorting of the nation's most-educated citizens may be among the factors driving economic stagnation—and declined social capital—in certain areas of the country." The committee report pointed to the threat posed to a state by brain drain. "To the extent that some states become home to large numbers of college graduates while non-graduates come to reside disproportionately in other states, social segregation across regions of the country worsens."[6]

For several decades, Louisiana leaders have lamented and warned about the state's brain drain. "Poor people are not leaving; elderly people are not leaving," then-commissioner of higher education Joe Savoie said in 2001 in response to then-governor Mike Foster's "brain gain" initiative. "The most productive section of our population is leaving in numbers that are alarming." Eight years later, in New Orleans, a New Orleans Civil District judge, Michael Bagneris, spoke to a group of young professionals about the same issue, one that only grew worse after Hurricane Katrina in 2006. "New Orleans has and continues to have a serious brain drain," Bagneris said. "The only way we're going to be able to keep young folks here is to let them know about opportunities available in the city. We, as a city, haven't offered those opportunities to young people." In 2002, the *Baton Rouge Advocate* spent months investigating and documenting the state's brain drain. Among other things, it polled 750 registered Louisiana voters and found that 45 percent of those with some college education wanted to leave the state.[7]

More than twenty years later, the problem and the debate about it persist. Despite decades of speeches, white papers, plans, and legislation aimed at keeping young professionals and other skilled workers in Louisiana, it appears that most of the progress Louisiana will see in creating a more hospitable climate for its young people—at least in the short-term—has been accomplished. The next administration may return to the well-worn playbook used by leaders in most states, but to near perfection in Louisiana: recruit jobs, regardless of their environmental or social impact, by offering generous corporate or personal tax incentives. The evidence suggests that this does not work. If it did, Louisiana would have the most vibrant economy in the nation, and any talk of "brain drain" would have ceased decades ago.

To the contrary, as studies by Together Louisiana (a liberal public-advocacy group) and other organizations have shown, in recent years, no state has awarded business and industry more tax incentives per capita—all ostensibly aimed at job creation and worker retention—than Louisiana. Data from the organization Subsidy Tracker—collected and analyzed by Together Louisiana—suggest that no state awarded more in state and local tax exemptions to corporations, per capita, between 2011 and 2014, than Louisiana: $2,857 per resident in corporate subsidies versus $89 per resident in Texas during the same period; $334 in Mississippi; $221 in Alabama; $102 in Arkansas. The second-most-generous state from 2011 to 2015 was Washington State, with less than half the subsidy of Louisiana per resident, $1,293.[8]

Additional data from Subsidy Tracker, which collects and aggregates public data from state government sources, show the extent of Louisiana's relative generosity to industry. Since 1995, Louisiana has awarded $25.665 billion in state and local tax exemptions to business and industry (the majority that since 2012). Put in perspective, Louisiana has given up more than four times as much tax revenue as California, a state with almost nine times as many residents (4.5 million versus 39 million). Since 1995 (mostly since 2012), California has award $5.464 billion in state and local tax exemptions. The most generous state in actual dollars since 1980 is New York, which has 18.8 million residents and awarded industry $42.826 billion. On a per capita basis, however, Louisiana was far more generous than California or New York.[9]

None of this resulted in robust economic growth over the past decade. Instead, Louisiana's average economic growth has been anemic, at best. Up to this point, many state leaders have operated mostly out of a mindset that our economic and social problems are entirely the result of tax policies that discourage business from locating or thriving here. Despite the pervasive myth promulgated by the business lobby that Louisiana is a high-tax state, Louisiana has for decades worked hard to help businesses avoid and evade taxes. The record is clear: if lower taxes was the cure for our ills, Louisiana would be in almost perfect economic health.[10]

Given the likelihood that, in the next administration, Louisiana will revert to the days of generous tax breaks for industry, we can expect two outcomes: Louisiana will return to fiscal crisis, but its economic health will remain as anemic as usual. If all Louisiana leaders will do to improve the state's social and economic life is adjust tax rates around the margins, it is reasonable to expect only minor change. But change is coming, just not what state leaders desire. And soon, all the economic adjustments in the world may not be enough to rescue Louisiana from the implications of the economic and environmental changes now occurring and, in some cases, accelerating.

Most debates about Louisiana's brain drain have focused on providing the economic incentives that might persuade young, college-educated residents to remain in the state. Chief among them is increasing job opportunities for recent college graduates and guaranteeing them and their employers low state and local tax rates. Debates about the cause of brain drain rarely extend to other factors that, within a few years, may become as or more significant than employment and taxes and may only accelerate the out-migration of college-educated young people.

One factor that policy makers concerned about brain drain might consider is the impact of the new state law that criminalizes abortion, even in cases of rape and incest, and permits it only in narrowly defined cases. Already, Louisiana has seen hospitals refuse to provide services to pregnant women with life-threatening complications. As cases like these continue to be reported in the press and individuals, particularly women of child-bearing age, begin to assess their rights under the law, it is possible we may see increased out-migration of women, particularly those who can afford to choose where they live and work. Physicians who provide care to pregnant women may also leave the state or choose not to relocate here for fear of being charged with a crime. It is also possible this law could make it harder for universities to recruit women to leave states that guarantee reproductive freedom for faculty and staff positions in a state that not only lacks such freedom but that makes medical professionals vulnerable to criminal prosecution in the case of a miscarriage, or that makes it difficult for them to obtain emergency obstetrical care. It is also possible that universities, like Tulane University, that attract widely from out of state will find their student recruiting efforts complicated and hindered by Louisiana's antiabortion law.

Major corporations may also discover that the law inhibits their ability to attract top talent to Louisiana. State officials may also find abortion laws a point of contention when recruiting business to relocate or expand in Louisiana. The *New Orleans Times-Picayune* reported in May 2019 on what the business community expected in Louisiana if the US Supreme Court overturned *Roe v. Wade*: "Business owners, particularly those in the tech sector, say New Orleans' image could suffer among the younger workers they hope to attract, making it harder to hire good people." The newspaper quoted Michael Hecht, president and CEO of Greater New Orleans Inc., saying, "This legislation [the trigger law that took effect after *Roe* was overturned] has the potential to impact economic development in Greater New Orleans, as we have heard concerns from companies both considering our region and those already located here." As one tech executive said in an interview with the newspaper, "I don't need any more roadblocks and challenges when I'm trying to bring people here to work with us." Another tech executive remarked, "If I'm trying to recruit people to a state that has legislation on its books that is hostile to women and their autonomy over their own bodies, I imagine that would be very difficult. There are other places I can open an office."[11]

Concerns about the impact of a state's antiabortion laws on economic development are not confined to Louisiana. After Indiana passed a similarly restrictive antiabortion law in 2022, Michael J. Hicks, the director of the Center for Business and Economic Research at Ball State University wrote: "Hoosier employers will be selectively disinvited from job fairs across the country. More importantly, college students will actively look in places with more mainstream legislation, or seek remote work from those business." Hicks added, "Businesses located in states with highly restrictive abortion laws are at a significant hiring disadvantage." As Sandy Baruah, president of the Detroit Regional Chamber, wrote in the *New York Times* in July 2022: "An extreme response is not in the state's competitive interest. To the extent that the data shows today that young professionals care about this issue, I don't want to give young professionals a reason not to come to Michigan to work for Michigan companies." In North Carolina, Democratic governor Roy Cooper said he believed "an abortion ban would have a negative effect on economic growth here in our state."[12]

While the state's abortion laws can and may change year to year, there is another factor that may hasten out-migration, and one that cannot be prevented by state laws, at least in the short-term. A large swath of coastal south Louisiana is threatened by the inexorable impact of sea-level rise, coastal wetland loss, and land subsidence, a potential triple whammy that makes Louisiana among the most vulnerable places on Earth to the effects of climate change. And effects of sea-level rise and warming temperatures might not be limited to low-lying communities threatened by ever-strengthening hurricanes that batter the coast from year to year. By one estimate, 100 million Americans—most of them in the Mississippi River basin from Louisiana to Wisconsin—will someday face humidity so intense that outdoor work or recreation during the summer months will be dangerous or impossible. Another factor already threatening communities along the coast is saltwater intrusion that makes it harder for many cities and towns to guarantee their residents safe drinking water. All of this and more might eventually force hundreds of thousands of Louisiana's residents, many of them along the coast, to move north or leave Louisiana altogether.[13]

Any talk about a potential mass exodus from Louisiana, especially from coastal and southern Louisiana, must reckon with the fact that the exodus is already occurring, albeit slowly and in fits and starts. In August 2022, for example, the *Baton Rouge Advocate* documented the wholesale relocation of the residents of Isle de Jean Charles, a spit of land amidst marsh and coastal prairie about forty-five miles south of New Orleans and, until recently, settled by the Jean Charles Choctaw Nation. As Craig E. Colten, an emeritus professor of geography at Louisiana State University, has noted in a concise summary of recent literature about out-migration in coastal Louisiana:

> Louisiana coastal residents have been moving inland for more than a century, and resettlement [because of sea-level rise] is an obvious option. Young people are leaving their home towns and relocating to urban centers farther from the coast. This has been a slow, multigenerational process without government assistance. After Hurricane Katrina, there was considerable relocation away from some of the most severely damaged neighborhoods in New Orleans. Additionally, the "immovable industries"—minerals, fishing, and shipping—no

longer rely solely on local employees. Workers on offshore platforms commonly commute from states well removed from the coast. Fishing and shipping employees, likewise, can drive longer distances than in the past, even if just from neighboring parishes.[14]

Until recently, the out-migration in southern Louisiana was confined mostly to smaller towns and villages. And, while the reasons for leaving might be the rising seas or the rising threats posed by monster hurricanes, the population decline in towns in rural America is not unique to coastal Louisiana. Until the past two decades, it seemed that cities such as New Orleans, Houma, Lafayette, and Lake Charles were mostly immune from the worst effects of hurricanes and climate change. But hurricanes such as Katrina, Rita, Gustave, Laura, and Ida have changed that equation. Because of the disappearance of the coastal marshes that once helped sap these storms of their worst punch before they reached places like Baton Rouge—and the increase in the severity of these storms as they approach the coast—communities a hundred miles or more inland are no longer immune from the severe effects of a hurricane. After Ida, the residents of many south Louisiana communities realized that the infrastructure they once thought could withstand a hurricane could not do so. Hundreds of thousands of residents across south Louisiana—in cities and towns, alike—were without power for weeks after Ida hit in August 2021. Communities in and around Lake Charles experienced the same after Laura in 2020. Residents in Baton Rouge understand they may have been sparred a similar fate when Ida tracked in a northwesterly direction after landfall. These residents, however, know it is only a matter of time until their community is hit with a devastating blow.[15]

No storm demonstrated the impact a hurricane can have on the willingness or ability of residents to remain in a city or region more than Katrina in 2006. As Jean-Marc Zaninetti and Craig E. Colten have observed, "Clearly, Hurricane Katrina has caused an unprecedented population shock in the history of American cities. Though the city of New Orleans's population has been declining since 1960, its demographic loss was balanced by its expanding suburbs until 2005. The storm caused the entire metropolitan area to shrink, at an unprecedented scale." As Zaninetti and Colten noted, Orleans Parish had an estimated population in July 2005 of 454,085, down by more than 172,000 during the preceding forty-five years. Between 2006 and 2012, New Orleans lost another 111,000 residents. "The long decline of the City of New Orleans is not an exception in the United States," the authors noted, "but its scale is comparable to some of the most extreme rust-belt industrial cities, which are mostly located in the Northeast or in the Middle West, and not in the American South."[16]

After Katrina, and before Laura and Ida, it may have been possible for those in south Louisiana to rest easy in the belief that the exodus from New Orleans, post-Katrina, was a once-in-a-thousand-year event. While it may have had cataclysmic effects, it was not likely to happen anywhere else and especially not in New Orleans after the federal government strengthened the levee and flood-control system around the city and throughout the region. But those who rest in the knowledge that their communities are surrounded by federal or other levees may soon find that that these "protections" do not guarantee their safety as much as they might hope, nor do they protect them from the whims and economic pressures of the flood and homeowners' insurance markets.

While it is true that many communities have adapted to climate change as best as possible—and the state and federal governments have made significant investments in shoring up levees and funding other prevention and mitigation efforts—continued adaptations may prove too expensive in the face of the predicted sea-level rise of one to three feet between now and 2050. Already, Louisiana residents along the coast are on the move, and as hurricanes worsen and sea-level rise continues, that movement will continue and may accelerate. Many Louisiana residents will move further inland, but many others will leave the state in search of better jobs or to escape the near-yearly disruption and pain of hurricane season. Such large-scale movements of people in response to economic or social conditions are not unheard of in the United States. For example, the migration of as many as 2.5 million people from the American Midwest during the 1930s in response to the Dust Bowl; the exodus of more than 6 million Black people from the South from 1915 to 1965; and, most recently, the massive relocation of the residents of New Orleans after Hurricane Katrina. Now, in the face of accelerating climate change, the World Bank estimates that more than 200 million people around the world could migrate by 2050 to escape climate effects. In a lengthy 2020 report on US internal migration because of climate change, *ProPublica* estimated "some 162 million people—nearly 1 in 2—will most likely experience a decline in the quality of their environment, namely more heat and less water." The report cited a 2018 study in the *Journal of the Association of Environmental and Resource Economists* that suggested 6 percent of Americans in the South will move toward California, the Mountain West, or the Northwest over the next forty-five years because of climate influences alone. It would be folly for political leaders and policy makers in Louisiana to pretend that such a mass exodus from Louisiana would be impossible given the right economic and environmental conditions. As an official with the National Oceanic and Atmospheric Administration said 2013, "today's flood is tomorrow's high tide."[17]

There is another factor in this equation that may trump the impact of rising seas, increased humidity, saltwater intrusion, and strengthening hurricanes: the inability of homeowners and business owners in coastal Louisiana to obtain or afford flood and/or property insurance on their homes or businesses. As *ProPublica* said in 2020, "Perhaps no market force has proved more influential—and more misguided—than the nation's property-insurance system. From state to state, readily available and affordable policies have made it attractive to buy or replace homes even where they are at high risk of disasters, systematically obscuring the reality of the climate threat and fooling many Americans into thinking that their decisions are safer than they actually are." In Louisiana, homeowners can expect to see, on average, a 122 percent increase in their flood insurance premiums over the next few years. This has led to fears that skyrocketing flood insurance rates will prevent many homeowners in coastal Louisiana from insuring their homes against hurricane damage resulting from rising water. From June 2021 to June 2022, the number of Louisiana flood insurance policies fell by 7.8 percent. In registering their concerns about the impact of rising flood insurance rates, US Senators Bill Cassidy and John N. Kennedy of Louisiana told FEMA in July 2022, "In five to 10 years, we will start to see a sizable number of Americans who can't afford to pay for [national flood insurance] . . . and remain in their homes."[18]

The problem is not limited to the rising cost of flood insurance. Increasingly, companies that write homeowners insurance policies in Louisiana are leaving the state or declaring insolvency. Since summer 2020, almost two dozen insurance companies writing homeowners policies in Louisiana have gone out of business or have notified the Louisiana Department of Insurance of their decision to stop writing policies in Louisiana. State Commissioner of Insurance Jim Donelon has called the situation a "crisis." Because the state cannot always find a buyer for these policies, thousands of homeowners now rely upon the state-supported "Louisiana Citizens" plan to provide them expensive, temporary, scaled-back coverage. In many cases, the premium for this lesser coverage is twice what the homeowner was once paying. In September 2022, Citizens applied for a 63 percent rate hike on new or renewed residential policies. "It could completely change the face of lower portions of Lafourche and Terrebonne parishes because people won't be able to afford to live there," Representative Jerome Zeringue of Houma told a reporter in 2022. "A lot of people are already choosing to relocate. They just won't be able to afford to live here."

"If more big providers leave the state in the coming years," one analysis of the situation by the publication *Grist* concluded, "it could trigger a downward spiral in the housing market. Not only would Citizens struggle to stay afloat as more customers seek public-option coverage but individual costs for homeowners on the private market would also soar as companies sought to maintain profit margins." As *ProPublica* observed, "In an era of climate change ... such policies amount to a sort of shell game, meant to keep growth going even when other obvious signs and scientific research suggests that it should stop." Such a scenario is unfolding in Florida, *Grist* noted, adding, "Farther down the road, lenders might hesitate to write [mortgage] loans in areas where they know the insurance market is thin, which would make it more difficult for many buyers to secure mortgages." As *ProPublica* noted, Florida taxpayers by 2012 had assumed $511 billion in publicly provided homeowners' insurance policies, seven times as large as the state's budget. In response, the state scaled back its aggressive self-insurance program. It is possible that Louisiana will eventually be forced to do the same.[19]

The risk of all this to the future of coastal Louisiana is clear. If homeowners cannot insure their houses, they cannot obtain a mortgage. If a home cannot be sold because it is uninsurable, that home's price will drop in value, if not evaporate. As *New Orleans Times-Picayune* columnist Bob Marshall wrote in May 2019, envisioning the impact of the collapse of the state's insurance market, "So, what do you think this means to the future business opportunities, mortgage rates and all other costs of living in south Louisiana—an area this state already admits is one of the riskiest places to climate change impacts in North America? You don't have to be a stable genius to figure this one out."[20]

Under Governor John Bel Edwards's administration, Louisiana government began trying to slow down the damage climate change will do to the state. Edwards supported coastal restoration and public-works projects aimed at protecting coastal cities and towns. He backed alternative energy sources and worked to attract carbon-neutral industry to the state. But the state's political leaders have not followed his lead. While US Representative Garret Graves is a leader on this issue on the Republican side, there is little evidence to suggest that other GOP leaders desire any substantive government action to combat climate change. Graves, himself, has essentially toed his party's line on the desire to double down on fossil fuels as a foundation of Louisiana's economy. Other state leaders are even more aggressive about the need to reinvest in fossil fuels to the exclusion renewable energy sources.[21]

While Louisiana's legislature and its congressional delegation cannot do much to affect global climate, they could acknowledge the existential threat that climate change and sea-level rise pose to Louisiana. While many of them are fighting for lower flood-insurance prices, there are other roles the federal and state governments can take to increase the resilience of local communities to sea-level rise. This might include even greater investment in flood protection. They could support more public-works projects, such as those funded by the Inflation Reduction Act of 2022, which included $2.6 billion projects supporting natural resources in coastal and marine communities, including wetland restoration. Louisiana and federal government leaders could also create an updated home appraisal process that rewards hazard-resistant construction. Federal and state funding could be used to spark investment into resilient home retrofits that reduce home insurance rates.[22]

Louisiana leaders might also awaken to the signal that the state's political and social policies send to highly educated young Louisiana residents, especially women, who have the means to move elsewhere and the skills thrive in a more progressive state. They might also awaken to the ways that Louisiana's official posture on climate change, reproductive rights, and a host of other issues say to those considering bringing their skilled labor here that it is only their labor, and nothing more, that are desired.

For all the aforementioned reasons, and more, Louisiana is on a path that could render it an even poorer, depopulated, partly submerged state whose leaders in the early part of the twenty-first century were focused on loyalty to dying industries and strict adherence to backward and highly discriminatory social policies. This writer would love nothing more than to conclude that his words of warnings from 2017 were misguided or premature, but little in the state's recent past or its near-certain future suggests that this is true.

NOTES

1. Robert Mann, "Louisiana's Young People Are Asking, 'Should I Stay or Should I Go?,'" *New Orleans Times-Picayune*, January 3, 2014.

2. Robert Mann, "Let's Face Fact: Louisiana Is Sick and Dying," *New Orleans Times-Picayune*, September 8, 2017.

3. "Survey Examines Children," *Shreveport Times*, May 23, 2002; "2022 Kids Count Data Book: 2022 State Trends in Child Well-Being," Annie E. Casey Foundation, August 8, 2022, https://www.aecf.org/resources/2022-kids-count-data-book; "In Louisiana's Child Welfare System, Senate Testimony Reveals 'Every Day Is Excruciating,'" *Baton Rouge Advocate*, September 9, 2022.

4. "Losing Our Minds: Brain Drain across the United States," *Joint Economic Committee-Republicans, US Senate, SCP Report No. 2-19*, April 2019; "Leaving Louisiana with a Degree: College-Educated Residents Going to Texas, And It's Getting Worse," *Baton Rouge Advocate*, November 28, 2019.

5. Johnathan G. Conzelmann, et al., "Grads on the Go: Measuring College-Specific Labor Markets for Graduates," NBER Working Paper No. 30088 May 2022, http://www.nber.org/papers/w30088; "The Movies Most Often Assigned in College, and More!," *Washington Post*, September 9, 2022.

6. "Losing Our Minds: Brain Drain across the United States."

7. "Foster Wants to Plug 'Brain Drain,'" *New Orleans Times-Picayune*, October 26, 2001; "Initiative Focuses on 'Brain Retain,'" *New Orleans Times-Picayune*, February 7, 2009; "State Brain Drain Easing?" *New Orleans Times-Picayune*, September 22, 1990; "Some Good News About 'Brain Drain,'" *Baton Rouge Advocate*, May 12, 1998; "Measures Aim to Keep 'Brains' in Louisiana," *Baton Rouge Advocate*, February 1, 2002; "Work Force Key to La. Future," *Baton Rouge Advocate*, October 14, 2007; "Louisianians Like It Here and Plan to Stay," *Baton Rouge Advocate*, January 13, 2002.

8. Together Louisiana, "Wealth, Poverty and Property Taxes," August 2018, 33, https://d3n8a8pro7vhmx.cloudfront.net/togetherbr/pages/2319/attachments/original/1543526419/2018-8-21_Session1_ITEP_Final_Print_version.pdf?1543526419.

9. Subsidy Tracker, "State Totals," https://subsidytracker.goodjobsfirst.org/state-totals.

10. FRED Economic Data, St. Louis Fed, https://fred.stlouisfed.org/series/LANGSP; "Best and Worst State Economies," *WalletHub*, June 6, 2022; "GDP by State," Bureau of Economic Analysis, US Department of Commerce, https://www.bea.gov/data/gdp/gdp-state.

11. "Backlash over Louisiana's Abortion Law? Business, Tourism Officials Brace for 'Fallout,'" *New Orleans Times-Picayune*, May 30, 2019.

12. Michael J. Hicks, "Abortion Ban Will Be Deeply Damaging to Indiana's Economy," *Greater Fort Wayne Business Weekly*, August 16, 2022; "States with Abortion Bans Risk Losing Their Economic Edge," *New York Times*, July 11, 2022.

13. "Hurricane Ian Is No Anomaly. The Climate Crisis Is Making Storms More Powerful," *The Guardian*, September 30, 2022; "Mississippi River Levels Are Dropping Too Low for Barges to Float," *Washington Post*, October 12, 2022; "Study Finds Climate Change Is Bringing More Intense Rains to U.S.," *Washington Post*, October 11, 2022; Colin Raymond, et al., "The Emergence of Heat and Humidity Too Severe for Human Tolerance," *Science Advances* 6, no. 19 (May 8, 2020), https://www.science.org/doi/10.1126/sciadv.aaw1838.

14. Craig E. Colten, *State of Disaster: A Historical Geography of Louisiana's Land Loss* (Baton Rouge: Louisiana State University Press, 2021), 143.

15. "The Last Days of Isle de Jean Charles: A Louisiana Tribe's Struggle to Escape the Rising Sea," *Baton Rouge Advocate*, August 28, 2022; "'Can't Take In': Living Conditions Deteriorate in Lake Charles Public Housing," *Baton Rouge Advocate*, September 25, 2022.

16. Jean-Marc Zaninetti and Craig E. Colten "Shrinking New Orleans: Post-Katrina Population Adjustments," *Urban Geography* 33, no. 5 (2012): 675–99.

17. "Climate Migration and Climate Finance: Lessons from Central America," Brookings Institution, November 19, 2021; "Climate Change Will Force a New American Migration," *ProPublica*, September 15, 2020; Qin Fan, Karen Fisher-Vanden, and H. Allen Kaibler, "Climate Change, Migration, and Regional Economic Impacts in the United States," *Journal of the Association of Environmental and Resource Economists* 5, no. 3 (July 2018); "Climate: 'Today's Flood Is Tomorrow's High Tide,'" *Summit Country Citizens Voice*, January 18, 2013, https://summitvoice.wordpress.com/2013/01/18/climate-todays-flood-is-tomorrows-high-tide/.

18. "Flood Insurance to Rise 122% on Average in Louisiana, Data Show," *New Orleans Times-Picayune*, August 27, 2022.

19. "Louisiana Homeowners, Insurance Brokers Seeing Premiums Skyrocket Amid Marketplace 'Crisis,'" *New Orleans Times-Picayune*, August 3, 2022; "Eighth Louisiana

Homeowners Insurer Goes Under, Stranding 10,300 Policyholders," *New Orleans Times-Picayune*, August 5, 2022; "Ninth Insurer In Louisiana Goes Under," *Baton Rouge Advocate*, September 26, 2022; "Insurance Meltdown Leaves Homeowners without Policies and at Risk," *Bloomberg*, July 1, 2022; "Louisiana Insurance Crisis Could Crush Home Ownership Dreams in Coastal Regions," *Houma Today*, September 22, 2022; "Louisiana's Insurance Market Is Collapsing, Just in Time for Hurricane Season," *Grist*, July 24, 2022; "Insurer of Last Resort Prepares for Worst," *Baton Rouge Advocate*, August 17, 2022; "Louisiana Citizens Wants 63% Rate Increase for Homeowners' Policies amid Failures," *Baton Rouge Advocate*, September 13, 2022; "Climate Change Will Force a New American Migration," *ProPublica*, September 15, 2020.

20. "Attention Louisiana Climate Deniers: Insurers Say Climate Change Now Biggest Risk," *New Orleans Times-Picayune*, May 12, 2019.

21. "Where the New Climate Law Means More Drilling, Not Less," *New York Times*, September 14, 2022.

22. "Billions in Climate Deal Funding Could Help Protect U.S. Coastal Cities," *New York Times*, September 20, 2022.

ABOUT THE CONTRIBUTORS

JANET ALLURED, PhD, retired professor of history and director of women's studies at McNeese State University in Lake Charles, Louisiana, is currently adjunct professor of women's history at the University of Arkansas. She has authored numerous peer-reviewed articles on southern women and has coedited several volumes in Louisiana history, including one in the University of Georgia Press's series on southern women entitled *Louisiana Women: Their Lives and Times* (2009). *Remapping Second-Wave Feminism: The Long Women's Rights Movement in Louisiana, 1950–1997* was also published with Georgia (2016). She is currently editing a collection of biographies on southern Methodist women who were agents of progressive change and is writing a monograph on the same subject.

CRAIG E. COLTEN, PhD, is a professor emeritus of geography at Louisiana State University and a senior advisor to the Water Institute of the Gulf. He has carried out research on Louisiana's environmental historical geography for more than twenty years. His most recent books include *State of Disaster* (2021) and *Southern Waters* (2014). He will be Landhaus Fellow at the Rachel Carson Center in Munich, Germany, this coming winter.

MARCUS S. COX, PhD, serves as dean of the College of Humanities and Social Sciences and professor of history at Fayetteville State University, Fayetteville, North Carolina. He is author of over two dozen articles, reviews, and book chapters in peer-reviewed journals and academic publications on the history of African American military figures, Black higher education, and military training programs at Black colleges and universities. He is also author of *Segregated Soldiers: Military Training at Historically Black Colleges in the Jim Crow South*. He currently serves as a Fellow at the Jenny Craig Institute for the Study of War and Democracy at the National WWII Museum in New Orleans, Louisiana, member of the Veterans Rural Health Advisory Committee to the US secretary of veteran affairs, and former Advisory Committee member for the Roundtable Discussion on Diversity and Inclusion, United States Army Training and Doctrine Command.

PEARSON CROSS, PhD, is director of the School of Behavioral and Social Sciences at the University of Louisiana at Monroe, where he teaches political science. His most recent book is *The Party Is Over: The New Louisiana Politics* (2022). His current research focuses on the politics of education during the Jindal administration.

JOHN BEL EDWARDS is a graduate of the United States Military Academy at West Point and a US Army veteran. He served two terms in the Louisiana state legislature. He is currently completing his second term as governor of the state of Louisiana.

ADAM FAIRCLOUGH, PhD, is Professor Emeritus of American History at the Leiden University Institute for History (Leiden University Chair of the History and Culture of North America, from 2005 to 2016) and is author of the following four books: *Race and Democracy: The Civil Rights Struggle in Louisiana, 1915–72* (1995); *The Star Creek Papers: Washington Parish and the Lynching of Jerome Wilson* (1997); *The Revolution That Failed: Reconstruction in Natchitoches* (2018); and *Bulldozed and Betrayed: Louisiana and the Stolen Elections of 1876* (2021).

KEITH M. FINLEY, PhD, is assistant professor of history at Southeastern Louisiana University and assistant director of the Center for Southeast Louisiana Studies. He is author of the award-winning book *Delaying the Dream: Southern Senators and the Fight against Civil Rights, 1938–1965*.

SAMUEL C. HYDE JR., PhD, is Leon Ford Endowed Chair, professor of history, and director of the Center for Southeast Louisiana Studies at Southeastern Louisiana University. He is author of multiple books, including the award-winning *Pistols and Politics: Feuds, Factions, and the Struggle for Order in Louisiana's Florida Parishes, 1810–1935*, and is screenwriter for five docudrama films including *American Crisis, American Shame: The National Consequence of Coastal Erosion*, recipient of a Gold Medal at the New York International Independent Film and Video Festival.

JOHN A. LOPEZ, PhD, previously worked in coastal restoration for the US Army Corps of Engineers and Pontchartrain Conservancy and currently works with the Center for Sustainable Engagement and Development to formulate alternatives to sustainably manage the Lower Mississippi River. He supervised the reconstruction of the New Canal Lighthouse and is the coastal scientist who developed the Multiple Lines of Defense System. He is soon to publish a novel set in New Orleans titled "Blind in Two Eyes."

ROBERT MANN, MA, holds the Manship Chair in Journalism at the Manship School of Mass Communication at Louisiana State University. He is author of critically acclaimed political histories of the US civil rights movement, the Vietnam War, American wartime dissent, and the 1964 presidential election. His newest book, *Kingfish U: Huey Long and LSU*, published by Louisiana State University Press appeared in 2023. Mann's op-eds and essays have appeared in the *New York Times*, the *Washington Post*, the Boston *Globe*, *Politico*, *Salon*, *Vox*, and *Smithsonian* magazine. From 2013 to 2018, Mann wrote a weekly political column in the *New Orleans Times-Picayune*. In the early 1980s, he covered Louisiana politics as a reporter for the *Shreveport Journal* and the *Monroe News-Star*. Before joining the Louisiana State University faculty in 2006, Mann spent more than twenty years in the political arena as a senior aide to three United States senators and a Louisiana governor.

INDEX

Alario, John, 203
Alexander, Avery, 11–12
Allured, Janet, xii
Amite City, Louisiana, 104, 106–7, 174
Apodaca v. Oregon, 92
Appel, Conrad, 203, 206–9
Ascension Parish, 180–82, 184
Aymond, Kayla, 72–74

backcountry justice, 101
Baptist Message, 23–28
Baton Rouge, Louisiana, ix, xvi, 17, 23, 49–50, 53, 81, 117, 160, 163, 180–82, 200, 216
Baton Rouge City Court, 76
Blanco, Kathleen, 121, 154
Bogalusa, Louisiana, 6, 49, 53, 177–78
Boggs, Lindy, 121
Brian, Hardy, 97
Brown, Jim, 74
Brown v. Topeka Board of Education, 5, 23, 29
Burke, E. A., 67
Butler, Ben, 67

Calhoon, Soloman S., 91
Canellos, Peter, 12
Carter, Hodding, 101
Cassidy, Bill, 134
Cawthorn, Lynn, 82
Chenoweth, Erica, 116
Citizens Committee, 8
Citizens' Council, 24–25, 28, 33
civil code, viii
Clay, Henry, 12

Cody, John P., 33–35
Colten, Craig, xiv, 221–22
Comite River Diversion, 183
Congress on Racial Equality (CORE), 53–54, 56–57
Costello, Frank, 68
Covington, Louisiana, 8, 10
Cox, Marcus, x
Criswell, Wallie Amos, 25
Cross, Pearson, xv
Cunningham, M. J., 102

Deacons for Defense and Justice, x, 54–55
Deepwater Horizon (DWH), xiii, 155, 157, 161
Denham Springs, Louisiana, 182
Dillingham, Kate, 12
Dobbs v. Jackson Women's Health Organization, 125, 133–34, 136, 137
Dodd, Bill, 65, 81
Double V campaign, 46
Draughon, Avery, 105, 107–8
Draughon, R. L., 100, 108
Dred Scott, 9, 13
Duke, David, 72

Edmonson, Michael, 81–82
Edwards, Edwin, 72, 74, 83
Edwards, John Bel, viii, xvi, 134, 216–17, 225
election of 1896, 96, 98, 101, 106
Ellender, Allen, 24

Fairclough, Adam, x, xi
Farmer, James, 56–59

INDEX

Federal Bureau of Investigation (FBI), xi, 68, 69, 74, 75, 77, 78, 80, 81, 109
Ferguson, John, 8–9, 11
Finley, Keith, ix
Florida parishes, xiv, 6, 98, 167–68, 171–72, 175, 184
Foster, Mike, 154, 218
Foster, Murphy J., 6, 97–98, 104, 107
Fourteenth Amendment, 9–10, 93, 95, 123
Fowler, Jerry, 74
Friedman, Milton, 196

Gagliano, Woody, 152–53
Gallot, Rick, 79
Gill, James, 83
Gordon, Spiver, 57
Grambling State University, 26
Great Southern Lumber Company, 6, 177
Gremillion, Jack, 68
Gulf Intracoastal Waterway, 150

Hair, William Ivy, 67
Hammond, Louisiana, 102, 174
Hannan, Philip, 32, 35
Harlan, John Marshall, 9, 11, 13
Harlan, Robert J., 12
Harvey, H. H., 124
Hayes, Rutherford B., 11
homeowners' insurance crisis, 224
Houma, Louisiana, 222, 224
Hurricane Katrina, xiii, 75–76, 153–56, 158–59, 162, 218; relocation of population after, 221–23
hurricanes, impact of, 222–23
Hyde, Samuel C., 6
Hyde Amendment, 137

Industrial Tax Credit system, 216
Ironclad Oath, 94

Jackson, Katrina, 132, 135–36
Jefferson, William, 72
Jemison, T. J., 15, 17–18, 21, 36, 49, 51–52

Jindal, Bobby, xv, xvi, 76, 78–79, 81, 196, 200–210; cuts to education, 216
Jones, Johnnie A., 21–22, 48–49, 52
Jonesboro, Louisiana, 53–54
Jumel, Allen, 107

Kellogg, William Pitt, 67
Kentwood, Louisiana, 176
King, Martin Luther, Jr., 15, 22, 49
Kleckley, Chuck, 202–4, 209–10
Kruttschnitt, E. B., 91, 98–100
Ku Klux Klan, 52–54

Lafayette, Louisiana, 222
Lafourche Parish, 224
Lake Charles, Louisiana, 222
Lake Charles Port Commission, 73
Lake Maurepas, 180
Lake Pontchartrain, 8, 167, 181
LeBlanc, Fred S., 20
Leche, Richard (Dick), 68
Lechtreck, Elaine, 16
Lee, George A., 25–26, 28
Liebling, A. J., 66
Livingston Parish, 180, 184
Long, Earl, 68
Long, Huey, 68
Long, Russell, 24
Lopez, John, xiii, 154
Louisiana Association of Business and Industry, 129, 202, 205
Louisiana Constitution of 1845, 94
Louisiana Constitution of 1852, 94
Louisiana Constitution of 1868, 94–95
Louisiana Constitution of 1879, 95, 97
Louisiana Constitution of 1898, xi, 6, 10, 90–91, 96, 100, 107–9
Louisiana elected officials, 69–70; convicted of corruption, 76
Louisiana Lottery Company, 67
Louisiana sheriffs, convicted of corruption, 70–71
Louisiana State University (LSU), 123, 150
Lynch, Bill, 72, 83

Maginnis, John, 65, 68
Mann, Robert, xvi, xvii
Marcello, Carlos, 68, 80
Marshall, John, 11
Martinet, Louis, 8
Martiny, Danny, 79
Mayfield, Irvin, 76
McClendon, W. H., 104
McKeithen, John, 118
McMichael, Pleasant P., 102–3
Mid-Barataria Sediment Diversion, 162
Miller, Dorie, 47
Mississippi River, xiii, 150, 159–64
Monroe, Louisiana, 53
Moore, Henson, 175
Moore, Ronnie, 57–58
Morel, Harry, 77
multiple-lines-of-defense strategy, xiii, 154–56
multiple-streams framework (MSF), 197, 199, 205, 210
Murray, Edmund, 11

NAACP, 33, 49, 53, 56
Nagin, Ray, 72, 76
National Organization for Women (NOW), 117–18, 122
New Orleans, xiii, 8, 10, 27, 35–36, 57, 74, 78; impact of hurricanes in, 222–23; police department corruption, 81, 100, 107, 117, 156, 158–59, 163, 218
Nichols, Francis T., 8

Orleans Levee Board, 73
Orleans Parish School Board, 74–75, 81

Palmieri, Stafford, 203, 206–8
Parks, Rosa, 10
Percy Quin State Park, xiv, 174–75
Perez, Leander, 31–36, 68
Pharr, John, 97
Plaquemines Parish, 32
Plessy, Homer, ix, 5, 8

Plessy v. Ferguson, 5, 8–10, 13
Poché, Justin, 16
Ponchatoula, Louisiana, 174, 176
Populism, xi, 96–100
Port Vincent, Louisiana, 181

Rainach, Willie, 25, 30, 33
Ramos v. Louisiana, 92
Rapides Parish, 100
Reconstruction Acts of 1867, 94–95
Reed, Walter, 77, 82, 84
Rhodes, Tom, 102–3
Roemer, Charles (Buddy), 72
Roe v. Wade, 122–23, 125, 133, 220
Rummel, Joseph, 29–36
Ruston, Louisiana, 25–26

Selma, Alabama, 17, 48
Semmes, Thomas J., 100
Shreveport, Louisiana, 117
Sinclair, Ricky, 76
Slidell, Louisiana, 173, 177, 179
Southern Baptist Convention (SBC), 23, 27
Southern Christian Leadership Conference (SCLC), 16, 22, 48–49, 56
Southern University, 49–50, 52–53, 55, 72
St. Bernard Parish, 33
St. Helena Parish, 102
Strauder v. West Virginia, 93
Street, Stephen B., 76–77, 84
St. Tammany Parish, 102, 171, 180, 184

Tangipahoa Parish, 6, 100–102, 104–5, 107, 171, 176
Tauzin, Billy, 65
tax exemptions to industry, 218–19
Taylor v. Louisiana, 121
Terrebonne Parish, 224
Thomas, Ernest, 54
Tinnin, Finley, 24–25, 27–28
Title IX, xii
Together Louisiana, 218
Tourgée, Albion W., 8

United Defense League, 20–21, 51–52

Warmoth, Henry C., 67
Washington Parish, 6, 104, 106, 184
Watershed Initiative, 168
Watson, Tom, 97, 99
Webb, Jesse, Jr., 20–21
Weeks v. Southern Bell, 118
West Feliciana Parish, 49, 97
White, Edward D., 10
Wilson, Jerome, 6
Wright, Skelly, 24, 30

Zurick, Lee, 84

www.ingramcontent.com/pod-product-compliance
Lightning Source LLC
Chambersburg PA
CBHW022005220426
43663CB00007B/963